W9-BBS-166

AMERICAN LITERARY REALISM, CRITICAL THEORY, AND INTELLECTUAL PRESTIGE, 1880–1995

Focusing on key works of late nineteenth- and early twentieth-century American literary realism, Phillip Barrish traces the emergence of new ways of gaining intellectual prestige – that is, new ways of gaining cultural recognition as unusually intelligent, sensitive, or even wise. Through extended readings of works by Henry James, William Dean Howells, Abraham Cahan, and Edith Wharton, Barrish emphasizes the differences between literary realist modes of intellectual and cultural authority and those associated with the rise of the social sciences. In doing so, he also greatly refines our understanding of the complex relationship between realist writing and masculinity. Barrish further argues that understanding the dynamics of intellectual status in realist literature provides new analytic purchase on intellectual prestige in recent theory. Here he focuses on such figures as Lionel Trilling, Paul de Man, John Guillory, and Judith Butler.

PHILLIP BARRISH is Assistant Professor in the Department of English, University of Texas, Austin. He has published essays in such journals as *American Literary History*, *Victorian Studies*, and *Diacritics*. This is his first book.

AMERICAN LITERARY REALISM, CRITICAL THEORY, AND INTELLECTUAL PRESTIGE, 1880–1995

PHILLIP BARRISH

CAMBRIDGE
UNIVERSITY PRESS

PUBLISHED BY THE PRESS SYNDICATE OF THE UNIVERSITY OF CAMBRIDGE
The Pitt Building, Trumpington Street, Cambridge, United Kingdom

CAMBRIDGE UNIVERSITY PRESS
The Edinburgh Building, Cambridge CB2 2RU, UK
40 West 20th Street, New York NY 10011–4211, USA
10 Stamford Road, Oakleigh, Melbourne 3166, Australia
Ruiz de Alarcón 13, 28014 Madrid, Spain
Dock House, The Waterfront, Cape Town 8001, South Africa

http://www.cambridge.org

© Phillip Barrish 2001

First published 2001

Printed in the United Kingdom at the University Press, Cambridge

Typeface Monotype Baskerville 11/12.5 pt   *System* QuarkXPress™   [SE]

A catalogue record for this book is available from the British Library

Library of Congress Cataloguing in Publication data

Barrish, Phillip.
American literary realism, critical theory, and intellectual prestige, 1880–1995 / Phillip Barrish.
p. cm.
Includes bibliographical references and index.
ISBN 0 521 78221 X
1. American fiction – 20th century – History and criticism.   2. Realism in literature.   3.
American fiction – 19th century – History and criticism.   4. American fiction – History and
criticism – Theory, etc.   5. United States – Intellectual life – 20th century.   6. United
States – Intellectual life – 19th century.   I. Title.

PS374.R37   B36   2001
813′.50912 – dc21   00-062144

ISBN 0 521 78221 X hardback

In memory of my mother
and
in honor of my father

Contents

Acknowledgements

In one way and another (and frequently in more ways than one), the following people helped to make this book possible.

Mark Seltzer, Cynthia Chase, Debra Fried, and Harry Shaw helped to guide my early thinking and writing about the topic. More recently, astute readings were given to portions of the manuscript by Brian Bremen, Evan Carton, Ann Cvetkovich, Alyssa Harad, Theresa Kelley, Jeff Nunokawa, Samuel Otter, Margit Stange, Warwick Wadlington, and Michael Winship. Amanda Anderson made insightful suggestions at various stages of the project. For having read the whole manuscript and helping to shape the book as it stands, I am greatly indebted to Sabrina Barton, Lisa Moore, David McWhirter, Ross Posnock, Julie Rivkin, and two anonymous readers for Cambridge University Press. For invaluable research assistance, I thank Rayce Boucher, Laura Broms, and Michael Martin. Without the latter, I don't know if I could have gotten through the final months of manuscript preparation. At several pinches along the way, Lisa Brown's generosity with her time gave me much-needed extra hours of work.

The University of Texas at Austin helped to support this project by awarding me a Dean's Fellowship and two summer research grants, as well as providing funds to pay my research assistants. I am grateful to James Garrison for helping to facilitate that support. I also thank the University of California at Davis for important aid at earlier stages of the project. A version of chapter 3 appeared in *American Literary History*, and I appreciate their permission to reprint it.

Sabrina Barton is my best reader, my best interlocutor, and my best friend. Elijah Barton Barrish is awesome. Both make me feel luckier than I can express.

Introduction

Up to this time I had written only a few poems, and some articles descriptive of boy life on the prairie, although I was doing a good deal of thinking and lecturing on land reform, and was regarded as a very intense disciple of Herbert Spencer and Henry George – a singular combination, as I see it now. On my way westward, that summer day in 1887, rural life presented itself from an entirely new angle.

> Hamlin Garland, 1922 "Author's Preface" to *Main-Travelled Roads*
> (first edition of *Main-Travelled Roads* published in 1890)

There would be a thousand matters – matters already the theme of prodigious reports and statistics – as to which I should have no sense whatever, and as to information about which my record would accordingly stand naked and unashamed. It should unfailingly be proved against me that my opportunity had found me incapable of information, incapable alike of receiving and imparting it; for then, and then only, would it be clearly enough attested that I *had* cared and understood.

> Henry James, "Preface" to *The American Scene* (1907)[1]

This book explores how certain key works of American literary realism articulate within themselves new ways of gaining intellectual prestige or distinction – new ways of gaining, that is, some degree of cultural recognition as unusually intelligent, discerning, sensitive, alert, knowledgeable, or even wise. Recent scholarship on American literary realism has concentrated on realism's correlation with a wide range of professional discourses – social-scientific, reformist, juridical, managerial, and others – that were all closely associated with the new middle classes' rise to hegemony in late nineteenth- and early twentieth-century America. Focusing on what Nancy Bentley calls "convergences" between literary realism and other emergent discourses and disciplines such as social work, city planning, and anthropology, this historicizing work has in part

been inspired by a Foucauldian impulse to locate forms of power operating within arenas that are not explicitly political. We have learned, for
example, that literary realism and ethnography both strove to produce
an "expert observation . . . that give[s] the observer mastery over a cultural territory."[2] Scholars including Bentley, Mark Seltzer, June Howard,
Howard Horowitz, Eric Sundquist, and others have shown that "realist"
frameworks structured a wide range of the new middle classes' participation in, and responses to, the period's remarkably rapid changes.[3] Yet
Henry James and Hamlin Garland, in prefacing works that treat many
of the same aspects of American reality that, for instance, sociologists
and reformers also investigated, are at pains to distinguish their
approaches from precisely those others.

James not only admits, he even boasts of a paralyzed incapacity in
relation to "reports and statistics," which at the turn of the century were
rapidly becoming the most privileged forms of knowledge in "an
American culture defined increasingly by the emerging disciplines of
social science." Indeed, James designates that cognitive incapacity as
primary proof of the special value that readers should accord to his perspective: "for then, and then only, would it be clearly enough attested
that I *had* cared and understood." So too, Garland's description of
gaining an "entirely new angle" on rural life, the angle from which, as
he implies, *Main-Travelled Roads* would be written, is accompanied by a
self-ironic reference to his own previous viewpoint, which he now recognizes as deriving from an immature, even incoherent, set of allegiances
to the sociologist Herbert Spencer and the radical land reformer Henry
George.[4] The centrality that these two authors give to differentiating
their own writing's "angle" from the angles of other emergent
approaches begins to indicate the need for us to pay closer attention to
the specificity of literary realist claims to intellectual authority. Recent
criticism's project of elaborating literary realism's consanguinity with
other cultural practices roughly contemporary with it has enabled us to
recognize importantly overlapping assumptions, methodologies and
goals, as well as pervasive cultural imperatives towards, for example, the
investigation and mapping of social spaces. Yet this same historicist
emphasis on revealing connections among cultural endeavors traditionally thought about in separation has, I believe, caused us to move too
quickly past the particular complexities characterizing claims to privileged intellectual status by and within literary realist texts themselves.[5]

REALIST DISPOSITIONS

Literary realist works elaborate new forms of intellectual prestige, which are, in various cases, identified with an authorial persona, personified through a fictional character, instantiated in a text's narrating voice, and/or implicitly proffered to readers. Claims to what we might call "realist prestige" exhibit at their center the assertion of a paradoxical relationship – comprising a unique degree of emotional and cognitive intimacy with, yet also controllable distance from – whatever category of experience a given literary work posits as the most recalcitrantly *real*, most intransigently *material*, that life has to offer.[6] As we will see, however, what comes to count in turn-of-the-century American literary realism as most irreducibly material (as, that is, the *realest* real thing) not only changes from work to work but also shifts within individual works.

Categories of human experience put forward as the realest reality at different moments of literary realist texts include, for instance, physical suffering, life in the slums, money and sex (or, at some moments, desire as such), people's overriding need for social converse, death, and the class hierarchies of American society. At other moments, American realist works also position linguistic events, whether regionally marked speech or facets of the actual scene of writing, as "most real" in the implicit hierarchies of realness that they set up. Finally, that which occupies the category of most resistantly *there* in American realist writing can even be not-strictly tangible notions such as, for instance, the impossibility of justice, or the ironies built into being a middle-class radical; I will turn to this category in chapter 1 (which focuses on William Dean Howells).

The reader will notice that, compared to virtually all other recent book-length studies of American literary realism, my book spends relatively little time discussing contemporary events or written sources outside of the literary texts that I read. This was not my intention when I first became interested in writing about literary realism and intellectual prestige. I imagined continually comparing explicit and implicit claims to intellectual status that I found within literary realist works with roughly analogous claims in social-scientific and other writing, all the while as I also explored the interrelating sets of historical institutions and circumstances in which these various bids for prestige emerged. As I worked, however, I became more and more convinced that the detailedly attentive reading permitted by concentrating on a relatively small selection of literary texts would be methodologically necessary, at least for me, if I wished to follow the layered operations and many vicissitudes

involved when powerful, self-conscious works of literature engage in any
sort of cultural work, let alone in a concerted attempt to develop new
modes of intellectual distinction.

Despite its relative absence of historicist trappings, however, I nonetheless believe that the present study works responsibly within an historical framework. Indeed, I would contend that the argument I pursue
throughout the book – an argument about the elaboration of specific literary realist methods of asserting intellectual distinction – is itself important for any attempt to achieve a detailed understanding of middle-class,
professional American culture since the Civil War.[7] We still have much
to learn about the fascinating intricacies of "internecine struggles within
the middle classes" over different modes of asserting cultural status. If
the professional–managerial middle classes achieved cultural hegemony
during the late nineteenth century, certainly it is crucial for us to understand how the literature most prominently identified with them helped
them to define themselves, as a grouping, in relation to other groupings,
such as working-class immigrants. Thus, studying the role that literary
realism played in helping the new middle classes differentiate themselves
from people of "lower" (and, to a certain extent, of "higher") socioeconomic status has been one of recent scholarship's most central concerns.[8] But, if only because the professional–managerial middle classes
are still culturally hegemonic in America, it is equally important that we
strive to understand *intra*-class differences and competitions. Internecine
struggles over cultural status among different middle-class fractions and
even sub-fractions, such as literary and social-scientific intellectuals, play
just as central a role (and often a more immediate one) in defining
various middle-class identities and cultural positions as *inter*-class
conflicts do. The examples of what might be called "realer-than-thou"
one-upmanship that this book attempts to dissect in literary realist works
(and, in the book's final portion, in recent literary-critical and theoretical writings) are almost entirely middle class in origin as well as aimed *at*
middle-class competitors. This is true even when immigrant slum life, for
example, is the ostensible referent of literary claims to have a more intimate grasp of the really real.

At the risk of trying the reader's patience, I must emphasize a bit
further what this book does not do. It does not seek to describe the intellectual status or cultural prestige given to "literary realism" as a genre in
turn-of-the-century American culture.[9] Neither does the current study
attempt to characterize the status acquired by individual "realist" writers
– whether Henry James or Abraham Cahan – in the world outside of

their texts. Nor, finally, does the book's governing interest center on the portrayal of those fictional characters whose activities make them easy to label as "intellectuals" – writers, for instance, or scientists.[10] I desire, rather, to capture a particular "realist disposition," exploring how selected works of literary realism both articulate and valorize its intellectual authority.

"Disposition" is a useful term for me because it encapsulates several of the most important specificities that I have found in literary realist claims to intellectual distinction. First, "disposition" connotes not only mood and personal temperament, but also general outlook on, as well as characteristic modes of interaction with, the world. "Disposition," moreover, moves towards the large semantic category of taste. Constructions of intellectual status within literary realism self-consciously emphasize personal preferences and opinions, emotional responses, and both physical and psychological postures.[11] This contrasts markedly with the attempts at systematized objectivity stressed in turn-of-the-century social science.

Second, the *dis-* in "disposition" helps point to the prominence of paradoxical embraces of negativity – embraces of specific incapacities (such as those Henry James boasts of in *The American Scene*), of blockages, painful ironies, and other forms of limitation and frustration – in literary realism's favored styles of intellectual prestige. The intellectual distinction attached to recognizing the effective reality of these modes of negativity constitutes another key difference from intellectual status in the more openly confident social–scientific, reform, and managerial discourses of the period. In chapter 5, I will suggest that American literary realism's conferral of distinction on an intellectual orientation towards various sorts of negativity can be understood as one anticipation within American literary culture of the significant prestige that poststructuralism's emphasis on absence and aporia would come to carry in the US literary academy during the 1970s and 1980s.[12]

Finally, the *-position* in disposition signifies that to talk about prestige is to talk about relational positions and positionings.[13] Rather than trying to understand the biographical positions of particular authors on a variety of social and institutional axes, however, my readings will explore the establishment of certain textual positions *within* realist works. These textual positions (or, rather, "*dis*positions") accrue intellectual status and prestige for themselves through asserting an exclusively proximate relationship with, yet also a signifying distance from, life's most nitty-gritty dimensions.

I tend to use "prestige" and "status" more or less interchangeably with "distinction," but the latter term is probably most apt and it deserves particular emphasis here. Each of the realist writers with whom this book deals regularly employed "distinction" when referring to recognizable manifestations of a privileged status. (Abraham Cahan's David Levinsky, for instance, refers to a suit giving its wearer "an air of distinction.")[14] In addition, "distinction" evokes difference or separateness, which is an important component (sometimes taking the form of isolation) of the realist dispositions that the current study explores. At the same time, however, distinction remains more syntactically dependent than either prestige or status on prepositions such as "between," which helps to stress that both it and its possession can only be defined in relation to something or someone else. Moreover, as a term distinction seems better able than status or prestige to encompass forms of recognition that, like those treated here, tend to be informal or new, and which do not easily align with institutional or other long-standing hierarchies.

I most wish to foreground the term "distinction" here, however, because it references the writing of Pierre Bourdieu, above all his remarkable study, *Distinction: a Social Critique of Judgments of Taste*. This is a work whose theoretical and methodological implications I rely on but also seek to challenge and refine throughout.[15] Bourdieu's *Distinction* draws on extensive interviews, surveys, and other data from France during the 1960s and early 1970s in order to map the ins and outs of cultural prestige. Although Bourdieu sometimes seems to use some of his own terminology a bit loosely, the term "distinction" in his work refers most specifically to one form of the larger category "symbolic capital." Symbolic capital encompasses any aspect of an individual's status, authority, privilege, honor, or socially effective reputation that does not directly equate with his or her material wealth. The version of symbolic capital that Bourdieu calls "cultural capital" has sometimes struck me as the category most appropriate to the forms of realist prestige that I seek to understand, and thus I do make some use of the term. But, as John Guillory points out, in Bourdieu's work "cultural capital" often refers to specific "knowledge, skills, or competence" that can be certified by "objective mechanisms," such as university diplomas.[16] "Distinction," by contrast, eschews official certification because it depends on the ineffable aura attached to "cultivation," "refinement," and, most of all, "taste."

An individual's "distinction" registers his or her place within one or more intangible, but nonetheless socially meaningful, cultural hierarchies. Familiar hierarchies of distinction include, for just a few classic examples, the ability (or lack of ability) to appreciate fine wines, the degree of abstraction that an individual is comfortable with in modern art, and a preference for "high" literature over popular fiction.[17] Distinction is characteristically demonstrated through acts of taste. One earns distinction through exhibiting a nuanced ability to *distinguish among* art objects, consumption choices, and lifestyle practices alike. Taste classifies the external world, but, as Bourdieu powerfully demonstrates, it also "classifies the classifier" (p. 6).

What determines whether a particular taste or practice will earn "distinction" for its possessor? For Bourdieu, cultural distinction defines itself first and foremost via its inverse relationship to those necessities imposed on us by "crudely material reality" (p. 196). Distinction in modern Western culture functions above all to show (or show off) one's "objective distance" from needing to worry about "the demands of biological nature," such as, for example, the body's requirements concerning nourishment and shelter (p. 255). Socially prestigious modes of dining – for instance, serving meals in discrete, leisurely courses – stress formal features of the experience over and against any direct need to satisfy bodily hunger, a dynamic that also explains why the "finest" restaurants proverbially serve the smallest portions. In Edith Wharton's *The House of Mirth*, Lord Hubert's recommendation of a particular restaurant as "the only restaurant in Europe where they can cook peas" renders emphatic how far those who frequent it are (or wish to be seen as) from any need to treat eating as putting sufficient food inside their stomachs.[18] "Distinction" can also accrue, Bourdieu observes, through demonstrating distance from "the necessities of the . . . social world" (p. 5). In *The House of Mirth*, the Duchess of Beltshire's impregnable social status not only allows for, but is also reinforced by, the bravado with which she swerves from social conventionalities that others feel bound to obey. When Lily Bart is accused of sexual misconduct, for instance, her friend Carry Fisher feels compelled to follow "the other women's lead" and shun her. But the Duchess of Beltshire publicly and "instantly" sweeps Lily "under her sheltering wing," and makes with her an "almost triumphant progress to London."[19] Equally pertinent here is Michael North's observation that "bad grammar has long been the privilege of the upper classes, who demonstrate their superiority to social constraints by slipshod speech."[20]

MATERIAL CLAIMS

Bourdieu's insistence that cultural distinction constitutes itself through the form of its relationship with material or social reality would seem to make his work particularly resonant for a discussion of prestige and literary realism. Indeed, each of my chapters relies in one way or another upon his central insight: that what he calls "strategies of distinction" (which may be consciously or unconsciously practiced) shape themselves through displaying a relationship with the real (p. 65). Yet I have also found Bourdieu's notion of the relationship between "distinction" and "reality" to be limiting in significant ways. Most obviously, where Bourdieu assumes that displaying distinction requires exhibiting a *distance* from the "basely material" (p. 196), the literary realist dispositions that I will explore claim special *intimacy* with materiality. Realist dispositions insist upon their own privileged access to hard, irreducible realities.

In addition, as will be developed more fully in chapter 3 on Abraham Cahan's *The Rise of David Levinsky*, I have found Bourdieu's writing too reductively literal-minded about what reality is, and where one should look for it, to capture the workings of distinction in American literary realism. For Bourdieu, strategies of distinction may be mobile, subtle, continuously reinvented, often multi-leveled, as they seek to distinguish their possessors within an ever-competitive field of practices (p. 230). But he almost always takes for granted that the "crudely material reality" against which strategies of distinction shape themselves is just stably there, easy to point to. Bourdieu analytically dissects different exhibitions of *freedom* from certain hard material realities of life, but implies that those realities themselves are what they are, and that one can simply refer to them in the course of studying distinction.[21]

Because of the constitutive roles that language and representation play in all human experience, however, the "real" is only ever available via mediating contexts and constructions. Directly accessible, easily delimitable "material reality" must be recognized as itself a construction. For the works of American literary realism explored in the following chapters, the "material reality" in relation to which distinction defines itself acts as a far more mobile category than Bourdieu's work ever considers. Moreover, the position of "the real" in realist texts is more variable, more flexible, than has been assumed by recent critical work on the period. As noted above, what comes to count as most real not only changes from literary work to literary work but also shifts within individual works.

I have found Judith Butler's account of *materialization* extremely suggestive for reckoning with the shifting nature of those categories, whether in literary realism or in critical theory itself, that come to count as bottomline, irrefutable reality. By "materialization," Butler means the processes by which various discourses "materialize a set of effects" and thereby produce what will appear within those discourses as unconstructed, prediscursive *matter*.[22] Like Butler, I believe it crucial that we try to trace how, and with what implications, that which is "considered to be most real, most pressing, most undeniable" gets textually defined and positioned.[23]

The present study, therefore, follows Bourdieu in his insistence that "taste" and other modes of manifesting distinction involve dynamics of self-situating vis-à-vis "crudely material reality." Yet my exploration of different modes of prestige in American literary realism also demonstrates, I believe, that Bourdieu's sociological insights are most analytically productive when combined with a poststructuralist sensitivity to the role played by discourse and representation in constituting the hard facts of reality as such.[24] Conversely, however, I try to show as well, in chapter 5, that the understanding Bourdieu's work helps us to gain about intellectual status in realist literature also illuminates a central facet of intellectual distinction in recent critical and theoretical writings, including Butler's (and also including John Guillory's currently influential applications of Bourdieu). From deconstruction to cultural studies, it is fair to say that the recent critical scene has been permeated by versions of "realer-than-thou" claims.

A diverse range of competing bids for intellectual authority center on claims to provide readers with new analytic access to – or at least superior glimpses of – an underlying level of materiality. Even poststructuralist critical approaches, which tend to be regarded as eschewing realist frameworks, actively participate in these contests to be more materialist than alternative perspectives. Thus, I will contend that, just as recent poststructuralist insights can help us to an improved understanding of how certain constructions of and orientations towards the nitty-gritty real operate to assert prestige within literary realism, so too understanding prestige in this earlier context gives us a new analytic purchase on poststructuralism's own dynamics of intellectual prestige. The supposedly more *material* materialities staked out by poststructuralist writing include, for example, American deconstruction's (Paul de Man's) necessary yet also disfiguring acts of linguistic positing, as well as recent Lacanian critics' (for example, Joan Copjec's and Juliet Flower MacCannell's) appeals to a "non-symbolizable" real.

I will be interested throughout the following chapters in how claims – whether they appear in realist literature or in critical theory – to a privileged representational intimacy with hard "reality" or irreducible "materiality" operate as bids for intellectual prestige. Here, however, I wish to broach the problems that I have had in trying to negotiate what Joseph Litvak aptly calls the "inexplicit but unmistakable effect of sardonic unmasking, along with the strong, lingering odor of bad faith" that frequently inheres in Bourdieu-influenced analysis.[25] It is difficult not to seem as if one is muckraking (and with a fairly indiscriminate rake, at that) when setting out to uncover a range of distinction-gaining practices that have not previously been acknowledged as such. Granted that, like other hierarchical relations involving symbolic capital, intellectual prestige might disappear altogether in some for now unimaginable future that has managed to eliminate the unequal distribution of social "goods" as such.[26] In the mean time, however, I view late nineteenth-century American literature's new emphasis on the "real" over and against the ideal as, for the most part, a positive, democratizing development. Similarly, I believe that late twentieth-century criticism's pervasive investments in what might be called an "are-we-being-materialist-enough-yet?" paradigm is much more of a good thing than a bad thing.[27] During both periods, sustained focus on the "real" or the "material" has brought into discursive presence people, things, categories of experience, dimensions of the social order, various sorts of textual and other relationships, that were previously underrecognized within the traditions of writing involved. However different writers, then and now, describe "material reality," it no doubt deserves all of the flexible, creative, complex attention that intellectuals can give it, and more as well.

Nonetheless, although I very much admire many aims of both the realist and the critical-theoretical works here discussed, I think it crucial that we recognize the multiple achievements of realism as fully and honestly as possible. In particular, we should strive to make ourselves as aware as possible of the role that "material claims" have played and continue to play in the dynamics of intellectual distinction within late nineteenth- and twentieth-century American literary culture – just as, of course, structures of prestige and distinction also operate in most other cultural arenas.[28] To investigate these dynamics in literary realist writing does not mean to dismiss the social and moral value of bringing focused literary attention to areas of American life excluded or treated with light ignorance by most previous American writing. As a genre, realist writing strove to move the overlooked into mainstream view, or, alternately, to treat with more penetrating honesty that which may have been depicted before but insufficiently explored. Yet such endeavors simultaneously served other, sometimes oblique or unconscious, purposes. Indeed, any significant cultural practice is, by definition, overdetermined, as it functions in more than one register and with more than one valence. I will argue that literary realist texts, inseparably from the other things that they do, also explore, experiment with, and embody modes of *competing* within what they themselves ask us to recognize as a narrow and specific context: that of the culturally insecure, ever-jockeying for status and distinction, new middle and upper-middle classes of turn-of-the-century America.

In exploring the "realist dispositions" that the literary works studied below seek to promote, I hope also to suggest a need to keep refining the questions that we ask about masculinity in/and realist literature. In his excellent and often-cited *The Problem of American Literary Realism*, Michael Davitt Bell argues that male realists were anxious about prevalent cultural assumptions in nineteenth-century America linking artistic activity with femininity.[29] In response, even novelists of manners such as James and Howells strove to construct their own writing as what Bell calls "masculine realism." Their literary practice should be understood not in opposition but rather as connected, albeit indirectly, to the "cult of virility" that was developing in turn-of-the-century America. Bell does make a valuable move in recognizing that the high realism of late nineteenth-century America can be linked not only with Victorian discourses of civilized "manliness," as is suggested by most other studies touching on realism and masculinity, but also with the period's emerging fascination with virile "masculinity."[30] My own sense, however, is once again that in the impulse to make literary works line up with what we already know (or think we know) about broader historical developments — whether it be Victorian formations of "manliness" that stress self-discipline or the emergent cultural emphasis on so-called "primitive" masculinity — we risk moving too quickly past some of the wrinkles and folds that distinguish (if you will) literature itself.

Perhaps because masculinity studies is still a relatively new practice within literary criticism (and perhaps also because it emerged in a 1990s literary-critical context dominated by historicism), we are still learning to allow for the variousness and vicissitudes of masculinity's literary constructions. I mean here not only masculinity's inseparability from other constructs such as race, class, and region, but also the multiply different ways in which even middle-class white masculinity's privilege can operate – or fail to operate – in American literary language, as well as within discrete works. (By contrast, consider the rich array of often conflicting or surprising critical readings produced over the past few decades on how the category of "femininity" functions in, for instance, just Kate Chopin's relatively short novel *The Awakening*.)[31] In an essay that considers the potential usefulness of a Bourdieu-influenced perspective for feminist analysis, Toril Moi suggests we should assume that "in most contexts maleness functions as positive and femaleness as negative symbolic capital." But at the same time, as she goes on to argue, "one of the advantages of Bourdieu's theory is that it . . . permits us to grasp the immense *variability* of gender as a social factor."[32] Because gender identities are structurally pervasive, yet also constitutively slippery and flexible, they can manifest their positive or negative symbolic capital – that is, the different sorts of prestige (or the lack thereof) attached to masculinity or femininity – with great variety.

Judith Butler's account of *materialization* does not engage with Bourdieu or with any Bourdieu-ean analyses of distinction, but it nonetheless supports Toril Moi's insight about the potential for diverse shiftings in how gender and cultural prestige relate to each other. Butler asserts that the textual construction of matter always yields a differentiated hierarchy of cultural status. This status hierarchy also always involves categories of gender and sexuality, *but in ways that are neither absolutely fixed nor predeterminable*. For Butler, "'materiality' is formed and sustained through and as . . . regulatory norms that are in part those of heterosexual hegemony." Yet, she insists, "to say that there is a matrix of gender relations that institutes and sustains the subject is not to claim that there is a singular matrix that acts in a singular and deterministic way . . ."

Moi's insight about the many different ways that gender and "symbolic capital" may relate with one another, and Butler's insistence that processes of "materialization" both transpire within and also produce gendered and sexualized matrices, but never in any "singular and deterministic way," correlate with what I have found in American literary realism. Although intellectual prestige does tend to figure as male in turn-of-the-century realist works, the specific economies and configurations involved vary surprisingly. As the chapters to follow make clear, no single paradigm (such as, for instance, the notion that in realism *knowing* is gendered male while *objects-to-be-known* are gendered female) can suffice to capture the various configurations to be found in these literary works of masculine privilege, cultural prestige, and claims about materiality.

In the novels of William Dean Howells, for instance, much of the low-key bantering that runs throughout his famous portrayals of middle-class marriage involves husbands figuring their wives *either* as overly literal-minded *or* as caught up in romantic illusion (or sometimes both). In either case, portraying their wives as having only a one-dimensional relationship to American realities allows the husbands in these novels more sharply to define the sophistication of their own orientation towards those same realities. For Henry James, by contrast, Merton Densher's bachelorhood – more specifically his lack of a publicly binding commitment to any other person – helps shape the intellectual prestige that he accrues in *The Wings of the Dove*. Densher is distinguished by his ability to "shut . . . out" of his consciousness, at will, specific female bodies, even as his cognitive, emotional and physical intimacy with those same female bodies adds significantly to his cultural status. Densher's realist prestige, moreover, is first registered within the "circle of petticoats" that constitutes both his most immediate and his most evaluatively powerful public. In Cahan's *Yekl* and *The Rise of David Levinsky*, women epitomize the "ethnic real." An intense but not full identification with this feminized ethnic real helps to constitute prestige for the male ethnic intellectual. Further, the relative inability of Yiddish-American women in Cahan's writing to, as it were, master the hyphen between Yiddish and American provides continual opportunities for displaying intellectual superiority on the part of male-identified textual positions.

These works by Howells, James, and Cahan bear out Toril Moi's assumption that, in most contexts, maleness will be aligned with "positive . . . symbolic capital." My fourth chapter turns to Edith Wharton's *Twilight Sleep*, however, which of the books considered here goes farthest in illustrating Judith Butler's insistence that the relation among "materialization," gender, and status ultimately allows for significant shifts. A surprisingly overlooked novel, the 1927 *Twilight Sleep* embodies Wharton's most intriguing fictional attempt to assign realist intellectual status to a woman. Like certain other intellectuals (such as Freud) struggling to make the transition after World War I from a Victorian to a modern world, Wharton strove to come to grips with what seemed to her the inescapable reality of destructiveness and self-destructiveness inhering within both modern civilization and modern psyches. *Twilight Sleep* distinguishes the flapper Nona Manford as uniquely able to grasp this horrific real, which manifests itself in the novel in gendered and sexualized terms as the incestuous drive of Nona's father. Both Nona and

Wharton associate the father's violently destructive passion with the prosecution and effects of World War I.

Alone among *Twilight Sleep*'s characters, Nona achieves a clear-eyed recognition (more so than her father, Dexter Manford, ever does himself) that the patriarch's incestuous drive acts within the novel's universe as its most powerfully determining reality. Although often "out of sight and under ground,"[33] the father's incestuous desires indirectly organize events, relationships, and various individual subjectivities. But despite Nona's unmatched level of insight into that which Wharton's novel considers "to be most real, most pressing, most undeniable" (borrowing Butler's formulation), it is hard to view her as culturally elevated by her knowledge. Nona remains a daughter who depends upon and loves her father. As such, gaining a controlled distance from the real – her father's intractable desires – that she sees with such uniquely intimate clarity is far more problematic for her than for any of the male-gendered "realist dispositions" developed in works by Howells, James, or Cahan. Nona ends the book literally prostrate, waiting to recover from an infected bullet wound incurred when she discovered her father in bed with her step-sister, Lita. Yet, as I will discuss more fully in chapter 4, the final scene of Nona lying alone hints that her prostration before the painful knowledge that she has come to recognize over the course of the novel may be yielding her a distinct cognitive and emotional power, as well as the possibility for artistic creativity.

It is certainly not shocking that, within the late nineteenth- and early twentieth-century American literary works examined here, realist modes of intellectual distinction should be much more smoothly accessible to men than to women. Yet the wide diversity apparent when one focuses closely on the gender dynamics surrounding this sort of prestige even during literary realism's heyday does underline the possibility of, to employ Butler's phrasing, "radical rearticulation of the symbolic horizon in which bodies come to matter."[34] Such would necessarily also mean a rearticulation of the horizon in which realist intellectual prestige is defined. In key respects, the American literary academy – even those theoretical vectors which may appear most set off from other American contexts – still draws upon historical terms and paradigms from American literary culture. Rather than a mere "sardonic unmasking," then, tracing the diverse routes through which privileged intellectual status has been claimed and granted within important works of American literature may put us in a better position to recognize positive "rearticulations" of intellectual authority on our own critical scene.

In the very last line of Wharton's *Twilight Sleep*, Nona teasingly suggests that she will join a convent – a convent, however, "where nobody believes in anything" (p. 315). Nona is in part trying here to scandalize her mother, who has just suggested (amazingly, given what has been transpiring with her own marriage) that Nona will only be happy when married. Nonetheless, Nona's vision imagines a group of women institutionally united and, at least in a certain sense, culturally distinguished by their shared project of dissolving patriarchal notions of that which (again using Butler's words) "is considered to be most real, most pressing, most undeniable." Nona's vision may obliquely remind us of the rise to critical prominence and professional influence accomplished by feminist and queer approaches to gender and sexuality.

CHAPTER ONE

William Dean Howells and the roots of realist taste

REALIST TASTE VERSUS PHILISTINISM

In the course of well-known critic James Cox's contribution to a 1991 collection of *New Essays on The Rise of Silas Lapham*, he makes a more-or-less parenthetic remark about the vernacular aspect of the book's protagonist: "Indeed there has always been a sense among cultivated readers of dialect that Lapham, in his swagger as well as in his speech rhythms, actually seems more Western than Northeastern."[1] While I do not wish to enter into the question of Western versus Northeastern swagger and speech rhythms, I do want to call attention to the group that Cox's comment both asserts and takes for granted: *cultivated readers of dialect*. This phrase does not evoke persons with scientific or professional knowledge of language variation, as for example a phrase like "sociolinguists" would. Instead, "cultivated readers of dialect" suggests people whose knowledge of dialect is informal, but nonetheless rigorous, as well as attained only after some experience. Because Cox specifically identifies its possessors as "readers," the knowledge in question would seem not to derive primarily from direct, person-to-person encounters with members of various American speech communities; but neither does it seem right to think of this knowledge as remote or sterile "book-learning," as if it had come from manuals, dictionaries or textbooks. "Cultivated readers of dialect" suggests, instead, those with a wide experience of *literary* depictions of colloquial American speech.

Moreover, insofar as this judgment about Silas Lapham's speech rhythms and swagger is grounded in what Cox calls "a sense" rather than in some explicit codification of facts, it is structured like a judgment of taste. The sense about Silas Lapham's speech that, as Cox says, there "has always been" among cultivated readers of dialect corresponds to the embodied, natural-seeming quality of most taste judgments. Cox's word "sense" evokes as well the tendency of taste judgments (whether about works of art, about home decoration, or about other people's table manners) to register first at a level below conscious ratiocination, to be experienced viscerally before verbally. Finally, as with all matters supposed to involve taste, there is an unavoidable implication in Cox's remark that those who fail to make the appropriate discrimination – those who fail to recognize that Lapham's vernacular is more Western than Northeastern – mark themselves as outside a certain circle of cultivation.

None of this is meant to challenge the validity of Cox's remark about Silas Lapham's speech. Rather, I want to emphasize how, in the 1990s, Cox is able to take casually for granted that literary dialect can serve as a terrain for readers to display certain specialized forms of taste and cultivation, or their lack. This chapter will begin by arguing that it was William Dean Howells himself who, a century ago, first elaborated what might be called *realist taste* – that is, a discriminating appreciation for literary representations of the nitty-gritty "real," including vernacular speech. In both his critical writing and his novels, Howells positioned realist taste as a form of cultural capital available to discerning members of the competitive, ever-jockeying for position, middle and upper-middle classes of the late nineteenth century.[2]

Understanding Howells's proffer of realist taste as a way for *some* middle- and upper-class readers to claim cultural superiority over *other* middle- and upper-class readers may help, first, to mediate between two seemingly incompatible critical accounts of Howells's cultural and political significance. The first generation of academic researchers to devote sustained attention to Howells portrayed him as the leading figure in what Edwin Cady called a "realism war." For Cady and other scholars, Howells waged a courageous campaign for "literary democracy," but nonetheless for most of his career remained something of a David confronting the genteel elitism and overwhelming conventionality of a Goliath-like literary establishment.[3] By contrast, more recent critical accounts have tended to place Howells not in honorable opposition to the dominant social and cultural forces of his period but rather as a sort of agent *for* what Richard Brodhead calls America's "postbellum elite," which Brodhead sees as exemplified by the audiences of the classy magazines that Howells edited and published in (such as *The Atlantic Monthly* and *Harper's Monthly*).[4] These "postbellum elite" audiences were drawn from such social groupings as new urban professionals, progressive-style government bureaucrats, and business executives and managers, as well as certain of the old antebellum gentry whose wealth still lay primarily in real estate.

Undoubtedly, earlier discussions of Howells such as Cady's were naive in not considering structural relations between his work and the new forms of socioeconomic hierarchy that became predominant after the Civil War. Yet in implicitly rejecting Cady's picture of Howells as a brave battler against his age's most powerful interests, more recent studies have failed to substitute a good explanation for the discourse of conflict in Howells's writing – the sharply polemical feel of his magazine criticism, in particular – that led Cady to title the culminating second volume of his biography: *Realist at War*. If Howells, rather than fighting *against* his period's most powerful cultural formations, can in fact be squarely identified *with* them – and I agree with recent scholars that Howells should indeed be so identified – a question remains, why need he employ such a sharp edge? Where's the battle?

Amy Kaplan is surely right when she argues that Howells's writing strove to define and protect the lines that separated the middle classes from frightening social groups literally adjacent to them, especially in cities like New York.[5] But at least in those moments where his writing is most directly involved with developing realist taste – an aesthetic prefer-ence whose valence I will further explain below – the exclusionary lines that Howells draws seem directed not primarily against "the other half," but against blocs of readers belonging to the very same urban middle- and upper-class groupings with whom recent critics have taught us to align his work.

We should not forget that for Matthew Arnold himself, even the later Matthew Arnold of *Culture and Anarchy*, culture with a capital C func-tioned as a mark of division most pertinently *within* what Arnold called "my own class, the middle class." Aesthetic cultivation could indeed help to take some philistines, as Arnold put it, "out of their class," but not in the material sense of changing their socioeconomic status – Arnold insists that he himself always remains a "philistine, son of a philistine." Rather, aesthetic cultivation could help some members of the middle classes to join that "certain number of *aliens*, if we may so call them," whose most energetic claims to inner distinction take shape in opposi-tion to the bland homogeneity of their own socioeconomic peers.[6] Arnold's middle-class aliens are still, socioeconomically speaking, philis-tines, but their rigorous aesthetic commitments separate them from philistin*ism*.

Howells explicitly condemned elitist uses of Culture to bolster an exclusionary hierarchy, a paradigm that he associated with Matthew Arnold and with Arnold's American devotees.[7] Further, Arnold's own criticism had been dismissive towards the literary potential of everyday life and talk, especially that derived from outlying regions, which Howells championed. (For Arnold, Robert Burns's use of the "world of Scotch drink, Scotch religion, and Scotch manners" counted aesthetically "against the poet, not for him" because that Scotch world was essentially ugly).[8] Yet despite Howells's negative opinion of what he took Arnold to stand for, Howells's development of realist taste provided an adaptive framework that in effect helped certain Arnoldian paradigms, paradigms for privileging the cultured few over the bathetic many, seem more consonant with America's democratic ethos. Realist taste, with its polemically democratic scaffolding, would enable some members of the middle and upper classes still to invoke rigorous aesthetic discernment as the guarantor of their cultural superiority even as they simultaneously reaffirmed their American disdain for aesthetic pomposity.

For instance, in a September 1891 "Editor's Study" column devoted to Hamlin Garland's just-published *Main-Travelled Roads*, Howells writes that "Mr. Garland's work . . . is a work of art, first of all, and we think of fine art; though the material will strike many gentilities as coarse and common."[9] Howells follows the Arnoldian imperative to separate what is art, and above all what is truly *fine* art, from other categories of expression, and also to privilege the few who do know the difference over the many who do not. In Howells's formulation, however, only those readers astute enough to recognize the "fine-art" potential of commonplace, even coarse, material earn the desirable status of being distinct from the many – of being, that is, *un*common. For Howells, the realism war ultimately meant trying to convince enough representatives of post-Civil War America's dominant socioeconomic strata – strata whose members, as I believe Brodhead fails sufficiently to stress, felt constitutively insecure – that acquiring an informed liking for the flavor of American realist literature could help to mark positively their own aesthetic taste relative to *other* members of their own social groupings.

I will turn in a moment to *The Rise of Silas Lapham*, which often served as a synecdoche for American literary realism in magazine and other discussions of the late 1880s and early 1890s. As we'll see, the 1885 novel is full of discussions of taste – on topics ranging from polite social protocols, to architecture, to the different varieties of tea available in late nineteenth-century America – with much additional punning on words associated with taste, such as palate, savor, and so on. First, however, I want briefly to discuss some of Howells's own critical considerations of literary dialect in his very influential columns. Howells's magazine criticism poses the question of literary dialect as one that, to be approached properly, requires special kinds of aesthetic discernment; hence, evaluations of literary dialect – its general artistic validity as well as the specific qualities or effects of individual instances – will distinguish among those doing the evaluating just as much as among the writing that is being evaluated.

Howells is anything but alone in post-Civil War America when he suggests, in an early article in *Round Table*, that the ability to produce valid aesthetic judgments should be considered as (in his words) "at once the attribute and the indication" of "an educated and refined literary taste"; but it *is* he who first tried to establish that educated and refined literary taste could be demonstrated through one's judgments of literary dialect.[10] When Howells asserts, in a *Harper's Weekly* column, that George Washington Cable's "ever-delightful use of the Creole accents and forms" remains "the most delicately managed of all the experiments in dialect which our prose authors have made,"[11] he is also making an assertion about his own taste that pertains both to his taste's "education" (Howells is familiar with a wide range of American prose authors' representations of dialect) and to his taste's "refinement" (he values "delicacy" in aesthetic objects).[12]

Here I should emphasize how my approach differs from several recent considerations of the roles that dialect writing played in American literary culture during this period. Where an earlier generation of scholars emphasized the democratizing implications of including non-standard English in high-culture literature,[13] more recent studies tend to stress how dialect, especially when it was textually juxtaposed with a standard-English narrative voice, could encourage a work's middle-class cosmopolitan readers to join with the author in feeling different from and superior to vernacular characters, and by implication to the marginalized social groups from which such characters were drawn.[14] I believe, however, that in concentrating on how literary dialect may have helped to emphasize differences between clearly dominant and clearly subordinate groups, we risk losing sight of subtler ways in which the *framing* of literary dialect played a role in what Christopher P. Wilson has described as the late nineteenth and early twentieth centuries' "internecine struggles within the middle classes to define the style of their cultural legitimacy."[15] Howells's critical discussions of dialect in American literature exemplify the complexity of literary realism's role in these internecine middle-class struggles over modes of style, taste, and aesthetic experience.

Howells often uses his magazine discussions of American literary works with dialect in them to imply differences among his *readers* – readers perusing the very same magazines as one another – in their capacity to participate in what he describes as the "sensitive" judgments necessary to evaluate literary dialect. In *Harper's Weekly*, Howells voices a suspicion that "the general reader does not . . . know what dialect is."[16] The general reader, Howells explains, probably does not see any difference between, on the one hand, those sloppy, heavy-handed gestures toward colloquial speech associated with humorous newspaper figures such as Artemus Ward and Petroleum V. Nasby (which rank low on the scale of "serious artistry" because, among other reasons, they rely too heavily on what Howells calls "orthographic buffoonery") and, on the other hand, "the subtly shaded accents of the vernacular" included in the works of "truly artistic" dialect writers such as Cable, Page, Riley, Murfree, Wilkins, and of course Twain.[17] Like Matthew Arnold's cultural philistines, the general reader, in Howells's words, may be "numerically . . . important," but "he is not worth minding, aesthetically." Arnold defines his privileged aliens by their "love and pursuit of perfection," which "dwells among high and steep rocks, and can only be reached by those who sweat blood to reach her."[18] The lack of exactly this sort of impassioned and disciplined aesthetic commitment prevents Howells's "general reader" from appreciating the "exquisite" "fineness" of literary dialect "of the genuine sort." Thus William McClennan's French-Canadian sketches have been unpopular, according to Howells, because "of the conscience with which the work was done." "[T]he general reader," Howells writes scornfully, "could have borne with a few sentences of dialect here and there, but was impatient of a perfection veiled from him in the strange locutions which formed the whole texture of the little stories."[19]

Howells's review columns, especially in the mid-to-late 1880s, sometimes suggest that the use of dialect in regionalist literature offers to discerning American readers the opportunity to claim special forms of intellectual prestige more encompassing even than that he accords to middle-class authors of regionalist literature, in particular some of the women regionalist writers whose careers and work he himself promoted. Consider the September 1887 "Editor's Study" for *Harper's Monthly* that Howells devoted to Mary E. Wilkins's *A Humble Romance, and Other Stories*. One hundred years before James Cox positions himself as speaking for a group of sophisticated readers who share Cox's sense that William Dean Howells's best-known vernacular character, Silas Lapham, sounds more Western than Northeastern, Howells's own editorial "we" posits a community of judiciously informed opinion about Wilkins's use of dialect. Howells's editorial "we" begins by conceding that Wilkins does have some "skill in rendering the Yankee parlance," but then adds "We have our misgivings, however, about 'thar' and 'whar' on New England tongues, though we are not ready to deny that Miss Wilkins heard them in the locality she evidently knows so well."[20] At first, the nuts-and-bolts specificity of the question that Howells raises about Wilkins's use of dialect – are the words "thar" and "whar" truly appropriate on New England tongues? – may seem at odds with the slightly noncommittal air – "we have our misgivings . . ." – with which he introduces this potential qualification of Wilkins's skill. The term "misgivings," however, allows Howells's editorial "we" to disclaim from the start any interest in scholarly or pedantic debate even while asserting a casual mastery of the matter under consideration. "Misgivings" connotes disturbed taste; it registers a "sense" (again to use James Cox's term) that "thar" and "whar" are *off* in the Yankee context where Wilkins places them. In the sentence's next clause, Howells seems to qualify his own qualification about Wilkins's use of "thar" and "whar": "though we are not ready to deny that Miss Wilkins heard them in the locality she evidently knows so well." This second clause may sound like a retreat from Howells's position as evaluator of literary dialect, but in fact it merely emphasizes again that the editorial "we" has no desire legalistically to *argue* its "misgivings" at the level of first-order evidence: yes, yes, Wilkins may have heard "thar" or "whar" in New England – Howells's editorial "we" does not wish to claim an omnipotence that could discover whether anybody ever happened to utter those syllables in Wilkins's presence. The effect of his local concession, however, is to distinguish between two relations to dialect: a direct, but limited, knowledge associated with Wilkins, and a literary, hence broader, knowledge associated with the editorial "we."

Howells's column works to suggest that Wilkins may very well know a particular locality and its dialect quite thoroughly, and, unlike the characters in her fiction, no doubt *she* is in full control of how that dialect differs from standard English. Yet, if her knowledge has the virtues it also has the constraints of being based in what she has herself actually "heard," which means that she cannot possibly have the comparative perspective that would enable her properly to "place" individual samples. (Maybe, for example, the "thar" and "whar" that she heard on New England tongues issued from the mouths of two sisters who had picked the pronunciation up on an extended visit to a cousin in Indiana.)

Howells's "we" implies that a truly sophisticated knowledge of dialect can never come from first-hand, direct oral experience, even for someone who is fully a master of Standard English. Instead, a truly sophisticated knowledge of dialect can be developed only through the experiences of America that *reading* opens.

Turning back to James Cox's assumption about *who* possesses the right kind of taste for placing Silas Lapham's vernacular properly, I want to suggest that the first fully imagined versions of those "cultivated readers" of Silas Lapham's dialect to whom Cox appeals in 1991 can be found in Howells's 1885 novel itself.[21] Tom Corey and Penelope Lapham's marriage at the end of the novel does not cause any dramatic external rupture with either family, but, in the Arnoldian sense of the word, it *alienates* the couple from the *cultural* fields of both of their families. What is important is that both families – the nouveau industrialist Laphams, especially Penelope's younger sister Irene, and the genteel, longer-established Coreys, whose income derives from real estate and other investments – can be situated, at least loosely, within post-Civil War America's dominant socioeconomic groupings. Thus, the *taste* that Tom and Penelope share for, among other things, Silas Lapham's speech – their ability to enjoy it in just the right way – helps to differentiate the two aesthetically from close family members whose social status is otherwise quite similar to their own. Tom and Penelope's shared realist taste, moreover, forms a large component of Howells's positioning them, at the end of the novel, as the characters with the most promising future ahead of them.

Although they do not yet know it, the pair of scenes that immediately follows Tom and Penelope's first encounter with each other begins to establish for the reader their mutually compatible taste dispositions, which will ultimately result in the marriage that surprises most of the book's characters. In the scene preceding the two scenes that I will discuss, Tom Corey had accidentally come upon and then joined the Laphams as Silas was showing his family around the new house he has under construction. When the Laphams get home after this incident, Irene, the conventionally pretty sister who already has a crush on Tom, despairingly demands of Penelope, "Do you suppose he'll think papa always talks in that bragging way?"[22] Penelope's response separates her own enjoyment of Silas's "way" of talking from her sister's anxiety about it, even as she also emphatically differentiates her attitude toward Silas's mode of speech from any possibility of disdainful superciliousness on Tom Corey's part: "It's the way father always does talk. You never

noticed it so much, that's all. And I guess if he can't make allowance for
father's bragging, he'll be a little too good. *I* enjoyed hearing the Colonel
go on" (emphasis in original). By contrast to Irene, Pen is able, first, to
recognize Silas's talk as a characteristic linguistic mode. Second, Pen distinguishes her own appreciative enjoyment of that linguistic mode from
both her father's and her *sister's* lack of free, aware choice toward it: "It's
the way father always does talk. *You* never noticed it so much, that's all"
(my emphasis). Implicit is that Irene still has such an intimate relation to
her father's linguistic mode that she would not have registered it *as* a
mode except for the extreme social pressure induced by Tom Corey's
presence. When Irene does notice that her father even *has* a characteristic "way" of talking, her panic derives from her humiliating fear of being
too closely aligned with it. For Penelope, by contrast, Lapham's speech
has become a taste – a pleasure that she can choose to claim – rather
than a necessity: "*I* enjoyed hearing the Colonel go on."

In referring to her father by the Civil War title that he prides himself
on – "the Colonel" – Penelope is playfully citing an especially characteristic example of Silas's speech. This sort of affectionate *citation* constitutes the relation to Laphamesque vernacular that Pen develops
throughout the book. Not long after this scene, Penelope responds to her
sister and mother's nervous excitement about a visit from Tom with, "I
don't see any p'ints about that frog that's any better than any other frog"
(p. 78). Directly quoting Twain's *The Celebrated Jumping Frog of Calaveras
County* (initially published in 1865), she has recast her family's "natural"
relation to country dialect as a citational – and here explicitly a *literary* –
relation to it.

After their first encounter, Penelope worries that Tom may be a little
"too good," that is, that Tom's taste preferences may be too inflexibly
genteel. But Howells in the very next scene shows Tom concluding to his
father, Bromfield Corey, that "I don't believe . . . that I can make you see
Colonel Lapham just as I did" (p. 60). He adds "I 'took to' Colonel
Lapham from the moment I saw him. He looked as if he 'meant business,' and I mean business too" (p. 61). The internal quotation marks that
Howells puts around the colloquial phrases "took to" and "meant business" indicate that Tom purposefully employs tone and rhythm to set
those phrases off from the rest of his speech. Tom wants to leave no
doubt that he is quoting Laphamesque speech, not unselfconsciously
merging his own with it.[23] Indeed, the novel will continue to take for
granted that, although Tom may join Silas's firm, the two men will never
"mean" business in the same way. At least until the book's closing scenes,

Silas and business have a one-to-one correspondence; Silas and business mutually *signify* each other. By contrast, for Tom Corey, to mean business is not to stand for or to signify business, but to *intend* business, to choose it without being reduced to equivalence with it. The novel and Tom himself will continue to hold in sight the differences between Tom's correct English and Silas's vernacular as well as between the two men's modes of relating to business. But what I wish to stress is the more subtle distinction that emerges between Tom's and his father Bromfield's taste responses to the general "rawness," the "rude, native flavor," that both the Corey father and son take Silas and his vernacular speech to represent (p. 127). With this latter distinction, between Tom and Bromfield Corey, Howells differentiates the realist taste that he endorses from another taste mode by which members of the middle and upper classes might – and indeed did – aesthetically engage what he positioned as the rawer aspects of American life: by rendering them exotically picturesque. The closest that Bromfield can come to entering into his son's having "rather liked" Silas, even Silas's "syntax," is to conjure up what Bromfield calls "the romance, the poetry" of Silas's having gone so suddenly from poor to rich, as in a magic tale (p. 58). Throughout the novel, Howells portrays this picturesquing mode as a form of cultural out-of-it-ness, a benightedness that is inseparable from aesthetic laziness.[24]

Where Irene Lapham – Penelope's younger sister – remains too closely identified with Silas ever to make an informed taste-preference out of his "rawness," as Penelope does, Tom's sisters Lily and Nanny stick too unthinkingly to Bromfield's picturesquing mode ever to cultivate proper realist palates for Laphamesque "rude, native flavors." At the book's end, when Tom and Penelope move for a few years to Mexico, where they will work to open Latin American markets for the large US paint corporation of which Tom has become an executive, Nanny says she hopes that when Penelope "comes back she will have the charm of not olives, perhaps, but of *tortillas*, whatever they are: something strange and foreign" (p. 328). Nanny's desire to exoticize Penelope's flavor serves here as the opposite of an aesthetically disciplined gesture in its unashamed ignorance ("tortillas, whatever they are") as well as in its almost boastful lack of interest in separating different aesthetic qualities and effects from each other. Lumping together diverse sorts of untraditional "charm" under the sloppy rubric "something strange and foreign," Nanny here recalls that "general reader" whom Howells dismisses in his *Harper's Weekly* column on dialect, a philistine who neither "would nor could acquaint himself" with the differences among the various "strange locutions" to be found in written depictions of vernacular speech.[25]

Except for Tom, the Corey family fails to add to their otherwise valid panopoly of prestigious tastes an aesthetically disciplined appreciation for the flavors of the American real with which Howells's novel aligns the Laphams. From the first day that the question of the Laphams arises in the Corey family, Bromfield claims that for such representatives of what he calls "the salt of the earth" to yield *any* pleasurable "savor" to long-established society people, "some sort of sauce piquante" must be, as it were, stirred in with them (pp. 59, 122). Early in the book, Bromfield can fantastically medievalize the thought of socializing with Silas as "carousing with the boon Lapham" (p. 85). At the book's close, when the Laphams have moved safely back to Northern Vermont, Bromfield takes pleasure in (as we might put it) Norseifying them, imagining them as "far off in their native fastnesses" (p. 328).[26] But this hodgepodge of picturesquing moves becomes less accessible to Bromfield in the moment that he first learns of Tom's marriage and the long-term regular contact with the Laphams that the marriage will likely mean: "It's a perspective without a vanishing-point," he complains (p. 245). Not having cultivated any disciplined mode of taking aesthetic satisfaction in the Laphams' rawness, Bromfield is forced to recognize how close to the surface his own "core of real repugnance" is. "I find that, while my reason is . . . acquiescent," he tells Mrs. Corey, "my nerves are disposed to – excuse the phrase – kick." That Bromfield's very nerves seem to rebel – to "kick" – even against his reason emphasizes Howells's portrayal of taste as an *embodied*, and hence as a deeply characterizing, mode of relating to objects in the world. In the context of the novel, the inability of Bromfield's nerves to tolerate contact with the Laphams tells us more about his own taste limitations than it does about Silas or Persis.

"Kick" is also a colloquialism that in the late nineteenth century was still visibly tied to its rural roots (that is, balky farm animals). "Kick"'s tie with colloquial rurality explains Bromfield's awkward disowning of the term (" – excuse the phrase – ") even as he incorporates it into his speech. Bromfield's wrinkled-nose framing of this bit of Laphamesque talk contrasts with Tom and Penelope's unembarrassed liking for Silas's phrases. Just such an explicitly reluctant acceptance of the still-countrified Laphams is what Bromfield sees the Corey family facing: in the same conversation where he asks his wife to excuse the phrase "kick," he also wonders with her what "our excuse" will be for Tom's marriage to a Lapham (pp. 237–8).

It deserves strong emphasis that Howells is at pains in this novel not to generalize his indictment of Corey taste beyond its failure to acquire an appreciation for flavors of the real (again excepting Tom). For Howells, developing an aesthetic liking for the sort of "rawness" that the Laphams personify is by no means incompatible with other prestigious taste preferences, including several that fall on the side of "high culture" in a period increasingly concerned with separating high and low as part of demarcating lines of cultural authority. Howells certainly approves the Coreys' preference for the correct kinds of architecture – architecture that shows classic "Italianate" influences, such as "slender, fluted columns" and delicately molded cornices (the Corey's own house is designed "in perfect taste") (pp. 171, 175). Howells depicts positively the Corey family's ability to recognize the significance of "true . . . artistic music" (pp. 169–70). Bromfield's knowledgeable affection for how certain Italian Renaissance painters used color, not to mention his penchant for reading the highbrow *Revue des Deux Mondes*, is all to his credit on the novel's implicit cultural ledger.[27]

Howells's novel in fact might be used to further illustrate historian Lawrence Levine's most fully developed example of how late nineteenth-century America opened a "chasm" between "high" and "low" cultural experiences, which, he argues, had previously not been as clearly divided.[28] Levine shows that in the eighteenth and early nineteenth centuries Shakespeare's plays were staged all over the country, very often on the same programs with burlesque skits, comic songs, animal acts and other broadly enjoyed forms of entertainment. But during the final decades of the nineteenth century Shakespeare started to be made into "a literary classic," whose plays were more appropriately read in good editions than watched in theaters. For instance, a *Harper's Monthly* critic asserted in 1882 (just three years before Howells would start writing his "Editor's Study" columns for that magazine) that it was becoming increasingly understood "that Shakespeare off the stage is far superior to Shakespeare on the stage." Those who associated themselves with "high" culture came to scorn, as Levine puts it, the "ignorant audiences and overbearing actors" who had heretofore been the primary agents of the playwright's popularity in America.[29]

In *The Rise of Silas Lapham*, Howells has Irene tell Tom that she is "perfectly crazy" about Shakespeare and then ask him, "Weren't you perfectly astonished when you found out how many other plays of his there were? I always thought there was nothing but 'Hamlet' and 'Romeo and Juliet' and 'Macbeth' and 'Richard III' and 'King Lear' and that one that Robeson and Crane have" (p. 104). (Robeson and Crane were two popular American actors who toured the country with scenes from "A Comedy of Errors.")[30] Tom's dry response to Irene's list of Shakespearean works – "those are the ones they usually play," he says – indicates Howells's assumption that realist taste could and should go hand in hand with a high-culture recognition of Shakespeare's entire oeuvre as literary monument, rather than simple entertainment. Realist taste should be recognized, Howells wants to suggest, as one element in the period's developing repertoire of culturally prestigious aesthetic preferences.

Tom's quiet indication that he, at least, recognizes a difference between, in John Quincy Adam's phrasing, "the true Shakespeare," whom one *read*, and that "spurious Shakespeare often exhibited upon the stage,"[31] is part of the novel's insistence that Tom and Penelope, the figures the novel privileges for their realist taste, are loyal readers of the emergent high-culture canon – the same "standard authors" who are explicitly endorsed by Bromfield Corey (p. 103). By contrast to "the vast majority of people," Tom and Penelope, like Bromfield, read "with some sense of literature," which, as Tom explains, means striving always to keep, while reading, a conscious awareness both of "the difference between authors" and of the importance of "deciding upon their quality" (p. 102). The Laphams other than Penelope have no such "sense of literature." Irene "gayly" admits to Tom that, in school, she used to get major authors "mixed up with each other" (p. 103), while Persis is vaguely worried about the focused determination with which Penelope reads ("I don't want she should injure herself" [p. 123]).[32] When Irene hazards to Tom that she guesses the library in the Lapham's new house "ought to have *all* the American poets," Tom must gently correct her lack of discrimination: "Well, not all. Five or six of the best" (p. 103).

The major difference between Bromfield's self-conscious mode of reading on the one hand and Tom and Penelope's on the other is that Tom and Penelope are able to extend something very close to the admirable "sense" for literature that they share with Bromfield in directions beyond his purview. They even can extend it towards second-order signs of the Laphams' rawness, by which I mean moments where the Laphams display their own aesthetic taste. The Laphams' fondness for excessive artifice becomes, in Howells's novel, an integral, if paradoxical, facet of their "simple rude" identities. Indeed, throughout the book one indication that a character is aligned with the raw American real is that character's preference for the culturally overcooked, like Irene, who spends hours at her toilet every day, dressing not merely well but, as the narrator puts it, "too well" (p. 25). In *The Rise of Silas Lapham*, alignment *with* the simple and the natural always precludes any preferential taste *for* the simple or natural. Silas announces in the book's very first scene that he's baffled by all the fuss some city people have begun to make about preserving nature areas, "as if we were all a set of dumn Druids" (p. 14). Later, the narrator tells us that the Coreys' elegant house looks "bare to the eyes of the Laphams" (it is significant that Penelope, who can appreciate a sophisticated aesthetic of simplicity, is absent from this scene) (p. 171). Except for Penelope, the Laphams themselves prefer houses stuffed full of what Howells calls "the costliest and most abominable" of everything, and decorated with "black-walnut finish, high-studding, and cornices" (pp. 23, 36). This "crude taste" that the Laphams have, their unfailing attraction to what the narrator dubs "obstreperous pretentiousness" (pp. 31, 283), correlates with, for instance, a vulgar bookkeeper's animalistic appetite for overly complicated figures of speech: "Walker began to feed in his breaded chop with the same nervous excitement with which he abandoned himself to the slangy and figurative excesses of his talk" (p. 239).

Yet Tom Corey shifts his habitual dining hour so as to be able to lunch with and listen to this bookkeeper. So, too, Penelope Lapham likes going to the vaudeville shows that her father favors because she enjoys watching *him* "roar" at the contrived comedy (p. 258). By contrast to Irene, Penelope has "a simpler taste" in dress, yet she loves to be present at Irene's complicated costuming rituals (p. 24). When Penelope regards the "massive" "imitation" and "gilt" furnishings set next to the confused group of allegorical statues that her parents have chosen for their Boston drawing room, she gives a "smile that broke into a laugh" (pp. 196–7). Penelope and Tom both take a quiet pleasure in witnessing exercises of "crude" taste. By contrast, Bromfield and Anna Corey, Tom's parents, are almost paralyzed with discomfort the first time that they are exposed to "the full brunt" of the Laphams' home décor (p. 317). After her future in-laws visit the Lapham home, Penelope is "able to report to Corey that when she entered the room his father was sitting . . . a little tilted away from the Emancipation group, as if he expected the Lincoln to hit him . . .; and that Mrs. Corey looked as if she were not sure but the Eagle pecked" (p. 305). Just as Penelope and Tom bond over discussions of George Eliot novels, so too they bond over Penelope's report of this scene. In *Strange Gourmets*, a study exploring sophistication as such, Joseph Litvak has argued that one powerful way "to outsophisticate the other is

to incorporate . . . the other's way of incorporating."[33] The enjoyable
charge that Tom and Penelope share here derives from their merely pic-
turing together the juxtaposition of their respective parents' vastly
different aesthetics.

In these moments, Tom and Penelope's realist taste opens into a sort
of "meta-taste," a taste for tastes. Just such a proclivity for the juxtaposition of different taste universes was – and is – virtually a prerequisite
for finding pleasure in the late nineteenth-century American novel of
manners (the plural is crucial), which characteristically displays the confrontation of new cultures with longer-standing ones. Furthermore,
however, Tom and Penelope's taste for tastes, especially for tastes that are
positioned as "lower," combines with their more traditional high-culture
orientations, including the knowledge of romance languages that Tom
gets from his father's immersion in European art and literature, to make
the couple seem exactly qualified for the imperial project that they take
on at novel's end. They leave Boston for Latin America, where their task
will be to "push" US paint products. In the late nineteenth century, such
"pushing" of new markets often involved the threat or use of US military force, especially in the Southern hemisphere, but it also integrally
involved an engagement with diverse tastes and modes of consumption.
Critics have tended to read Tom and Penelope's departure for Mexico
as a mere "authorial convenience," designed to avoid portraying the
inevitable in-law messiness by placing the couple off stage "in a kind of
social limbo." Rather than a contrivance "without relevance to the basic
situation," however, I would argue that going to Mexico to "push"
American paint represents both a narratively and a historically logical
culmination of Tom and Penelope's partnership, which has all along
drawn its energy from their shared taste for tastes.[34]

"ALL THAT'S IMPOSSIBLE NOW"

The rest of this chapter will briefly consider how the category of "realist
taste" modulates in novels that Howells wrote in the years following *The
Rise of Silas Lapham*, in the late 1880s and in the 1890s. During this period,
Howells became more and more painfully conscious of facets of
American reality that he found himself compelled to regard certainly as
less "simple," but also as less "honest" and even "natural" than the vernacular figure Silas Lapham.[35] Much has been written about how
Howells's relation to both life and literature darkened after such epochal
events as the hanging of the Haymarket anarchists in 1887, which he

alone among well-known American intellectuals publicly opposed, and his daughter Winnifred's mysterious decline and then death in 1889. Howells, in Kenneth Lynn's apt term always an "ambidextrous" writer, continued to pen light farces, children's literature, and so on, but his novels showed a newly intense awareness of social and personal deformations, especially those attributable, in his view, to the shape of American capitalism.[36] These post-*Lapham* novels do continue to model for their readers an appreciation of what I have called "Laphamesque" aspects of the American "real," including regional vernaculars. But in the novels that Howells wrote during the decade after *Lapham*, the most valorized forms of cultural distinction accrue to those characters – and authorial perspectives – who establish a taste relationship with a less empirically specifiable reality, which is best characterized by abstract nouns with a component of negativity: intractability, impossibility, irony.[37]

The intractabilities, impossibilities and ironies given prominence in Howells's late 1880s and 1890s novels cluster around America's socioeconomic system, what Howells calls "our conditions." But the concrete facets of America's socioeconomic conditions that we habitually think of in conjunction with 1890s realism and naturalism – slum life, for instance, or railroads, or new commercial phenomena (department stores, futures markets) – remain much less important for Howells's later elaboration of realist taste than do the postures his characters take towards certain abstract limitations that Howells sees as accompanying modern American "conditions," such as the *impossibility* of people of different classes truly understanding one another's lives, or the unavoidable *contradictions* lived by liberal/radical intellectuals (such as Howells himself) who criticize America's socioeconomic structures even as they continue to profit from them. Such intransigent limits – on inter-class communication, on internally consistent political practice – themselves become the "real" in realist taste: by displaying what Howells presents as the only genuinely tasteful stance one can take vis-à-vis painful and insoluble American difficulties, certain privileged middle-class characters in Howells's later work accrue distinction.

As Howells found it increasingly difficult to envision positive social change actually transpiring in America, his imagination of an ethically consistent society, as well as of individuals able to live ethically consistent lives, restricted itself to the realm of admittedly utopian "fable": his writing about the imaginary land of Altruria. In his proclaimedly "realist" novels, by contrast, the question of what posture a well-intentioned middle-class intellectual should take – not so much towards any specific detail or even towards the general texture of America's social conditions as toward the abstract but ineradicable *difficulties* that these social conditions presented – came more and more to the fore. In referring to an individual's "posture" towards a "real" of perceived limitation, I mean to evoke components of taste in its most capacious sense – including, for instance, moment-by-moment orientation (that is, where and how one's attention is directed), attitudes, ways of talking, and styles of wit. Above all, I want to retain here Bourdieu's notion of "taste" as a mode of relation that accrues cultural prestige to oneself.

Everyday "lifestyle" choices, however – how one eats, dresses, shops – which Bourdieu's studies position as central to "strategies of distinction,"[38] play only a peculiarly oblique role in the realist taste elaborated by Howells's fiction. In an often-cited 1888 letter, Howells tells Henry James that now, for him, "'America'" (Howells places the proper noun inside ironizing quotation marks)

> seems to be the most grotesquely illogical thing under the sun . . . [A]fter fifty years of optimistic content with "civilization" and its ability to come out all right in the end, I now abhor it, and feel that it is coming out all wrong in the end, unless it bases itself anew on a real equality. Meantime, I wear a fur-lined over-coat, and live in all the luxury my money can buy.[39]

Certainly Howells's fur coat operates to confirm a basic difference in money and status between himself and working-class Americans. But his letter implicitly takes as its most pertinent field of comparison those who can be assumed to have more or less the same material lifestyle as Howells himself does. Rather than try to distinguish his actual consumption choices from those of his well-off peers, Howells locates the difference between himself and them in his *attitude* toward those choices. Howells admits that, like most successful late nineteenth-century Americans, he takes advantage of an unfair, unequal system and lives in all the luxury his money can buy. But, the quoted passage implicitly continues, *I* clear-eyedly recognize how my fur-lined overcoat and other consumer luxuries are possible only because of my participation in a set of sickeningly unjust socioeconomic arrangements. Not only do I recognize that truth, but I have the good taste to set up an ironic juxtaposition that underlines the discrepancy between what I profess and what I practice.[40]

Another 1888 letter, this one to Edward Everett Hale, follows a similar sequence as the letter to James, juxtaposing Howells's despair about the wrongness of American conditions with a depiction of himself taking daily practical advantage of these same wrong conditions. After first exclaiming against America's divergence from principles of equality and fairness, Howells hastens to tell Hale that "I am neither an example nor an incentive, meanwhile, in my own way of living."[41] In both of these letters, Howells uses "meantime" and "meanwhile" as hinges that place into a single temporal moment two contradictory things: one, Howells's commitment to what he called "equality," which, for him, explicitly included not only political but economic and social equality, albeit only for white men,[42] and two, his "way of living," in which he strives to acquire as much "luxury" as he can for himself and his. I do not believe that Howells calls attention to this ironic lack of fit as an indirect way of confessing that his sociopolitical convictions are shallow or insincere. Those convictions had become a centrally defining, deeply felt aspect of his identity. At the same time, Howells regarded the daily consumption patterns attaching to one's "own way of living" in much the same way that William James regarded habit: not "natural" or inborn, but almost impossible to change once fixed in place. (The committed socialist Matt Hilary in *The Quality of Mercy* comes from a wealthy family and has worn "good clothes" all his life. Therefore, although "Matt had a conscience against whatever would separate him from his kind," he "could not help" dressing and "carrying himself like a swell, for all that.")[43] The juxtaposition set up by "meantime" and "meanwhile" in both of these letters involves two aspects of Howells's life that contradict one another but that nonetheless both count as solidly *there*: his sociopolitical convictions and his everyday "way of living."[44]

Howells's letters and first-person essays of this period return again and again to the irony of this specific disjunction: "As yet I haven't got to *doing* anything, myself," he concludes yet another letter that passionately criticizes social and economic inequalities. In 1891 he writes to his father that "Elinor and I live along like our neighbors; only, we have a bad conscience."[45] One couldn't quite say that Howells's letters and first-person essays convey a "taste" for finding clashes between his own sincere convictions and his daily practices if "taste" were taken to mean that he finds such clashes directly pleasurable. Indeed, a certain degree of self-disgust is always present. One can say, however, that this writing is drawn to, hovers around, indeed seems to seek out opportunities to chew over – for by definition they can't be swallowed – irreducible discrepancies between his sociopolitical beliefs and his way of life.

Part of the reason that Howells's repeated flaggings of his own failure

to make his "words, words, words" into "things, deeds" become something other than repeated confessions of personal hypocrisy is that he
also often points toward structural impediments that no strength of individual resolve could overcome.[46] For instance, Howells venerated
Tolstoy as "the most extraordinary instance of modern times" of a comfortably established intellectual who had taken radical steps to make his
everyday life correlate with his belief in equality. Tolstoy had famously
surrendered his comfortable luxuries in order to live as a peasant. Yet
even Tolstoy, Howells emphasized, ultimately found it structurally
impossible, as a member of the well-off classes, really to "*do*" the right
thing: "Tolstoi believes unquestionably in a life of poverty and toil and
trust; but he has not been able to give up his money; he is defended
against want by the usual gentlemanly sources of income; and he lives a
ghastly travesty of his unfulfilled design."[47]

The gap between what remain the actual facts of Tolstoy's life (his
property, investments, and literary royalties are carefully tended by his
wife and agent) and Tolstoy's "design" for completely refashioning his
life in accord with his political ideals produces a "ghastly travesty." This
ghastly travesty of a design – in addition to everything else that it is –
becomes an aesthetic error. Most crucial here is that Tolstoy's aesthetically ugly mistake does not lie in the clash between what he *believes* in
doing and what he *does* do, but rather in his failure to show that he *recognizes* the inevitability of such a clash.[48]

Throughout Howells's realist novels of the 1890s, the language of aesthetic error appears when the single-minded pursuit of some social or
political vision comes up, even if, or rather especially if, the vision is one
that Howells himself sympathizes with. Most of the radical activists who
play supporting roles in these novels – both Conrad Dryfoos and Lindau
in *A Hazard of New Fortunes*, for instance, as well as Hughes in *The World
of Chance* and the Reverend Peck in *Annie Kilburn* – do not recognize the
complexities that surround their passionately pursued projects. They
thereby render themselves aesthetically "flat" – as Howells has a
painter/sculptor put it – with "no relief and no projections."[49] The
unbroken smoothness in how radical activists relate to their own political visions makes them, in the words of one of Howells's writer characters, "always the easy prey of caricature." But even without a malicious
caricaturist at hand, "real reformers" tend to seem "very like the burlesque reformers."[50] One way of understanding the challenge faced by
late 1880s and 1890s Howellsian protagonists is as how to oppose pervasive social injustices wholeheartedly without rendering themselves as

"flat" or caricature characters, which would be a stylistic error both on their own part and on the part of their realist author. Giving a character awareness of an irreconcilable division between that character's own genuinely felt political commitments and the same character's practical, everyday adherence to the status quo – a division that can then manifest itself in a self-ironic stance on the part of the character – provides an effect of internal layering that, for Howells, helps to separate psychological realism from the vulgarly simplifying genres of caricature and burlesque.

The Boston minister David Sewell, who plays a supporting role in *The Rise of Silas Lapham*, becomes the protagonist of Howells's next novel, *The Minister's Charge* (1886). *The Rise of Silas Lapham*'s closing scene had employed Sewell for a final illustration of the earlier version of realist taste that that book elaborates. After Tom and Pen have departed for Mexico, the novel moves to a sort of epilogue in which Sewell visits Lapham because of an "intense . . . interest" in "the spectacle which Lapham presented" back on the "plain" Vermont farmstead to which the bankrupt industrialist has returned.[51] Sewell's "burning desire to know exactly how" Lapham is living and feeling in this rural context (p. 321) ends the 1885 work by compactly modeling for readers a passionate but disciplined Arnoldian commitment to "see the object as in itself it really is," where the object is not a work of art but a vernacular American figure.

Yet as if undoing something that retroactively feels too pat in this closing scene of *The Rise of Silas Lapham*, *The Minister's Charge* opens with Sewell returning to Boston from deep in the New England countryside, this time "evasive" about his interaction with the farm boy Lemuel Barker. Barker, who lives in an "unpainted wooden house" and has a "granite-soul," immediately recalls the Silas Lapham whom Sewell was visiting as the previous work ended (pp. 24, 261). Yet what Sewell wishes to evade in this opening scene of *The Minister's Charge*, but almost immediately owns up to, is the hard fact that, because of their social differences, neither he nor any of his established Boston friends can really understand, communicate with, or do much to help Lemuel Barker. Sewell articulates this frustration to his wife as early as the second chapter:

If I could only have got near the poor boy . . . If I could only have reached him where he lives, as our slang says! But do what I would, I couldn't find any common ground where we could stand together. We were as unlike as if we were of two different species . . . We understand each other a little if our circumstances are similar, but if they are different all our words leave us dumb and unintelligible. (p. 26)

Sewell assigns to this distance between himself and Barker the facticity of biology itself: "as unlike as if we were two different species." The gap, he frustratedly admits, is one no mastery of American colloquialisms could help him to close. After emphasizing the gap's unyielding, irreducible nature, the central question that Sewell must then negotiate, however, is how to bear himself in relation to it. By contrast to the model provided in *The Rise of Silas Lapham*, the "real" most at issue in *The Minister's Charge* is not figured by the vernacular character Barker, but instead consists of a structural blockage that Sewell and the novel itself find in any attempt, whether by Sewell or by other "comfortable" Bostonians, to connect with Barker.[52] In the later novel, Sewell's most significant move towards a realist aesthetic does not come in some consummating moment when he sheds the picturesquing rose-colored glasses with which he had initially encountered Lemuel Barker and his farm.[53] Instead, it comes when he recognizes an inescapable lack of transparency that will always remain in his relations with Lemuel. The minister can and does shed a sequence of distorting illusions about the farm boy, but what he comes to see most clearly of all is that because of their class difference he will always wear distorting lenses of one sort or another when looking at Lemuel. Sewell's clear sense of this inevitable distortion earns him intellectual credit, both from other characters and from Howells.

The reappearance in *The Minister's Charge* of Bromfield Corey, Tom Corey's father (Tom and Penelope, we are informed, are still in Latin America, where they have already made a pile of money), helps to indicate why Sewell's developing some new parameters for what will count as "realist taste" might be desirable within the intra-class jockeying for distinction that continues to play a large role in Howells's fictional universe. Bromfield and his portly cousin Charles Bellingham (yet another figure who recurs from *The Rise of Silas Lapham*) show signs of beginning to catch on to the more straightforward version of realist taste developed in the earlier novel. The problem this presents is that, when Bromfield Corey (of all people) starts taking "delight in a bit of new slang" (p. 261), then that particular mode of aesthetic delight can no longer suffice to represent what Andrew Ross, in another context, has called "the ever-changing front of hip."[54]

In Howells's earlier novel, Bromfield mostly displayed distaste for Silas

Lapham and the vernacular American real that Silas was made to represent. Bromfield's only way of taking some incidental pleasure in Silas Lapham relied on facile picturesquing gestures. By contrast, in *The Minister's Charge* Bromfield actively cultivates a deeper, more informed taste for Lemuel Barker's Laphamesque "rustic crudity and raw youth." Bromfield goes so far as to arrange for Barker to live in his house and to read novels out loud to him, including such writers as the American regionalist Bret Harte. Bromfield "liked to hear Lemuel talk, and he used the art of getting at the boy's life by being frank with his own experience" (p. 257). Although at first he "could not repress some twinges at certain characteristics of Lemuel's accent," Bromfield soon "seemed, in a critical way, to take a fancy" to Barker's voice. In the growth of his "critical" appreciation for Barker's renditions of Bret Harte stories, Bromfield has finally come to enjoy mediated representations of American regional dialects – he has joined the group that critic James Cox, a hundred years later, would matter-of-factly refer to as "cultivated readers of dialect." Meanwhile Charles Bellingham enthusiastically explores a hospital in Boston's South End where Lemuel becomes a patient, explaining that "he had found it the thing to do – it was a thing for everybody to do; he was astonished that he had never done it before" (p. 301). In short, several of the facets of the realist taste that Tom and Penelope had modeled in Howells's 1885 novel seem, even by the 1886 *The Minister's Charge*, already to have become more generally accessible among representatives of Boston's upper-middle classes. Hence, Tom and Pen's style of realist taste has only a reduced ability, on its own, to distinguish its possessors as having a uniquely discerning aesthetic sensibility.

I suggest that the Reverend Sewell's response to the "enthusiasm" that his friends Bromfield and Bellingham come to display for Lemuel Barker – "all that's impossible now," Sewell tells them (p. 301) – is at least partly driven by cultural competitiveness.[55] For Sewell, it is not Barker, nor the rustic crudity of Barker's background, nor even the urban-poverty scenes that Barker's Boston life brings Sewell in contact with, but the *impossibility* of a meaningful relation with Barker that now constitutes the "real."[56] The minister's "charge," like the charge of several of Howells's protagonists over approximately the next ten years, is to establish a distinctive stance – distinctive, above all, relative to his nearest social competitors – towards the intransigent contradictions, the negativities that characterize modern American society.[57] After yet another frustration, Bromfield Corey confesses that he and Bellingham are utterly nonplussed by the stubborn resistances they keep encountering as they try to get closer to Barker and his life. Bromfield asks Sewell why "these things can't be managed as they are in the novels." Howells writes that all three of the men "laughed, Sewell ruefully" (p. 302). I will return in a moment to the specific importance that rueful laughs and wry smiles have for the realist posture of Howells's later protagonists, but will here point out that adding the adverbial tag "ruefully" to differentiate Sewell's laugh from that of the other two men already suggests that Sewell has a richer "take," or at least one requiring more descriptive refinement, than they do on their now jointly acknowledged inability to enter fully into Lemuel's experiences. When Bromfield Corey and Charles Bellingham realize that Sewell is correct about this "impossibility," they move on to other interests; Sewell, by contrast, turns toward the impossibility itself.

The most basic feature of realist taste as it is presented in the middle–late Howells involves just orienting one's attention toward the irreducible complexities and ironies, as such, of America's social problems.[58] Consider Basil March's interest in the violent streetcar strike that occurs in the last portion of *A Hazard of New Fortunes*. March finds the streetcar strike's "negative expressions as significant as its more violent phases." In the first weeks of the strike, March returns in office conversations to the spectacle of the State Board of Arbitration admitting itself unable to resolve the strike. When asked what he himself would do, March laughs: "Do? Nothing. Hasn't the State Board of Arbitration declared itself powerless?" (pp. 357–8). Later, March spends an afternoon wandering the streets not because he is drawn toward observing the "war" between the strikers and management but because he "interested himself in the apparent indifference of the mighty city" (p. 358). The mere turning of March's "interest" towards the strike's "negative expressions" – the big city's indifference to the strike's "riotous outbreaks"; the seeming impossibility of anyone's resolving the strike, let alone dealing with its underlying causes; and ultimately the strike's futility – itself signals a taste orientation that distinguishes him from the other middle- and upper-class characters in *Hazard*, who each toss off firm but simplistic proposals for ending the strike.[59]

March's having cultivated his attention to the frustrating negativities that American society presents comes in handy during small moments of implicit cultural competition such as, for example, when he and Isabel have to travel with the friendly but self-important Mr. Eltwin, a sort of Ohio forerunner to Sinclair Lewis's Babbit, who shares the Marches' first-class status on a boat to Europe at the start of *Their Silver Wedding*

Journey. One afternoon Basil and Mr. Eltwin find themselves together looking down over a railing at the "shabby and squalid" people in steerage. The sight makes both men somewhat uneasy, especially since they themselves have just finished lunch in the ship's "uncommonly good" first-class dining salon. As they look over the railing, March conversationally informs Eltwin that living in New York gives one "opportunities to get used to" such contrasts; March then goes "on to speak of the raggedness which often penetrated the frontier of comfort where he lived in Stuyvesant Square." Eltwin's own attempts "to have March realize the local importance he had left behind him" are here effectively outmaneuvered, as he must "restively" admit that "I don't believe I should like to live in New York much."[60]

March himself does not actively *like* living near the disturbing "frontier" between comfort and raggedness in New York's Stuyvesant Square, at least not in the same straightforward sense that Penelope Lapham's realist taste means that she *likes* hearing her vernacular father "go on." Nonetheless, the habit of smiling, even occasionally laughing, as one demonstrates one's quiet, unsurprised familiarity with just *how* intransigent American problems are, constitutes another defining component of the realist taste that Howells's later novels elaborate. The rueful but nonetheless "amused" smiles issued by Basil March, David Sewell, *Annie Kilburn's* Dr. Morrell, and other Howells protagonists of the period must be differentiated from the "flippant gayety" that characterizes vulgar newspaper reporting about social problems. In Boston newspapers such as the *Sunrise*, as Sewell explains to his wife, such gaiety is "odious" because of how it minimizes the seriousness of urban tragedies. Where news reporters' tones of flippant gaiety seem of a piece with how their coverage often "rather blinked" the city's truly "worst cases," the wry smiles of Sewell, March, and Morrell attest to the clear-eyedness that they bring to hard realities (*Novels, 1886–1888*, p. 75).

When a sick and poor infant whom Annie Kilburn had philanthropically sent to the seaside dies there instead of getting better, Annie "hysterically" announces to Dr. Morrell that she is a "murderess." Dr. Morrell's "severity" with Annie soon modulates towards a sort of rigorous pleasure as he tries to make her see that there was *nothing* that anyone could have done for the sick baby. Given all of the medical factors involved, she has no reason to blame herself so excessively. He "allowed himself to smile" when he comes to the end of his explanation, and then to "smile once more, and, at some permissive light in her face, he began even to laugh": "All the tears in the world wouldn't help; and my laughing hurts nobody. I'm sorry for you, and I'm sorry for the mother, but I've told you the truth – I have indeed; and you *must* believe me" (pp. 748–9). Especially when placed next to Annie's "reeling" and "hysteric" reaction, Dr. Morrell's repeated smile and then his laugh suggest more than the superiority of his medical knowledge. The smile and concluding laugh operate here as a bodily index of the balance and perspective Morrell brings to bear on the "sorry" situation (a sick baby whom nothing could have saved, a ridiculously self-accusing woman), a situation whose painful "truth" (in his word) he sees both steadily and whole. In addition, Morrell's insistence that his laughing has no functional consequences, that it cannot make any sort of positive or negative impact on the situation, helps to give his laugh something of the feel of a specifically aesthetic judgment in the sense that Kant elaborates – Dr. Morrell's laugh announces itself as transpiring in a "pure" realm, detached from instrumental motivations or effects.

CONTINGENCY, IRONY, AND CONJUGALITY

It is Basil March, whom Howells recalls from his initial appearance in *Their Wedding Journey* (1872) to serve as organizing consciousness in several 1890s works, who best demonstrates different possibilities for accruing cultural prestige by weaving several various versions of realist taste together, as well as by adding these different versions of realist taste to more conventionally prestigious "high culture" tastes. As a couple, Basil and his wife Isabel take "credit to themselves" for Europeanized preferences in literature and the visual arts, "tastes which they had not always been able to indulge, but of which they felt that the possession reflected distinction on them." Their home contains more "good pictures" and books than the Marches can afford, but they feel, "with a glow almost of virtue, how perfectly it fitted their lives and their children's . . . that somehow it expressed their characters – that it was like them" (pp. 22–3). Yet Howells implies that, within certain social strata in both Boston and New York, these sorts of claims to "distinction" have become somewhat trite: just about everyone in the circles that Howells characteristically portrays seeks to distinguish his or her taste and self from those whom Matthew Arnold called philistines, and whom *A Hazard of New Fortunes* refers to as "the vast prosperous commercial class, with unlimited money and no ideals that money could not realize . . . the culture that furnishes showily" (p. 262). Describing what he aptly calls a "culture boom" in late nineteenth-century America, Jonathan Freedman has noted

an increasing public awareness of, and interest in, high culture – not only high culture conceived as a magisterial space of aesthetic contemplation, but also high culture experienced as a site of intense social competition. What was at stake in this competition, of course, was a sense of cultural competence; being cognizant of or versed in the works privileged by the gentry provided a power-ful means for the newer elites to grant themselves an equivalent status.[61]

Howells depicts, for instance, a virtual industry in art courses taught by European-trained artists and enrolled in by the wives and daughters of economically successful men who wish to transcend mere showiness. As earlier moments in this chapter have pointed out, Howells's work does indeed still participate in the large-scale project of the late nine-teenth century's upper-middle and upper classes of using canonically defined "high culture" to demarcate lines of cultural distinction. At the same time, however, Howells also presents additional taste strategies for accruing specialized forms of distinction *within* those upper-middle and upper-class strata. Such strategies operate on the same "battlefield," as Freedman describes it, "of high-cultural tastemaking."[62] The Marches' appreciation for fine art does enable "them to look down upon those who were without such tastes" for European painting and literature, that is, philistines (*A Hazard of New Fortunes*, p. 23). But the Marches' complex of tastes also includes specifically realist tastes that help them – especially Basil, as I will argue below – to stand out even from those who share their Europeanized appreciation of high art, such as, for example, the social-ite Mrs. Horn, who always invites a well-chosen selection of artists to her parties, or Kendricks, the young literary reviewer from a good family.

When Fulkerson, in *A Hazard of New Fortune*'s opening paragraph, says to March, "You ain't an insurance man by nature. You're a natural-born literary man; and you've been going against the grain," his portrayal of March's through-and-through literary disposition as alienating him from the philistine world of the insurance business (where March has been earning his living) touches a deep part of March's own self-image. But it also follows what Howells had come to recognize as a rather well-beaten path to claims of specialness, especially since Matthew Arnold's works had become so widely influential in America.[63] What distin-guishes Basil and Isabel March from the book's several other high-culture mavens who are eager to separate themselves from the stereotypical philistine is, first, the pleasure that the Marches take in

Fulkerson's use of American colloquialisms such as, in the above passage alone, "ain't," "natural-born," and "going against the grain." Throughout the book the Marches make teasing fun of, but also enjoy quoting, anticipating, and playfully experimenting with the plethora of vernacular Americanisms that issues from Fulkerson's mouth.

The book's setting in New York City offers the Marches special opportunities to evoke simultaneously aspects both of their Arnoldian high-culture tastes and of their realist tastes. On their cook's scheduled day off, the Marches become American literature's first – but by no means last – professional-class New Yorkers to make their knowledge of the city's cheap ethnic restaurants into a point of pride. Thus in Greenwich Village's immigrant Italian neighborhood, "the flavor of olives, which, once tasted, can never be forgotten" enables them to recollect their high-culture tours of Italy (where, no doubt, they acquired some of the afore-mentioned "good pictures" that hang on their walls) even as they pursue their newer cultural project of becoming "adept" in the diverse lifestyles of the city's poorer neighborhoods (p. 256).[64] Similarly overlapping two taste categories, March's renewed relationship with Lindau, his boyhood tutor in German literature, allows him to showcase his longstanding love for the German High Romantics, especially Goethe, who were so pre-stigious in late nineteenth-century Anglo-American culture, at the same time as the mixed "ethnical character" of Lindau's Mott Street neigh-borhood inspires him to compose a series of New York "local studies" for magazine publication.[65]

I want to conclude this chapter by considering how certain of March's jokes, especially what Isabel calls his "self-satires," signal the taste rela-tionship that March develops with the particular negative knowledge about American reality that Howells poses as most difficult to grasp: knowledge about the contingency of social conditions that seem natural. March issues a characteristic "smile" on an occasion when Fulkerson gets especially carried away and his "talk" starts to mix, willy-nilly, "American slang with the jargon of European criticism."[66] Here, March's smile indicates not simply his own pleasure in being able to rec-ognize and appreciate both European-flavored high-art speech and American slang, nor merely a sense of superiority at how Fulkerson can't quite keep these two discourses straight. Rather, March enjoys how Fulkerson's comical "mixture" of discourses foregrounds each *as* a dis-course, a "jargon" – as opposed to some sort of natural language with a direct relation to the world. Richard Rorty's *Contingency, Irony, Solidarity* has recently offered the useful definition of "ironist" as someone who recognizes the "contingency" not only of other people's or other cultures' "vocabularies" – by which Rorty means their entire discursive systems, including central values and beliefs – but of his or her own "vocabulary." For Rorty, the ironist realizes that all facets of a given culture, from language to widely accepted social practices to a specific individual's deepest commitments, are *contingent*. That is, they are produced by multiple factors of history and chance and hence cannot be legitimately grounded either in universal nature, in the supernatural realm (God), or in abstractions such as absolute justice.[67] Howells, I believe, makes it possible to recognize how the specific sort of ironic worldview that Rorty describes (and unironically privileges) can itself constitute a bid for intellectual distinction.

Basil March displays a taste – to which Howells attaches cultural prestige – for this sort of irony. More specifically, he displays a taste for contingency, which becomes American society's bottom-line "real" for him in two senses. First Basil recognizes, unlike any other characters in the novel, that social practices and beliefs, including his own, *really* are contingent all the way down – and thus that they might have been constituted differently.[68] When *A Hazard of New Fortune*'s German revolutionary Lindau demands of Basil, "How much money can a man honestly earn without wronging or oppressing some other man?" Basil answers in English, "I should say about five thousand dollars a year." He then adds, "I name that figure because it's my experience that I never could earn more; but the experience of other men may be different" (p. 166). "Amused," Basil admits that his answer to Lindau's earnestly objective question is inevitably shaped by contingent factors in his own personal history. Basil enjoys suggesting that if he had ever happened to have a slightly better year selling insurance or editing a magazine, the figure he would name as the most a man "might honestly earn" would undoubtedly be that much higher. A moment after answering Lindau, Basil "laughed outright." His laugh registers both the pleasure that Basil takes in emphasizing the contingency underlying his own answer to Lindau – that is, Basil's taste for irony in Rorty's sense of the term – and also the difference between Basil's own cultivated capacity to appreciate this contingency and Lindau's ardent belief in absolute truth.

Basil does not find quite the same sort of pleasurable amusement in calling attention to a second sense of contingency's realness, but he nonetheless often returns, with a rueful smile, to the paradoxical fact that identifying something as contingent does not give it any less practical solidity or weight. Recognizing a practice or belief as contingently,

rather than metaphysically, grounded does not make it any less real on
a pragmatic level, even for Basil himself. When Basil and Isabel's apart-
ment-hunt takes them through an impoverished quarter, Isabel
announces to him, "I don't believe there's any *real* suffering – not real
suffering – among those people; that is, it would be suffering from our
point of view, but they've been used to it all their lives, and they don't
feel their discomfort so much" (emphasis in original). Basil responds with
an exaggerated promptness: "I shall keep that firmly in mind" (p. 60).
Isabel is practicing what Wai-chee Dimock has aptly dubbed the nineteenth-century's "magical calculus" of pain, whereby those social
groups who have the most to suffer are considered to be, luckily for all
concerned, the least sensitive to such suffering.[69] The "self-satire" of
Basil's response to Isabel marks his more distanced relation to this
magical calculus, his willingness to see that indeed it is a piece of hocus-
pocus, derived only from a wish to curtail a feeling of what Dimock calls
"moral liability" for the suffering of the poor.[70] At the same time as Basil
points with irony to the contingent *motivations* of this self-deluding belief,
however, he makes at least as much practical *use* of it as Isabel or any of
his middle-class peers do. He makes it plain that he sees no choice but
still to *act* as if this magical calculus were absolutely objective. Its grounding in contingent ideological needs, rather than in neutral science,
doesn't give the magical gesture of *"they* don't feel it as *we* would" any
less practical force for him. Even as he points to the gesture's hocus-
pocus dimension, Basil turns with Isabel to go "home to their hotel"
(p. 60).

By contrast to Basil, Isabel March can never quite grasp this paradoxical aspect of contingency's realness. She can never quite grasp that
something's being contingent does not make it any less weighty, solid, or
real on a practical level. On those few occasions when she does get a
glimpse of the contingency of something whose natural, common-sense
status she had not previously thought of questioning, she then blithely
thinks that its contingency means it can just be swept away and replaced.
For instance, when Isabel has a moment of realizing that certain individual cases of poverty she sees in New York result from larger socioeconomic "conditions" in America that might theoretically be different,
she exclaims "Then we must change the conditions" (p. 61). (At a similar
moment in *Annie Kilburn*, Annie becomes so excited at the mere thought
of making a difference in painful social conditions that she behaves "like
a young girl with an invitation to a ball" [p. 748]). Basil's response to
Isabel, "Oh no; we must go to the theater and forget them. We can stop

at Brentano's for our tickets as we pass through Union Square," constitutes a realer-than-thou gesture (p. 61). His remark implies that he has
long noted what Isabel has only just discovered, that America's socioeconomic conditions are "really" contingent, instead of natural or universal.[71] Yet he also indicates that he has been able to accept a second, even
more difficult, reality: that is, simply recognizing that they are contingent does not make the conditions themselves any less there, any less
certain, any less stable.

Basil's implicit shrug of the shoulders here signifies his own sophisticated familiarity with the paradox of contingency's realness, even as the
lightly self-mocking aspect of his tone shows that he has the good taste
not to brag about his epistemological superiority in such a painful
matter. Moreover, although Basil's self-mockery does at least in part
derive from genuine frustration at what seems to him the impossibility
of doing anything to "change the conditions," his emphasis on the
impossibility of positive intervention, like Dr. Morrel's laugh that "hurts
nobody," has the effect of locating his attitude – indeed, his and Isabel's
whole conversation – in the realm of the aesthetic. Just as he presumably
would have done anyway, even had he not paused to nod at the contingency of American social conditions, Basil goes off to the theater that
evening.[72] There, he does "forget" about America's socioeconomic
inequalities, just as most of the theater's audience no doubt does. Unlike
the rest of the audience, however, Basil has earlier shown both Isabel and
the reader that he recognizes his "forgetting" as neither natural nor necessary. He "forgets" as the rest of the audience does, but he implicitly
claims credit for a more sophisticated stance toward that forgetting.

If, as Kenneth Lynn claims, *A Hazard of New Fortunes* constitutes "the
most revealing study ever made of sentimental American liberalism,"[73]
it is important to recognize that Basil both exemplifies the failings of
such liberalism and, simultaneously, himself accrues the realist intellectual credit of recognizing those failings. For Richard Rorty, the motivat-
ing crux of modern liberal commitments is "the imaginative ability to
see strange people as fellow sufferers." Therefore, anything that helps to
increase "our sensitivity to the particular details of the pain and humil-
iation of other, unfamiliar sorts of people" forwards the spread of liberalism, which is why Rorty celebrates imaginative literature.[74] Yet
Howells's late 1880s and 1890s novels have the effect, we might say, of
increasing our imaginative ability to see why someone such as Basil
March could come to have a keen sense that "unfamiliar sorts of people"
are suffering but still end up not trying to do much of anything about it

(such a person might even possess the "extraordinary moral sensibility and empathic imagination" that Edwin Cady ascribes to Howells himself).[75] Moreover, Howells uses Basil March to demonstrate how the very moment of empathizing with someone else's suffering ("I feel your pain") can be combined with a clear-eyed articulation of the structural impediments to taking action against the underlying causes, such that the combination yields a margin of intellectual prestige.[76]

Isabel's straight-man role in her interchange with Basil about American "conditions" is symptomatic: although she shares most of Basil's superior tastes for literature and art, and even acquires a competent ability to appreciate Fulkerson's American slang, Isabel is excluded from her husband's appreciation of the paradoxical realness of contingency. Indeed, she functions as a near-at-hand surrogate for those social peers of Basil who do not match his orientation towards this most difficult object of realist taste. By never smiling at contingency, Isabel helps to make Basil's taste for it more sharply defined. Howells's famous portrayals of professional-class marriages are permeated, in his late 1880s and 1890s novels, by scenes that stage contrasting relations to sociopolitical contingency. Much of the banter in which his husbands and wives – especially his husbands – take such endless low-key pleasure involves the wives' inability to see that truth is always "coloured and heated" by one's perspective, as Dr. Morrell smilingly explains to Annie Kilburn shortly before they marry: "I suppose no man, except the kind of man that a woman would be if she were a man – excuse me, Annie – is ever absolutely right" (*Novels, 1886–1888*, p. 845). Performing an important conjugal service, wives embody a contrasting exhibit for readers as Howells's husbands demonstrate their appreciation of contingency and irony. More obviously (and comically) than any one else, Howells's wives circumstantially shape and reshape their own convictions of what's true but without ever showing awareness that their convictions are not fixed.[77] The Reverend Sewell replies "you've got them" when his wife exclaims, "I can't think of what's become of your principles, my dear." "I really believe I have," she responds, "with that full conviction of righteousness which her sex alone can feel" (*Novels, 1886–1888*, p. 302).

Both Michael Davitt Bell and Scott Derrick have recently argued that, anxious about prevalent cultural assumptions in nineteenth-century America that linked artistic activity with femininity, male realists such as Howells strove to construct their own writing as what Bell calls "masculine realism." Bell emphasizes a continuity between the "cult of virility" that was developing in turn-of-the-century America and Howells's attempts to associate the realist, by contrast to the stereotypically effeminate artist, with "'masculine' normalcy." For Bell, "it requires no great leap to get from Howells . . . to a writer like Ernest Hemingway, with his compulsion to conceal 'artistic' sensitivity and true concern for style under a near-burlesque exterior of aggressive masculinity."[78] To fully understand the realist masculinity that emerges in Howells's writing of the late 1880s and the 1890s, however, one must note the privileged stature that Howells accords to that masculinity's repeated turn towards, even taste for, insoluble social and personal difficulties. Indeed, it is here that one can best grasp the line connecting the complex realist masculinity of a Basil March with the only seemingly simpler modernist virility of Hemingway's Jake Barnes or Nick Adams. A key part of the masculinity of Hemingway's male protagonists is their special, and often paralyzing, insight regarding the unfixable brokenness of both self and world.

Consider the unusually vitriolic review that Howells wrote after seeing Sarah Bernhardt's portrayal of Hamlet. Howells finds Bernhardt most to have "profaned" and "denatured" Hamlet's "vital essence" in her failure to capture what Howells calls "the large vibration of that tormented spirit."[79] Howells's review does draw from the vocabulary of masculine virility, but the "large" vibrating phallus that his language seems to accuse Bernhardt of castrating (of denaturing) is Hamlet's striking awareness of his impotence to resolve the tragic circumstances that define his own position. Hamlet's "tormented" awareness of his own impotence, including his awareness of the complications that continually prevent him from acting as he believes he should, are, for Howells, the "essence" of Hamlet's masculinity: "Hamlet is in nothing more a man than in the things to which as a man he found himself unequal; for as a woman he would have been easily superior to them. If we could suppose him a woman as Mme. Bernhardt . . . invites us to do, we could only have supposed him to have solved his perplexities with the delightful precipitation of his putative sex."[80] Rather than a blithe feminine dismissal, the version of realist masculinity that Howells privileges "vibrates" in tune with the immense "perplexities" inherent in an American society where so much (as in Denmark) is rotten. It can be said of Howellsian realist protagonists such as Basil March and the Reverend Sewell that, like Hamlet, they are "in nothing more" men than in their constant (sometimes tormented, but sometimes merely rueful) awareness of all that blocks them, internally and externally, from taking effective action.

CHAPTER TWO

The "facts of physical suffering," the literary intellectual, and The Wings of the Dove

Early in *The Wings of the Dove*, Kate Croy's Aunt Maud Lowder and Milly Theale's chaperone, Susan Shepherd Stringham, have a conversation about Merton Densher. In the words of Aunt Maud, whose "money and morality" make her the novel's embodiment of institutionalized judgment, Densher is "not good enough for my niece, and he's not good enough for you."[1] Densher is a journalist and would-be novelist, who has been raised "in strange countries, in twenty settlements of the English" and educated always "at the smallest cost, in the schools nearest; which was also a saving of railway fares" (p. 115). Although Mrs. Lowder and Mrs. Stringham decide to leave "in question – what Merton Densher 'in himself' was," he does fall definitively outside of the "great man" that Mrs. Lowder wants Kate to marry (pp. 327, 109). The novel repeatedly emphasizes that the wealthy Mrs. Lowder would accept as "great" a man who possesses either money or public status. Densher's problem is that he possesses neither.

Densher, as James writes, is "at all events, not the man wholly to fail of comprehension." He recognizes that "it was the plain truth: he *was* – on Mrs. Lowder's basis, the only one in question – a very small quantity" (p. 109). But by the close of the novel, as Kate informs him, he's "squared" Aunt Maud (p. 461). Densher has developed another "basis" for distinction, one which Mrs. Lowder respects even if she doesn't fully understand it. I will argue here that Densher's new cultural status derives from the paradoxical relation to Milly Theale's fatal disease that he elaborates, and that it represents an alternative version of the same realist prestige that chapter 1 discusses. Key characters in Howells's writing model "realist taste" in a manner that, as it were, proffers its various modes for adoption by members of his reading public. Indeed, the new forms of cultural distinction that Howells's novels elaborate come with the democratic scaffolding of their implied availability for any middle-class readers who can grasp them – cultivating realist taste would not even require any significant change in one's everyday lifestyle. The realist prestige that Densher develops in *The Wings of the Dove*, by contrast, centers on the utter uniqueness of Densher's relation with what that novel positions as the most really real, Milly's fatal illness. Taking off from the Romantic idea of the alienated artist, Densher's realist disposition defines itself against the experiences, reactions and orientations even of those characters within the novel whose approving recognition first ratifies his new status. The prestige that these characters (and, as we will see, many critics) accord Densher is, as James puts it, "all his own" (p. 502).

During the course of the novel, Densher arrives at a remarkably attuned grasp of Milly's "incurable pain," which stems from his high degree of felt connection with it (p. 441). His mode of apprehending her physical and mental suffering differs, however, from that of a scientific or medical professional. First, Densher pointedly does not seek the stance of emotional balance and objectivity that was becoming central to the professional personae of doctors around the turn of the century, and which is embodied in James's novel by the eminent specialist Sir Luke Strett. Second, he continually conveys that his unique relation to Milly's "consciousness, tortured, for all he knew, crucified by its pain" has come without any direct study, examination, or other purposeful effort on his part (p. 466). To that extent, it preserves a certain "amateur" status. Densher's understanding of Milly's experience differs also, moreover, from the "sympathy" associated with the sentimental tradition. It differs both from sentimental sympathy's unstinting desire for closeness to the suffering other as well as from the sentimental imperative towards open displays of strong feeling.[2] As I will be arguing below, Densher's most characteristic moves throughout the novel comprise his attempts to limit and channel his indeed unparalleled connection to Milly's "disintegration." Above all, however, by contrast both to sentimentalism and to the newly dominant canons of medical and scientific professionalism, Densher explicitly strives throughout to maintain targeted areas of determined ignorance about Milly, and especially about "the manner of her so consciously and helplessly dying" (p. 452).

Densher's paradoxical engagement with, yet also rigorously maintained ignorances about, Milly and her "facts of physical suffering" (p. 441) is responsible for his movement from a "not quite nobody" (p. 326) who cannot answer the implicit question posed him by Aunt Maud's very house – "what do you offer, what do you offer?" (p. 270) – into the possessor of a unique aura, which, as Aunt Maud herself intimates to him, will only continue "quite richly to ripen" (p. 464). What specific character does this aura have? Historian Thomas Haskell has argued that "disinterestedness" was "the central tenet" of Progressive America's ideology (one could almost say idolatry) of professional expertise.[3] Densher, however, helps to indicate some of the nuanced differences possible within this culturally privileged notion. He achieves a complexly paradoxical version of disinterestedness that, I would contend, is specific to literary realism's "realist dispositions." It is vividly articulated in the claim that James would later make for his own relation to the American scene, which consists, he says, of "that last disinterestedness which consists of one's getting away from one's subject by plunging into it, for sweet truth's sake, still deeper."[4] Here, in contrast to the positivist detachment of doctors, scientists or social scientists, the Jamesian "analyst" flamboyantly foregrounds his own cognitive and emotional involvement with his "subject." But rather than signifying any loss of his own autonomous status, as his language would initially seem to suggest, the personal immersion coloring this analyst's relation to his "subject" allows him to claim a more advanced form of detachment, and hence to claim a disinterestedness that ultimately is superior to all others ("that last disinterestedness . . .").

THE FACTS OF PHYSICAL SUFFERING

The new status that Densher achieves derives from the structure and the texture of his relation to Milly's experience of her illness, but only insofar as Milly's experience itself comes to count as the book's "greatest reality," as what the novel designates "the utter reference," that to which all else in the book refers. The details, the symptoms, and the course of Milly's disease, even its name, are alike left out of the text and out of the otherwise voluminously filled consciousnesses of its characters.[5] Yet despite our never learning how or where Milly hurts, her "facts of physical suffering" figure in several different ways as the most bottom-line level of reality in the world of the novel. It is because of the irrefragable reality attached to it that Milly's suffering presents Densher with what James calls "one of those chances for good taste, possibly even for the play of the best in the world . . . that are absolutely to be jumped at from the moment they make a sign" (pp. 35–6). Densher very pointedly makes no direct effort to achieve his nearness to Milly's experience, just as Basil March has not actively *sought* to live next to the ragged frontier of poverty in New York's Stuyvesant Park neighborhood. Nonetheless, the propinquity of both men to a site marked as overwhelmingly real proves essential to their elaborations of the "realist dispositions" that each of their respective novels will privilege.

Yet if Milly's "incurable pain" yields virtually no external signs (as Kate says, Milly does not "smell, as it were, of drugs . . . taste, as it were, of medicine" [p. 284]), then how does her pain come to take on the "intense" sense of material presence that it does? Milly's illness accrues much of the feeling of size, density, and identity-constituting force that is initially located in her "immense" fortune (p. 167). From early in the novel, the most visible dimension of Milly is her wealth, making of her a "princess," who is celebrated in "effigies, processions" (p. 164). It is "beyond everything . . . the mass of money so piled on the girl's back" that places her "on a scale and with a sweep that . . . required the greater stage" (p. 123). The "intense" "vision of her money" possessed by all of the characters in the novel (p. 346) turns Milly into a spectacle for the "flagrant" London tourists at Matcham to file by and view as naturally as, if more avidly than, they view the famous house itself (p. 194). With most "awfully rich young American[s]," the money would also make her, as the Matcham tourists assume, "by all accounts nice to know" (p. 195). Kate has earlier noticed, however, that one may *see* Milly "more than one sees almost anyone, but then one discovers that that isn't knowing her and that one may know better a person whom one doesn't 'see,' as I say, half so much" (p. 276; James's italics). Kate's observation points to, although it doesn't enter, the "extremely private" dimension of Milly that is her "incurable pain" (p. 353). These two most important elements of Milly's "situation" – her visibly vast wealth and her invisible but fatal disease, what Kate later registers as "the felt contrast between her fortune and her fear" (p. 340) – are constantly opposed, both by James's preface and by the novel itself. Ultimately, this opposition works to transfer the representational plenitude of Milly's wealth to her "invisible experience of physical suffering" (I borrow this phrase from Elaine Scarry's powerful *The Body in Pain*).[6] The transferring of the novel's locus of overwhelmingly forceful "reality" from Milly's "mass of money" to her private experience of illness is especially accelerated as her pain again and again shows itself to play a more materially determining role in her life than her wealth ever could.

In his 1908 preface, James says that he conceived the "dazzlingly" wealthy American girl, the "heir of all the ages," as bringing with her character "a strong and special implication of liberty, liberty of action, of choice, of appreciation, of contact – proceeding from sources that provide better for large independence, I think, than any other conditions in the world" (p. 38). "One would see her then," James explains, "as possessed of all things, all but the single most precious assurance" (p. 38). The absence of that single assurance, health, however, has the power so strongly to compress Milly's "range," to erode her "large independence," that the "all things" the rich Milly originally possesses shrink to the any and every "object the grasp of which might make for delay" in James's striking figure for his situation's "drama": "She had been given me from far back as contesting every inch of the road, as catching at every object the grasp of which might make for delay, as clutching these things to the last moment of her strength" (p. 39). Densher himself compares the fatally ill Milly to "some noble young victim of the scaffold, in the French Revolution, separated at the prison-door from some object clutched for resistance" (p. 468). Like Milly, the young noble clutches "some object" as a material vestige reminding him of the materially replete existence that he is on the verge of being forced to surrender even beyond its most fundamental element, his sentient body. Kate, early on sensing "the truth that was truest about Milly," tells Densher, paradoxically it seems to him at the time, that the rich girl "has nothing" (pp. 440, 283).

Milly's illness dramatically curtails the power and usefulness to her of her money and of her many material possessions. It thereby comes to usurp for itself the tangibility previously belonging to her fortune. John Goode's observation that "the effect of making Milly ill is to dramatize more actively the potentiality of her wealth" should be inverted: Milly's wealth illumines the material force of her illness.[7] In Book Three, Susan Stringham marvels over the pervasive signifying effects of Milly's wealth:

A less vulgarly, a less obviously purchasing or parading person she couldn't have imagined; but it prevailed even as the truth of truths that the girl couldn't get away from her wealth . . . it was in the fine folds of the helplessly expensive little black frock that she drew over the grass as she now strolled vaguely off; it was in the curious and splendid coils of hair . . . it lurked between the leaves of the uncut but antiquated Tauchnitz volume . . . She couldn't dress it away, nor walk it away, nor read it away, nor think it away; she could neither smile it away in any dreamy absence nor blow it away in any softened sigh. She couldn't have lost it if she had tried – that was what it was to be really rich. It had to be *the* thing you were. (p. 133)

But in James's image quoted above, Milly's final "grasp" and "clutch" of objects indicates how far "the road" whose every inch she contests will penetrate the folds and layers of material possessions that have heretofore defined her most inescapable reality. The "road," her illness, slices through the frock that shelters her body, through her elaborate hair coils, through even the leisure-implying paperback book that Milly carries around. Finally, her illness will cut through even the Venetian *palazzo* that Milly chooses as "the ark of her deluge." Although the ancient *palazzo*, "with all its romance and art and history" may seem to Milly to "set up a whirlwind around her that never dropped for an hour" (pp. 342, 361), still the illness will pave over it too – until the illness becomes "*the* thing" she is.[8] One realizes, then, that there is an ominous foreshadowing in the distinction Susan Stringham draws between Aunt Maud, who "sat somehow in the midst of her money, founded on it and surrounded by it" and Milly, "far away on the edge of it . . . you hadn't, as might be said, in order to get at her nature, to traverse, by whatever avenue, any piece of her property" (p. 181). Milly has already ceded so many inches, feet and yards to her illness that she teeters at the very edge of her material demesne.

Milly's illness assumes her money's previous status as "*the* thing" (p. 133, James's italics). It acquires the irrefutable presence, the space-occupying bulk, previously lodged in her "immense wealth." In a converse movement, her physical suffering further gains the status of "greatest reality" in the novel's world through an alignment that James sets up between the illness and the slum conditions whose determinations of character and narrative among the poor several of his naturalist contemporaries (including, for instance, Crane, Norris, and London) were exploring. James was and is often criticized for his apparent lack of interest – with a few vexed exceptions, such as *The Princess Casamassima* – in depicting the living conditions of turn-of-the-century poor people.[9] Yet in *The Wings of the Dove* he purposefully makes the effects of Milly's illness resonate with the sort of structurally inescapable poverty portrayed in such gritty texts as Crane's *Maggie: a Girl of the Streets*. Milly's experience of her illness thereby takes on some of the hard-edged realness that much literary discourse of the period, whether approvingly or disapprovingly, associated with slums.[10]

Milly first becomes certain that she is fatally ill in a decisive scene that James places in a "shabby" section of Regent's Park, which occurs almost exactly in the middle of *The Wings of the Dove*. Milly has just been for her second visit to London's most famous physician, Sir Luke Strett. Taking to an extreme the medical profession's assumption that knowledge properly belongs with the doctor, not the patient, Strett has continued to avoid telling her directly what he thinks of her condition. In answer to Milly's questions about her state, he has merely announced to her that one can always live if one wants to enough. When she reaches the park, Milly recalls the truism that she has always assumed about the poor – that they "could live if they would; that is, like herself, they had been told so: she saw them all about her . . . digesting the information" (p. 215). Thinking over her visit with her doctor, however, Milly gradually recognizes in this scene that, although Strett's words to her may seem "superficially . . . striking," they are like the "information" that the poor are asked to "digest" (as if instead of more substantial provisions). Milly decides that for the poor, as for herself, the truism's inverse has more pertinence: "they would live if they could." Milly is suddenly hit by a sense of herself as "just in the same box" with the slum inhabitants who surround her: "Their box, their great common anxiety, what was it, in this grim breathing space, but the practical question of life?" She then perceives as "a wave" the unspoken truth of her illness "directly divesting, denuding, exposing" (pp. 214–18).[11]

Before leaving the park, Milly "looked about her again, on her feet, at her scattered melancholy comrades – some of them so melancholy as to be down on their stomachs in the grass, turned away, ignoring, burrowing" (p. 217). The image evokes a graveyard. London's poor, scattered on their stomachs in the grass and burrowing, are not only "turned away" from injunctions to live but, foreshadowing Milly's own final days, during which, as Susan Stringham famously puts it, Milly has "turned her face to the wall," the poor seem actually turned into the ground (p. 421). It is at the beginning of this same paragraph that Milly "had been asking herself why, if her case was *grave* – and she knew what she meant by that – he [Sir Luke] should have talked to her at all about what she might with futility 'do'" (p. 217; my italics). If the "same box" Milly and London's poor share are different versions of the grave, different versions of material conditions so constraining as to negate "the practical question of life," one might indeed ask Milly's naturalist question of why anyone should talk about what they "might, with futility, 'do.'"[12]

THE REAL, THE RIGHT STILLNESS

How does Merton Densher make his own relation to Milly's "incurable pain" – to, that is, the novel's "greatest reality" – yield him a new cultural prestige, one that is registered by observers both inside and outside the book? In the novel's final scene, Densher fails to accept the "stupendous" fortune Milly has left him and, in so doing, also lets Kate Croy go

(p. 507). Commentators, beginning with James's own notebook entries from before he wrote the novel, have tended to perceive this as the moment when Densher finally achieves an ethically creditable position, which at least partly redeems his culpable willingness to allow Milly to think that he loves her in the service of Kate's and his "scheme" to get Milly's money. (Their "'game' as they say" has been for Milly to fall in love with and marry Densher so that when Milly dies her fortune will make it possible for Densher and Kate, who will have been secretly engaged all along, to marry each other [p. 436].) According to various of the book's critics, the final scene demonstrates that Densher has undergone a "change," a "conversion," a "transformation," a saving "upheaval," which is thus an "initiation . . . into the possibilities of a totally different mode of conduct."[13] If, in Densher's own "recovered sense" of his encounter with Milly, "he had been . . . forgiven, dedicated, blessed" (*Wings*, p. 469), many of his readers have agreed: Dorothea Krook writes that Densher has "been moved to repentance and expiation,"[14] while, for Peter Brooks, "Merton Densher's refusal to take Milly's legacy . . . achieves the status of a moral imperative."[15] David McWhirter's existential reading sees Densher as having at last attained "a full and responsible acceptance of the fateful power resident in his own acts and choices . . ."[16] The novel's last scene thus seems to have resolved very much to Densher's credit what James's initial introduction of him had noted as still uncertain: "the question of the final stamp, the pressure that fixes the value" (p. 86).

As ironic as some of them ultimately do judge Densher's "spiritual victory" to be[17] – given, that is, that Milly has already died, and died knowing of Densher's deceit – readers who find value in Densher's final stance have failed to recognize what its most significant meaning is. Even James's own early vision of the novel, in notebook entries, seems initially to have conceived of Densher's final stance as representing a break with his disingenuously selfish behavior, which most of the book would subtly yet incisively expose.[18] When it came to writing the novel's final scene, however, James made the *form* of Densher's reaction to Milly's gift follow exactly the *form* of the rest of his behavior. Throughout the novel, as at its close, virtually all of Densher's effective actions take the form of his being still, waiting, or "doing nothing." His final "action" itself, his failure to accept the money, consists of his statement to Kate, "I do nothing." Rather than officially declining the bequest, he will not even acknowledge having received notification of it. He repeats, "I do nothing formal" (p. 506). The "intensity" that pervades Densher's determined non-action in this last scene indicates the extent to which displays of such non-action shape his sensibility for the entire novel: Densher's having told her "you must choose," Kate "stood in his own rooms doing it while, with an intensity now beyond any that had ever made his breath come slow, he waited for her act" (pp. 507–8).

From Densher's conveying to Kate's Aunt Maud, "outside, afterwards," that "the essence" of what transpired during his time alone with Milly in Venice remains "too beautiful and too sacred to describe" (p. 469), to his tendency to present his journalist job as not involving active work, "I do nothing" serves as the kernel of the personal posture that he elaborates during the novel.[19] Densher's compulsive, at times almost hysterical, identification with non-action ultimately shares the same structure as the rueful recognition of impossibilities characterizing such Howells protagonists as Basil March and David Sewell, but it has a far higher affective charge. The realist prestige that Densher achieves depends, I wish to argue, on how he develops a disposition (a temperament, recall, but also a relational position) that combines this intensely invested "I do nothing" posture with his empathic grasp of Milly's painful "reality" (p. 352).

From early on in his life, Densher has bemoaned "the fact of his weakness, as he called it, for life – his strength merely for thought – life, he logically opined, was what he must somehow arrange to annex and possess" (p. 88). His desire to annex and possess "life" is what had first attracted Densher to Kate, for "the handsome girl" is "as strong as the sea": "It's in *her* that life is splendid" (pp. 285, 332). Instead of the dynamic energy and vibrant sexuality that Kate represents, however, it turns out to be Densher's association with Milly's experience of impending death that allows him to "annex" real life.

Densher's change in cultural status centers on the period that he spends alone with Milly in Venice, during which her "incurable pain" becomes a more and more tangible part of her existence. James's preface designates this Venetian time with Milly as "Densher's final position and fullest consciousness" (p. 44). By contrast, having excluded herself early on from this superior version of realist consciousness by announcing "from illness I keep away," Kate leaves Venice as Milly gets sicker. In Venice, Densher feels, if anything, "too real" because, as he later puts it to Mrs. Lowder – making his point through an unconscious pun on Milly's name – "he *had* been through a mill" (p. 464; James's italics).[20] In Venice, Densher comes so to empathize with Milly's experience that he feels Milly's "pass was now, as by the sharp click of a spring, just completely his own – to the extent, as he felt . . . [that] anything he should do or shouldn't do would have close reference to her life" (p. 410). Such a "close reference" does Densher construct between himself and Milly as "miserably, prohibitively ill" that towards the end of his stay in Venice, when he says back to Susan Stringham what she has just told him, that Milly is now indeed dying, Susan looks "at him a minute as if he were the fact itself that he expressed" (pp. 318, 423). Yet of course Densher is *not* himself "the fact" that he expresses – Densher is not dying. Although he, far more so than any of the book's other characters besides Milly herself, experiences "the drop, almost with violence, of everything but a sense of her reality," Densher does pass *through* the "mill" (p. 401). Unlike Milly, he finally does return to London.

Once back in London, the relationship that Densher established in Venice with Milly and, as he puts it, with "the manner of her so consciously and helplessly dying" begins to give him a certain distinction (p. 452). As Aunt Maud, Kate, Susan Stringham and the reader all register, Densher has developed a "connexion" that transpires "in a richer degree" than that of any character except the dying Milly herself to the book's "greatest reality" (pp. 477, 106, 46). It is Densher who has made the "nearest approach to the utter reference they had . . . avoided" (p. 447). At the same time, however, Densher has continued to indicate his separation from Milly's painful fate, a separation of course not available to Milly. If the real for James, as he famously puts it in his preface to *The American*, is comprised by "the things we cannot possibly *not* know, sooner or later" (his italics), then Densher and Milly come to represent very different ways of knowing Milly's irreversible illness.

From his first time hearing that she is ill, Densher has displayed a remarkable capacity to enter into Milly's experience of pain. This capacity is always matched, however, by his determination to maintain a sort of visceral distance from it. When Kate announces to Densher, "I think I'm free to say it now – she sees Sir Luke Strett" (the most eminent surgeon in London), her words make Densher "quickly wince. 'Ah, fifty thousand knives!' Then after an instant: 'One seems to guess.' Yes, but she waved it away. 'Don't guess'" (p. 285). Juxtaposed with Kate's immediate and almost automatic gesture of distancing, Densher's physical reaction of wincing is a sympathetic miming of Milly's pain, and his words give it more bodily tangibility, in this case through employing what Elaine Scarry calls "the sign of the weapon" (p. 17): "Ah, fifty thousand knives!" Repeatedly during the novel, Densher's body involuntarily indicates an awareness of Milly's suffering, which he then signifies with great vividness even as he also strives to curtail his own powerful response.

When he unthinkingly alludes to Milly's physical condition during a conversation with her, for example, Densher first winces, then winces again, and then, turning, "in his pain, within himself," he flushes "to the roots of his hair" (p. 406). This series of bodily reactions marks for the reader Densher's unique sensitivity to Milly's experience of her ill body. An instant later, however, in this case as in others, "he had found what he wanted": he fully regains his composure. James emphasizes Densher's determination to retain at least certain topoi of ignorance when, for instance, he tells us that Densher "positively wanted not to be brought with his nose up against Milly's facts."[21] The dark humor in the comment derives from how it images direct physical contact between the small and the great, respectively, of Densher's and Milly's bodily experiences (his "nose," the "facts" of her fatal illness), even as we learn that Densher regards as "positively . . . not" acceptable the unmediated cognitive encounter with Milly's suffering that the phrase's idiomatic meaning conveys.

In Venice, Densher tries to elaborate a sequence of linkages between, on the one hand, his eschewal of any attempts to gain knowledge of Milly's "facts of physical suffering" and, on the other hand, his cultural standing:

What better proof could he have that his conduct was marked by straightness? . . . [H]e hadn't even the amount of curiosity that he would have had about an ordinary friend . . . He was accordingly not interested, for had he been interested he would have cared, and had he cared he would have wanted to know. Had he wanted to know he wouldn't have been purely passive, and it was his pure passivity that had to represent his dignity and his honour. (p. 380)

Densher's almost ostentatious lack of curiosity about Milly's state serves here as an elemental instance of his more general "I do nothing" stance. So long as he remains incurious of, does not actively "want to know" about her experience (recall, however, that he again and again implicitly claims to know it better than anyone except her), his conduct will attain to "pure" passivity, which will serve as the best "proof" of his "straightness." His lack of cognitively desirous "interest" in Milly's own experience of her illness can thereby function as a sign proving his lack of self-serving interested*ness*. The two lacks together constitute "his dignity and his honour."

Upon Densher's return to London, the novel's last section works hard to render continuous his determined lack of interest in the details of

Milly's pain and the moral decision that has won him widespread validation from critics: his not accepting her "stupendous" financial bequest. Densher above all must foreclose any "monstrous supposition" that he has been "up to something in Venice . . . To some 'game,' as they say. To some deviltry [sic]" (p. 436). This entails, for one, differentiating his own Venetian experience with the dying Milly from that of "the hound," Lord Mark, who has quite openly sought "good for himself" from Milly's situation (pp. 454, 432). The cynical Lord Mark openly admits that he "works" everything "for all it's worth" (p. 169). Densher, on the other hand, must establish that his own relation with Milly was not "work," that it was not purposefully instrumental. Most crucially, he must retroactively demonstrate, to his own "recovered sense" as much as to anyone else, that the bequest which Milly announces in a letter timed for Christmas Eve (the "season of gifts") is truly a gift. He did not manipulatively provoke, he neither intended nor expected, the bequest of her money. His "proof" consists, repeating and amplifying his behavior throughout the book, of various forms of doing nothing. Not only, as mentioned above, does he fail to read the Christmas Eve "gift" letter from Milly, but he prefers to have the follow-up letter from her New York lawyers, which, as he and Kate guess, specifies the bequest's actual amount, returned unopened, "intact and inviolate," "the state of the envelope proving refusal . . . not to be based on the insufficiency of the sum" (p. 504).

Yet after the explicitness of Densher's discussion with Kate at Milly's party in Venice, where the two named directly their plan for acquiring her wealth, he cannot pretend to understand Milly's bequest to him as entirely gratuitous (p. 394). Hence his "tormented" condition upon receiving notice of it, as well as his bitter statement to Kate, "You must intensely feel that it's the thing for which we worked together" (pp. 485, 507). While Densher's comment does accept the possibility that Milly's posthumous gift has been "worked for," the comment's second-person address projects that possibility onto Kate. His earlier remark to Kate that "I'd rather not, you know. It's straighter," although it occurs in another context, summarizes how he will construct himself as "straighter" than Kate throughout the book by aligning himself with "not" doing (p. 119). Densher can accurately stress to Kate, regarding lies, for example, "I, my dear, have told none" (but he also hasn't told Milly the truth), just as he can say to her in the last scene, "I put you up to nothing" (pp. 377, 506). James's description of the moment when Kate burns the letter Milly had timed for Christmas Eve can serve as an illustration of Densher's entire practice, as well as of the division of labor in his and Kate's "dreadful game" to get Milly's money (p. 478). Densher "started – but only half – as to undo [Kate's] action: his arrest was as prompt as the latter had been decisive" (p. 497).

Densher on several occasions half "starts" with an impulse to undo Kate's actions regarding Milly, but "arrest" becomes his most character-istic posture, arrest that always has the effect of implicitly charging Kate as the actively guilty party. Thus, early in the book, when Densher first sees Milly alone after learning that both Kate and Mrs. Lowder have lied to her about his romantic availability, he is already asking himself what "*he* could do that wouldn't be after all more gross than doing nothing" (p. 300). Although he is conflicted, he remembers that "he had himself as yet done nothing deceptive. It was Kate's description of him . . . it was none of his own; his responsibility would begin, as he might say, only with acting it out" (p. 299). Certainly, Densher recognizes immediately that "the sharp point was, however, in the difference between acting and not acting: this difference in fact it was that made the case of con-science." Hence, "it had hung for him by a hair to break out with" the truth and explain to Milly that his affections are already engaged. But asking himself whether it wouldn't "be virtually as indelicate to chal-lenge her as to leave her deluded?" Densher says nothing (pp. 305, 299). As with the prompt "arrest" of his half start "to undo her action" when Kate burns the letter, Densher's "impulse to break out" with the truth to Milly "came and went quickly enough" (p. 305).

Later, when he has remained without Kate in Venice to maneuver for marriage with Milly, Densher "knew . . . pretty well" that

Milly herself did everything – so far at least as he was concerned – Milly herself, and Milly's house, and Milly's hospitality, and Milly's manner, and Milly's char-acter, and, perhaps still more than anything else, Milly's imagination, Mrs. Stringham and Sir Luke indeed a little aiding. (p. 402)

Moreover, Densher has told Kate that, though he stays in Venice in order to marry Milly, he will not propose to her but will wait for her pro-posal: "It will be for me then to accept. But that's the way it must come" (p. 397). In fact, when Densher and Kate are finally explicit about their plan, Densher frames both his options as forms of inaction. Either he will accept the plan by staying in Venice and waiting for Milly to propose to him, or, if Kate declines to come to his rooms and sleep with him, Densher will "do nothing." He repeats, "I'll do nothing. I'll go off before you. I'll go tomorrow" (p. 398). Whether he stays in Venice or leaves, participates in the plot to dupe Milly or doesn't, Densher will construct his behavior as a non-action. As Milly's death and the novel's end approach, Densher's assumption of this "I do nothing" posture becomes more and more affectively charged, taking on ever higher stakes. Densher feels "himself . . . shut up to a room on the wall of which something precious was too precariously hung. A false step would bring it down . . . He should be able to be still enough through everything" (p. 411). Personifying "action" in the passive act of hearing, Densher goes on to claim that "action itself, of any sort, the right as well as the wrong – if the difference even survived – had heard . . . a vivid 'Hush!' the injunction to keep from that moment intensely still" (p. 410).

It is important to understand that Densher does not merely "pretend" to do nothing while actually doing all sorts of bad things. If what Kate says about Lord Mark is even more true of Densher – "he has somehow an effect without being in any traceable way a cause" – that is because determinate non-action is how Densher participates in bringing effects about (p. 289). To describe Densher's mode in abstract terms, his intentional "I do nothing" functions as the negative element in a dialectic with its symmetrical opposite – Kate's "action" – and the dialectical system of action and its negation produces the result of Milly's being lied to and manipulated. The operation of Milly's "abysmal trap" can thereby be articulated in the passive voice, as in the sentence that ends a chapter in Book Sixth: "So Milly was successfully deceived" (p. 294).

It is equally important to recognize that Densher's ultimate cultural status depends on his separating his determinate negation of action from a weak or hapless inability to act. If, at Densher's first appearance, James notes that he might "have been observed to demean himself as a person with nothing to do" (p. 85), by the novel's close Densher has transformed the vaguely demeaning "nothing to do" into the far more creditable "I do nothing" (p. 85). Repeatedly throughout the novel, Densher tropes a drifting or indecisive paralysis into a definite choice for negative action. For instance, during a period when Milly's illness has gotten worse and Densher is miserably uncertain about whether he should leave Venice, he feels unable to "purge" his wandering, aimless days "of a smack of the abject. What was it but abject for a man of his parts to be reduced to such pastimes?" And yet, after three days, "when still nothing had come, he more than ever knew that he wouldn't have budged for the world" (p. 420). Once again reasoning that any sudden departure might cause a traumatic shock to Milly, Densher determines not to make any movement, no matter how bad he feels. He will "stay in spite of odium,

stay in spite perhaps of some final experience that would be, for the pain
of it, all but unbearable. That would be his one way . . . to mark his virtue
beyond any mistake" (p. 420). Densher's "abject" waiting has become a
forcefully virtuous decision to "stay."

In Howells's *A Hazard of New Fortunes*, Basil March announces that he
himself will suggest "nothing" in response to a streetcar strike whose
insoluble difficulty in any case makes the suggestions of those around
him seem simplistic and futile. So too, Densher repeatedly refigures his
own frustrating inability to do anything as a determinate negation of
action.[22] Only a few pages beyond the above passage, Densher takes an
experience shaped for him by various humiliating lacks – during his last
days in Venice he lives "in mean conditions, without books, without
society, almost without money" – but defined for him above all by the
disempowering sense that he has "nothing to do but to wait" – and reval-
ues it by concentrating on a profound "idea of waiting," indeed of
"waiting for the deepest depth his predicament could sink him to"
(p. 442).

James's phrase here, "idea of waiting," compactly indicates the connection that Densher forges between his "I do nothing" stance and
thinking. The connection serves as a constitutive element of this literary
intellectual's character. Indeed, the purposeful effort of mind that
Densher eschews when it comes to his apprehension of Milly's state
reappears with compensating force in his unceasing attempts to construe
himself as doing nothing. When Densher gives himself yet another
"injunction to keep from that moment intensely still," with almost the
same gesture "he thought in fact . . . of several different ways of his doing
so." What this thinking "luminously amounted to was that he was to do
nothing" (p. 410).

Densher is never simply or thoughtlessly confident about his non-
action. Instead, his constant, often agonized, awareness of "complications," which inevitably ends up meaning to him that "he had only to
wait" (p. 418), correlates with his drive for a privileged cultural position.
His penchant, in particular, for self-critical thought testifies to Densher's
cultural specialness, to his status as "complicated by wit and taste,"
which attracts Kate to him from the first (p. 116). Hearing Mrs.
Stringham observe that Lord Mark, Densher's rival, seems always to
have "such a good conscience," Densher snaps back "that's always the
inevitable ass" (p. 432). By contrast to Lord Mark as well as to Kate, who
"showed admirably as feeling none of them," Densher insists that "the
discrimination and the scruple were for *him*" (p. 365; James's italics).

Initially, however, James leaves open the implications of Densher's linking together non-action and intense thought. "Distinctly," James writes when first describing Densher to the reader, "he was a man either with nothing at all to do or with ever so much to think about; and it was not to be denied that the impression he might after all thus easily make had the effect of causing the burden of proof in certain directions to rest on him" (p. 85). Densher will operate throughout, however, to turn the opposition this sentence posits between "nothing at all to do" and "ever so much to think about" into an identity, and a strongly privileged one. As a result, at the book's culmination Densher can respond to the "burden of proof" laid on him by this introductory sentence with the "great deal of thinking" that finally leads him to "do nothing" in regard to Milly's bequest – and thereby to earn the praise of generations of critics (pp. 485, 506). His initial introduction notes that because most of Densher's work at the newspaper happens at night, during the day he maintains a slightly suspicious "sense, or at least an appearance, of leisure." During hours when people expect men with any sort of important business "to be hidden from the public eye," Densher wanders the city, openly practicing "behavior . . . noticeably wanting in point" (p. 85).[23] This apparent lack of purposive behavior in Densher's first appearance turns out, however, to anticipate his climactic choice not even to break the seal on Milly's letter. That climactic choice for non-action follows a "mercilessly wakeful" night – itself foreshadowed by Densher's nighttime newspaper hours – where "in the darkness, as the slow hours passed, his intelligence and his imagination, his soul and his sense, had never on the whole been so engaged" (p. 474).[24] Among the "all sorts of difficult and portentous forms" that action might always take, Densher succeeds by the book's end in collating publicly visible non-action with "his intelligence and his imagination" and in assigning a high cultural value to that collation (p. 485).[25]

"TOO BEAUTIFUL AND TOO SACRED TO DESCRIBE"

As I noted earlier, Densher's change in status centers on the time that he spends alone with Milly in Venice, which James's preface calls "Densher's final position and fullest consciousness" (p. 44). Densher himself, however, conveys that this period was "too beautiful and too sacred to describe" (p. 469). "I don't think," he announces to Aunt Maud, "I *can* quite tell you what it was, what it is, for me" (p. 452). It is important to understand this additional paradox in the new "basis" for cultural status that Densher develops: his experience with Milly's "incurable pain" takes much of its social worth from its figuration as private and personal. The social currency of Densher's new distinction depends on his successfully conveying that the "essence" of his relation to Milly cannot be communicated to others (p. 469). "I can't talk to anyone about her," he tells Susan Stringham (p. 429). Densher's contact with Milly's suffering is thus positioned as somewhat like the "taste" of the French avant-garde aesthetes that Bourdieu analyzes, which is more culturally valued the less widely comprehensible it is taken to be.[26]

By the novel's close, Densher has publicly established (at least among the novel's remaining characters) that the details and meaning of his final experience with Milly are unshareable. From the book's start, however, Densher has worked on constructing a peculiarly public kind of privacy, a privacy that calls attention to itself even as it seeks a greater and greater air of inviolability. The way in which Densher first affects Kate is "as detached, as it was indeed what he called himself – awfully at sea – much more distinct from what surrounded them than any one else appeared to be" (pp. 88–9). Densher's ostensibly secret relationship with Kate advertises its own privateness from the start. Beginning with his and Kate's initial introduction at a London "gallery" (where people, then as now, go to see and be seen) and their subsequent encounter on the London tube, the romance develops "essentially in presence – in presence of every one" (pp. 88, 371). The two practice privacy in a series of public locations, often within sight of those from whom they most need to keep their engagement secret: they have *sotto voce* conversations inside Mrs. Lowder's actual house, at parties (including the one in Milly's palace where they name their plan), across St. Marks Square from Mrs. Lowder and Mrs. Stringham, and even in Milly's London hotel suite while waiting for her to get a hat ("Milly's room would be close at hand, and yet they were saying things – ! For a moment, none the less, they kept it up" [p. 309]). Certainly, they derive an erotic charge from attempting to be secret where they are most in danger of discovery. But for Densher, at least, the public exercise of privacy goes beyond that. For him, publicizing that he possesses an exclusive private realm helps to demonstrate his cultural uniqueness, as when, at a dinner party, "suddenly . . . in the course of talk" (p. 364), he announces that he has left his large Venetian hotel, "choked . . . with the polyglot herd" (p. 359), and rented his own small set of rooms, "the humblest rococo . . . of a Venetian interior in the true old note" (p. 364). Even as Densher alludes to his rooms, he tries to discourage anybody from actually visiting there.

Once Densher returns to London from Venice, it becomes clear that the strategic secrecy of his engagement with Kate meant something other to him than the temporary necessity he claimed to chafe against. Densher almost seamlessly slips into the inverse of his previous practice of keeping from Milly the truth of his relationship with Kate. He keeps his emotions about Milly from Kate:

he had on several recent occasions taken with Kate an out-of-the-way walk that was each time to define itself as more remarkable for what they didn't say than for what they did . . . There was something deep within him that he had absolutely shown to no one – to the companion of these walks in particular not a bit more than he could help. (p. 499)

In the last analysis, Densher's privacy need not be materially objectified in a secret romance or even in a small set of rooms. Rather, he must both feel and convey that he possesses "*something* deep within him that he had absolutely shown to no one."

Shortly after Milly's death, Densher finds himself deeply sorry that he let Kate burn, unread by anyone, the letter that Milly wrote and addressed to him on her death-bed and that she timed to arrive on Christmas Eve. Densher can now "never, never know" the content of what he labels the inner "turn" Milly "would have given her act" (p. 503). Although the words "turn" and "act" refer locally to Milly's thoughts about the bequest, "turn" also evokes Milly's last movement toward death, earlier encapsulated by Mrs. Stringham's telling Densher that Milly "has *turn*ed her face to the wall," phrasing that Densher finds so striking he later quotes it to Kate (p. 421). Not having read the letter means to Densher that he has "missed forever" the opportunity to have a unique view of Milly's final "turn": he has missed the opportunity to grasp her feelings at what was virtually her moment of death.[27] Milly's moment of death represents the ultimate instance of what has been positioned throughout as the novel's "greatest reality," her irreversible illness. Significantly, because a full apprehension of Milly's last feelings is now forever unavailable, Densher's explicitly direct longing to know them does not contradict his book-long stance of never actively seeking his privileged grasp of her experience. Indeed, their unavailability by definition renders Densher's desire for Milly's last feelings impractical, even unachievable, which pushes his desire to know them away from any air of functionality and towards the aesthetic.

Moreover, as he thinks about the unread letter, Densher's focus shifts away from Milly's final experience to his own *loss* of the chance fully to grasp this experience, and then to his *regret* about the loss, regret that includes both self-blame and self-pity. Ultimately, Densher's "ache" of regret at having missed her final "turn" compresses, thus enabling him always to keep with him, like a portable package, key facets of his encounter with Milly and her "facts of physical suffering." As the book closes, the tastefully self-denigrating character of Densher's regret – as well as the peculiar relationship he maintains with his own regret: the "rare" "delicacy" with which he returns to it day after day – will allow him to prolong indefinitely the status that he finally achieves through his privileged relation to Milly's "incurable pain" (pp. 502–3).

As with Milly's illness, for instance, Densher's regret allows him to set up a charged connection between doing nothing and thinking. The regret is "only a thought," but because it is a "thought precisely of such freshness and such delicacy as made the precious, of whatever sort," Densher "guard[s]" and "cherish[es]" it "alone in the stillness of his rooms" (pp. 502–3). Although Milly is dead, Densher can continue his quest for "the real, the right stillness" by seeking to preserve the intensity of his sense of failure and loss (p. 444). Moreover, like his time with Milly in Venice, which is "too sacred to describe," Densher's retroactive "pang" becomes the object around which he organizes an almost fetishistic privacy. The ache of regret is "all his own, and his intimate companion [Kate] was the last person he might have shared it with. He kept it back . . ." (p. 502).[28]

Most significant of all, however, Densher tries to cast his regret into the same role of bottom-line, recalcitrant reality that Milly's illness has previously played in the novel. He tries to give his regret, or "aftersense," the status of "utter referent" through figuratively identifying it with a painfully suffering body, which cannot help but evoke Milly's own. Imagining his regret as kept in "soft wrappings" in a "sacred corner" of his room, Densher every day unwraps it, "handling *it*, as a father, baffled and tender, might handle a maimed child" (p. 503; James's italics). He further transfers to the "stiff reality" of his own regret attributes that have belonged to Milly's "ravaged" body when he stresses his regret's mortal frailty, its inevitable vulnerability to "the hunger of time" (pp. 46, 502). Finally, while in Venice Densher had had a moment of guilty self-consciousness about the moments in which he participated, "with every one else," in "actively fostered suppressions" of the "pain and horror" Milly must be experiencing. These suppressions, he had sardonically observed at the time, "were in the direct interest of every one's good manner" (p. 440). Now, back in London after Milly's death, it is his own *regret* that Densher poses as liable to suppression because its deep authenticity resists society's conventions of smoothing over tragedy. This conventional social "process," he fears, "would officiously heal the ache in his soul" (p. 503).

INTENSELY TO CONSULT AND INTENSELY TO IGNORE

Densher is at least twice associated imagistically with the parenthesis of a sentence (pp. 256, 290). Nonetheless, it would probably be reductive directly to link the late-Jamesian sentence's reliance on parenthetic phrases to Densher's status as emotionally inside, yet unmistakably set off from, Milly's experience. And it would probably also be too simple to align Densher's posture of waiting or doing nothing with the late-Jamesian sentence's ostentatious deferrals.[29] I would, however, like to recall the "attention of perusal" James, in a passage from the novel's preface, labels "our highest experience of 'luxury'" (p. 49). James designates that attention of perusal – which at least today the Master no doubt receives from most who read him – as "What I . . . absolutely invoke and take for granted." Calling forth the experience of luxury even as he assumes its presence, the novelist enacts the classic gesture of cultural upward mobility, which tries to give an always-already achieved status to its attainments during the very process of attempting them. The "attention" the writer both invokes and takes for granted shares a root with the French *attendre*: to wait. The "attention of perusal" that James's writing demands, then, might be considered a relative of the prestige that Densher ultimately gains by waiting, being still, and doing nothing.[30]

At key moments in *The Wings of the Dove* James does implicitly criticize Densher, and with severity. One can nonetheless point, though, to additional continuities between the novelist and his character, even in territory – Densher's ongoing deception of Milly – where James's irony toward him is especially harsh.[31] James's sarcasm is clear, for instance, when he has Densher scapegoat Lord Mark as "evil" for revealing Densher and Kate's concealed engagement to Milly. To Densher, Mark's telling Milly the truth about the engagement constitutes one of "the stupid shocks he himself had so decently sought to spare her":

Densher had indeed drifted by the next morning to the reflexion . . . that the only delicate and honourable way of treating a person in such a state was to treat her as *he*, Merton Densher, did . . . [T]he impression but deepened – this sense of the contrast, to the advantage of Merton Densher . . . (p. 419)

James implies here that it is self-serving hypocrisy for Densher to view his continual lack of openness with Milly as decent, let alone as delicate and honorable. Yet in the novel's preface, James claims a similar sort of credit for his own "merciful indirection" when dealing with the "sick young woman" (p. 50). "The author's instinct everywhere for the *indirect* presentation of his main image," his tendency "to approach her circuitously," James insists, "proceeds, obviously, from her painter's tenderness of imagination about her" (p. 50).

James's "tenderness of imagination" about Milly makes for a relationship to her "disintegration" that closely parallels Densher's own, not only in its tension between special access and scrupulously maintained distance but also, and more importantly, in how that particular tension transforms the "miserably, prohibitively ill" woman into a source of personal distinction for a male intellectual (p. 456).[32] Feeling himself as artist to be "invited and mystified alike" by the "formidable theme" that the "stricken" young woman constitutes, the author says that he has been "long . . . standing off from it, yet coming back to it" (p. 35). James emphasizes that to write *The Wings of the Dove* he knew that he would have to develop an "intimate relation" to the novel's "central figure," "at the whole course of whose disintegration and the whole ordeal of whose consciousness one would have quite honestly to assist" (p. 36). Resonating with Densher's continual claim to disinterestedness, James's phrasing here suggests that, as a writer, his "intimate relation" to Milly's "ordeal" was thrust upon him by the integrity of his realist "honesty," rather than by personal choice. He knew immediately that centering his novel on a young woman who "was to draw her breath in such pain" would offer a valuable chance to illustrate his virtuosity, insofar as it was "sure to prove difficult and to require much handling" (pp. 40, 35).

James goes on to explain that, for "her designer," taking full advantage of the opportunity that Milly's illness offered for showing "good taste, possibly even . . . the play of the best in the world" required him to make the literary "expression of her state" "discreet and ingenious." Therefore, he decided that his narrative strategy would be to "go but a little way with the direct – that is with the straight exhibition of Milly" and her facts of suffering (p. 50). The narrative point-of-view would "walk round and round" her experience. Once James has thus framed his artistic approach, then, even when the preface worries more about the topic's difficulty, asking "Why had one to look so straight in the face and so closely to cross-question that idea of making one's protagonist 'sick'?" James's personification of "idea" already serves to manifest his good taste. The "'sick'" Milly should not herself be looked straight in the face and cross-questioned.

I pursue this question of James's own "taste" relationship to Milly and her "facts of physical suffering" because I believe that it points to a more general – and also a crucially gendered – paradox in James's conception of "the very meaning of expertness" for the realist novelist. For James, just as important as a novelist's ability to observe the real is his ability to "ignore" it. In one of the most often quoted paragraphs from all of James's New York Edition prefaces (from the preface to *Roderick Hudson*, which is the first preface that he wrote), James asserts that "Really, universally, relations stop nowhere, and the exquisite problem of the artist is eternally but to draw, by a geometry of his own, the circle within which they shall happily *appear* to do so."[33] The artist must recognize that in the real world everything always refers to something else, so that one might keep following out chains of relationship without ever reaching an end point ("il n'y a pas d'hors texte," as Derrida would later phrase it). Yet to give his work form the artist must also circumscribe it, which means attempting to foreclose certain avenues of relation. The artist finds himself, thus, "in the perpetual predicament that the continuity of things is the whole matter, for him, of comedy and tragedy; that this continuity is never, by the space of an instant or an inch, broken, and that, to do anything at all, he has at once intensely to consult and intensely to ignore it."[34]

"Continuity" or endless relationality is, James here suggests, the most basic "matter" with which a novelist works. For the artist, *relationality* itself is the "utter referent," the real real. Relationality underlies the possibility of art. Yet even as the novelist must intensely consult this "matter" of relationality in creating his narratives, he must also intensely "ignore" it. With what James calls a "desperate discipline," he must suppress his interest in the same real that enables his achievement.

Dramatizing his own first confrontation with this "perpetual predicament" in the writing of *Roderick Hudson*, James depicts a development not only into professional maturity but also into manhood. (As has often been noted, in designating *Roderick Hudson* his "first attempt at a novel," James ignores the earlier *Watch and Ward*.) While working on the book, James, the "young embroiderer," discovers, to his "terror," that "the canvas of life" in fact consists of a "boundless number" of "holes" though which he might pass his needle. These "little holes" are the openings of an infinite number of relations and connections; that is, the little holes here become themselves the "whole matter" of continuity with which the young novelist necessarily works (the hole/whole pun reinforces the connection). The young embroiderer's "ache of fear" derives from his recognizing that

the very nature of the holes is so to invite, to solicit, to persuade, to practise positively a thousand lures and deceits. The prime effect of so sustained a system, so prepared a surface, is to lead on and on . . .

Facing a "cruel crisis," the embroiderer finds himself with no choice but, "by a difficult, dire process of selection and comparison, of surrender and sacrifice," to determine "intensely to ignore" most of the holes. It was here, James says, that he came to understand "the very meaning of expertness."[35]

Turning briefly back to *The Wings of the Dove*, Jonathan Freedman has observed that James's portrayal of Kate Croy, especially in her relation to Merton Densher, partakes of the aestheticist figure of the "belle dame sans merci." One might say the same of these luridly soliciting, deceitful "holes" in the *Roderick Hudson* preface. James's image of the holes, with their "prepared . . . surfaces," feminizes the "matter" of relationality, making that "matter" something to be penetrated by the writer, but only with a rigorous discipline, one that knows how "at once intensely to consult and intensely to ignore" such matter. David McWhirter has recently suggested that, in figuring his own writing as embroidery at moments such as this, James aligns it with femininity. If that is so, however, then the ruthless expertise with which the needle comes to penetrate the holes that it encounters re-phallicizes the embroiderer, indeed makes him Master.

This paradigm for the difficult but disciplined relation that the writer must establish between his own artistic rigor and what counts, for a given context, as "the utter referent" returns us to Merton Densher's relationship with Milly Theale. Like James writing his first novel, Densher distinguishes himself among the other characters by feeling the "drop, almost with violence, of everything but a sense of her reality" (p. 407). His own susceptibility to engulfment in this reality, however, means that he must strive, at the same times as he feels it, "to ignore" it: "The last thing he wished was to be unconscious of her," Densher thinks to himself at one point, "what he wished to ignore was her own consciousness, tortured, for all he knew, crucified by its pain" (p. 466). Densher also, however, applies a version of this same targeted "ignoring" to Kate's physicality at the same time as he consummates the sexual intimacy with her that he has sought since their engagement.

After they have, at Densher's demand, slept together in his rooms, Densher feels a sense of victory. Above all, he has begun to resolve the anxieties about his manhood raised for him through most of the book by his determined stance of non-action, which has contrasted itself throughout with Kate's vigorous purposiveness.[36] Having pressed her into having "come, that once, to stay, as people called it," Densher feels himself, for example, finally to have achieved the complete, possessive vision of Kate's body that he has long craved:

> Wherever he looked or sat or stood, to whatever aspect he gave for the instant the advantage, it was in view as nothing of the moment, nothing begotten of time or of chance could be, or ever would; it was in view as, when the curtain has risen, the play on the stage is in view, night after night, for the fiddlers. (pp. 399–400)

This sentence's shift in tone, however, evoking first eternal classicism and then interminable vaudeville, hints that what initially seems Densher's achievement of aesthetic and erotic fullness he quickly begins to feel as entrapping. His absolute vision of Kate's body soon becomes "something he couldn't have banished if he had wished" (p. 399). But Densher then discovers that by getting "a little away" from his rooms he can control Kate's body's presence or absence from his consciousness:

> What it came to, fortunately, as yet, was that when he closed the door behind him for an absence he always shut her in. Shut her out – it came to that rather, when once he had got a little away; and before he reached the palace . . . he felt free enough not to know his position as oppressively false. (p. 401)

What I wish to underline here is the centrality that James accords to Densher's feeling "free enough not to know . . ." As with Milly, Densher has achieved the ability to "shut . . . out" of his consciousness, at will, a woman's body, with which he also has attained an intimate connection that signifies privilege and prestige. The male literary intellectual's status derives here from his simultaneous intense knowledge of, but also rigorous determination "not to know," a real aligned with feminized materiality.

For Densher, as for James, realist prestige depends not only on displaying a powerful grasp of the real, it depends on attaining the arduous discipline to ward it off. As mentioned above, James's preface to *The American* famously describes the real as "the things we cannot possibly *not* know, sooner or later" (his italics). Using these terms, Densher illustrates the personal distinction to be gained through displaying an expert leverage over that italicized *not*, over, that is, when and how one knows "the things" that constitute the real. With such a leverage, the realist intellectual can manifest a relation to those irrefutable "things" that is closer *and* more distant, sooner *and* later.

CHAPTER THREE

The "genuine article": credit and ethnicity in The Rise of David Levinsky

"I was never snobbish. I care very little about titles; what I look
to is intellectual distinction."
"Combined with financial success."
"Why, that is what distinction means."
George Gissing, *New Grub Street* (1891)

Abraham Cahan was born in a Russian shtetl. In New York City, Cahan became best known as the long-time editor of a mass-circulation left-wing Yiddish newspaper, *The Daily Forward*. He also wrote well-received fiction in English, however, most notably a lengthy realist/naturalist novel called *The Rise of David Levinsky* (1917). This fascinating, semi-auto-biographical text narrates the immigration of a poor Talmud scholar to the United States, where he finds work in the garment trade and, through a series of brilliant (often unethical) business moves, ultimately becomes a wealthy industrialist. Like virtually all of Cahan's English-language fiction, *The Rise of David Levinsky* is set in the Jewish ghetto of New York's Lower East Side.

William Dean Howells praised Cahan's fiction in his columns and used his book-trade connections to help promulgate it, just as the powerful editor had done (albeit to a much greater extent, of course) with Henry James. Because Cahan might even be seen, at least in this sense, as one of Howells's many protégés, including a chapter on Cahan's literary realism in a book that also treats Howells perhaps needs no further justification. It might seem more counter-intuitive, however, to insert such a chapter directly in between two chapters that concentrate, respectively, on literary works by Henry James and by Edith Wharton. Both James and Wharton identified very strongly with Anglo-American and Western European high culture. Moreover, although each criticized French persecutions of Dreyfus, both James and Wharton were at least arguably antisemitic. During his 1904 trip to the United States, James

73

viewed the inhabitants of Cahan's Lower East Side neighborhood as threatening embodiments of cultural and linguistic barbarity. East Side intellectuals, in particular, represented to James "the agency of future ravage" on his own tradition of "letters." The Jewish intellectuals whom he overheard during a tour of East Side cafés struck him as poised to obliterate "the light of our language as literature has hitherto known it."[1] Cahan might be said to have come closer than any other single figure in twentieth-century America to personifying that ravaging agency that James feared. As editor of the *Daily Forward*, for instance, Cahan consciously used a style that blended English and Yiddish expressions. Moreover, he helped to shape a section of H.L. Mencken's *The American Language* that celebrated the growing interrelationship between Yiddish and "American English." With significantly less ambiguity than James, Wharton too expressed anxious hostility toward the very notion of Jewish intellectuals in America. As Wharton biographer Shari Benstock relates, when a New York-based scholarship fund solicited Wharton for a donation in 1923, she wrote to a friend that she had no interest in helping "female yids" go to college.[2]

How, then, does Abraham Cahan "fit" with these two figures? Rather than trying to use Howells's support of Cahan as a sort of biographical or institutional hinge with James, and maybe thus with James's close associate Wharton, and thereby attempting to set up a chain of extra-textual connections among the four diverse realists in my study, I argue for significant similarities in their textual dynamics. The work of these writers elaborates – and seeks to accord intellectual distinction to – a particular "disposition" towards hard reality. What such different figures as James, Wharton and Cahan share most centrally for the purposes of this study is not a professional or social connection with Howells. It is the structure of relationship that each writer goes about establishing among intellectual posture, cultural status, and the "really real." In the process, both James and Cahan, as we have already seen with Howells and will see with Wharton, invoke categories of negativity with such solidity as to make them seem actually palpable.

FINANCIAL CAPITAL, INTELLECTUAL CAPITAL

At the close of the first-person narrative detailing his rise from a Yiddish-speaking immigrant "with four cents in my pocket"[3] to "the height of . . . business success" as a ladies' garment manufacturer, the narrator and protagonist of *The Rise of David Levinsky* asserts that "my sense of triumph is coupled with a brooding sense of emptiness and insignificance, of my lack of anything like a great, deep interest" (pp. 3, 529). Similar announcements of a feeling of empty meaninglessness have followed each of Levinsky's financial leaps. A first question Levinsky's narrative suggests, then, might be: when an apparently contradictory element such as "a brooding sense of emptiness and insignificance" is "coupled with" his financial triumph, does the sense of emptiness somehow also serve within the narrative as a cultural mark of distinction, one that complements, or perhaps even helps to represent, Levinsky's business success? If so, how might one understand the forms of cultural distinction thereby accruing to Levinsky in the context of the literary-realist dynamics of intellectual prestige that previous chapters have described?

After all, Merton Densher participates dramatically in the thematics of sacrifice that appealed so often to his author's sensibilities. A key element in Densher's attainment of a privileged cultural status by *The Wings of the Dove*'s close is his climactic move (or, as Densher would cast it, non-move) *not* to accept the immense wealth that Milly Theale's bequest makes available to him; Densher's income and lifestyle will remain those of a middle-class literary intellectual. Similarly, William Dean Howells's Basil March and Reverend Sewell are disgusted by capitalism and its inequities (although both men also enjoy, with varying degrees of expressed discomfort, the relative luxuries that capitalism's unequal distribution of goods provides for them). In contrast to these middle-class intellectuals, whose self-definitions reject any role even resembling that of an actual capitalist who seeks to accumulate money, David Levinsky is a self-made millionaire. He owns large factories and operates ruthlessly in a highly competitive industry. Given that Levinsky, furthermore, has almost no formal education (except for some aborted Talmud study in Russia, and the night-school classes in which he learned English), as a character he is markedly distant from any such category as "literary intellectual." Any claims that Levinsky might make to intellectual or cultural distinction would seem as if they must necessarily be quite different in shape and thrust from the claims to such distinction that my two previous chapters have explored in James and Howells.

Many critics of Cahan's novel, however, have argued that the novelist, translator, and editor was closely identified with his fictional protagonist, despite their contrasting careers. Louis Harap's *The Image of the Jew in American Literature* contends, for instance, that "Levinsky is a thinly disguised Abraham Cahan."[4] Whether or not one accepts such assertions of an almost unmediated identity between author and character, Cahan does place his first-person protagonist in the signally literary position of writing a self-reflective narrative about his own *Bildung*. As narrator, Levinsky meditates upon his own shifting relationships to language, to religion and morality, and to the social world, all within a generically novelistic framework. Moreover, within his diegesis itself, Levinsky does act briefly as financial patron, or "angel," for a poet, has periods during which he spends time in literary cafés, and often regrets having abandoned his own humanistic studies.

Levinsky's shadow allegiance to literary pursuits, which accompanies his primary identification as a businessman, helps Cahan's novel to make manifest, first of all, that the mechanisms for claiming intellectual distinction that I have been aligning with a specifically literary "realist disposition" can also operate in spheres that would seem far removed from the domain of literary intellectuals. Indeed, as we will see, Levinsky's paradoxically doubled "taste" relation to categories that his narrative positions as base materiality, as well as the component of negativity that he brings to his own postures and orientations, play a big role not merely in how he gains intellectual and cultural capital, but also in how he generates his vast amounts of financial capital. This fact, that Levinsky's gains of financial and intellectual capital proceed in tandem and rely on precisely the same means, allows Cahan's novel in addition to counter an overly simple, precapitalist plus–minus assumption that still remains common in discussions of cultural prestige. Visible, for instance, as a tendency throughout Bourdieu's *Distinction*, this plus–minus assumption holds that *gains* in certain sorts of cultural capital, such as those usually associated with artists and intellectuals, must correlate with a corresponding *minimalization* in an individual's financial capital.[5] (I return periodically through this chapter to challenges that *The Rise of David Levinsky* presents to Bourdieu's work.)

The Rise of David Levinsky is still further instructive, moreover, for its implicit exploration of the twentieth-century Progressive assumption that in America *intellectual* capital, at least, should not be heritable, even if an individual might inherit money or social standing. The widespread attempts of early twentieth-century American intellectuals to break from New England's "genteel tradition" demonstrate an invigorated commitment to the Emersonian belief that intellectual status does not derive from an affiliation with past intellectual achievement, no matter how celebrated. It must be achieved, as it were, *ex nihilo*. Perhaps because of the value that Jewish culture has always accorded to intellect and learning, Jewish-American immigrant literature foregrounds, more so than other immigrant literatures, the male immigrant's loss upon arrival in America of anything that might previously have served him as intellectual capital. The just-arrived Jewish immigrant thus acts as an almost ideal illustration of the supposed necessity to earn one's intellectual capital for oneself in America.

Jewish-American immigrant writing often depicts, for instance, the sudden drop of Talmud scholarship's negotiable value in America, despite the fact that in Russia it constituted a form of intellectual distinction that could gain for "a man of learning" economic support from his family or even from an entire village. David Levinsky hears a typical lament his first afternoon in America from a former Talmud scholar whose wife "lo and behold! instead of supporting him while he read Talmud, as she used to do at home . . . persisted in sending him out to peddle" (p. 97).[6] Levinsky himself, when asked his "occupation" or "trade" by a more experienced immigrant, answers "confusedly": "I read Talmud." "I see," comes the reply. "But that's no business in America" (p. 91). Levinsky goes on, however, brilliantly to intertwine his business practices as a garment manufacturer with the very same mechanisms that he will also use to develop a privileged intellectual status.

I wish to argue that the specific *styles* of self-division characterizing Levinsky mean that, despite his active, and often blatantly exploitative, attempts to get richer and richer, he nonetheless accrues intellectual and cultural "credit" (adopting his own term), that is notably congruent with the versions of literary realist prestige that we have already examined. Acquired both from other characters within the space of his narrative and from the readers that his narrative implicitly assumes, Levinsky's financial and cultural "credit" alike derives from his paradoxical relation to a succession of different categories that he aligns with recalcitrant materiality. Throughout his career, Levinsky recurrently calls attention to two positions within himself. Although the actual contents of these two internal positions shift, their arrangement remains the same: one position is aligned with a material dimension – base, but necessary – of Levinsky's life, while the other is defined as somehow distinct from that material dimension. Levinsky's repeated stagings within himself of this same opposition, between materiality and a something else that is discordant with it, depend above all on his varying the element that occupies the slot of materiality. Levinsky alternately identifies as basely material, for example, his business successes and ambitions, his own bodily habits, his non-standard English, then later his too-eager showing-off of correct English, and even his own philanthropic giving.

This chapter first details how this particular version of a divided self – a self constituted through the clash between Levinsky's identifications with base materiality but also with a something supposed to be discrepant with that materiality – drives both Levinsky's financial and his cultural "rise." The chapter's second half considers Levinsky's placement of his own ethnicity into the category he aligns with materiality. He thereby produces another, "American" dimension of himself which he props upon – yet also makes distinguishable from – his identity as an immigrant Jew. The latter part of my discussion of Cahan's novel will thus implicitly address the question: what forms of capital – in Cahan's terms, what sorts of "rise" – become available to early twentieth-century ethnic Americans who acknowledge, even embrace, their ethnicity, even as they also register a position of difference from it?

To anticipate briefly: if intellectuals of the period, ranging from Mark Twain, to Charlotte Perkins Gilman, to W. E. B. Du Bois were drawn to tropes of self-division, so too the notion of a divided self must inevitably arise when considering the subjectivity of any "hyphenated American" (in the phrase to which John Dewey gave wide currency in 1916). The implications of such self-division are especially relevant, however, to those turn-of-the-century ethnic intellectuals, including Cahan, Du Bois, and also, although we don't often think of him as an intellectual, Booker T. Washington.[7] Such figures performed the task of articulating ethnic experiences from within. Their articulations were often performed for an ethnic community itself (Cahan founded and edited the *The Daily Forward*, at one time the largest circulation Yiddish newspaper in the world) as well as for a larger American audience. This sort of accomplishment by ethnic intellectuals had unquestionable social and ethical value: Cahan's writing, editing, and translating helped to ease the difficult transitions to America and modernity of hundreds of thousands of immigrants. Nonetheless, it is still crucial, if we wish to grasp as fully as possible the situation of ethnic intellectuals in early twentieth-century America, to explore the mechanisms by which at least a few such intellectuals achieved and maintained a relatively prestigious cultural status. Reading Cahan's work, for example, helps to suggest how an intimate knowledge of Eastern-European Jewish immigrant life could enable an immigrant to figure as a "natural" expert, while, conversely, his status as self-consciously analytic could simultaneously help him to seem culturally and intellectually distinct from the immigrant world his writing elaborated.

RAW MATERIAL

While traveling as a salesman "on a west-bound train" (p. 327), Levinsky thematizes as an important "discover[y]" about America his encounter with a rich wholesale butcher (p. 330). The butcher paradoxically represents an openly vulgar "business" at the same time as he emblematizes "cultured English and ways." Levinsky is "fascinated" by this "conflict" between a business based on "raw beef, bones, and congealed blood" and a "refined" personal appearance, manner, and above all language (Levinsky emphasizes the butcher's "vocabulary" and "English") (p. 330). This conflict repeats in exaggerated form the sense of "discrepancy" that marks one of Levinsky's very first observations in America when, walking into the Wall Street district, he had been struck by a disjunction between people's hurried preoccupation with business concerns and their "general high-born appearances" (p. 91). (In fact, David Engel counts the word "discrepancy" as occurring two dozen times in the novel.[8])

Sitting across from the butcher in a Pullman dining car, Levinsky's syntax mimics what he thinks of as a specifically American self-difference when he uses a reflexive idiom to describe it: "I said to myself, 'It takes a country like America to produce butchers who look and speak like noblemen'" (p. 330). Levinsky's idiom posits two distinguishable positions within him, "I" and "myself." Indeed his "eye" had already rehearsed the key incommensurability of the butcher's two dimensions when it noted an initial contrast between two men placed next to one another: the "gaunt, elderly" butcher, seated at an indirect slant from Levinsky, and a more grossly physical "fat man," whose body impinges more immediately also because he "occupied the seat directly opposite mine." Most important, however, is how at crucial moments during his encounter with the butcher and the other businessmen on the train Levinsky produces an internal opposition exactly analogous to the wholesale butcher's own. First, determined to impress the three "well-dressed American Gentiles" he is dining with by showing his ability to talk about national politics, Levinsky "entered upon a somewhat elaborate discourse . . . I was so absorbed in the topic and in the success I was apparently scoring that I was utterly oblivious to the taste of the food in my mouth" (p. 329). Levinsky's verbal assertions and the taste of his food both occur at the same physical location – his mouth – but Levinsky stresses his experience of them as entirely incompatible. The discordance between the food he chews and the "elaborate discourse" he speaks repeats in more compact form the distinction embodied by the butcher between the meat by which he makes his living and his "vocabulary . . . appearance and manner."

Likewise paralleling that structure is the conflict between Levinsky's "discourse" and his hands. The gesticulations that traditionally accompany the reading of the Talmud are a bodily "habit [that] worried me like a physical defect" (p. 327). While speaking about politics to the three gentiles on the train, Levinsky determines to keep his hands "so strenuously still that they fairly tingled with the effort, and, of course, I was so conscious of the whole performance that I did not know what I was talking about" (p. 329). These two moments might appear simply as symptoms of an "identity crisis" provoked for the Jewish immigrant by his encounter with successful gentiles, but in fact both moments follow the form of the gentile butcher's own seemingly divided identity: in both moments Levinsky's narrative emphasizes a marked incommensurability between something positioned as bodily or material (the food he chews, the "physical defect" of his uncontrollable gesticulation) and something else (Levinsky's "elaborate discourse") juxtaposed with it.

Pierre Bourdieu sees the staging of oppositions between materiality and what is distinct from it as central in constructing "relations of distinction" between members of different social classes and class fractions – in constructing, that is, differences in cultural capital. For Bourdieu, cultural capital is the category that displays the hierarchized relations between socioeconomic identities. Although cultural capital can sometimes be represented by such official certifications as diplomas, in many contexts its primary manifestation occurs through practices of distinction. Practices of distinction exhibit the bourgeoisie's "objective distance from necessity" (p. 155) through a series of opposed terms played out in systems of ostensibly apolitical aesthetic taste (pp. 169–78). The most pervasive assertion of the bourgeoisie's distance from the crude economic necessities governing working-class life is their aesthetic insistence on "the primacy of form over function," of "manner over matter" (pp. 3, 176). This aesthetic insistence, at its most elemental level, establishes a hierarchy between culture and the body, especially the body's needs and desires. Related oppositions – which are enacted at the dining table just as much as in art galleries – include "on the one hand, freedom, disinterestedness, the purity of sublimated tastes . . . on the other, necessity, self-interest, base material satisfactions" (p. 254).

Such oppositions primarily occur in *The Rise of David Levinsky* within single individuals, however, rather than regulating differences between socioeconomic groups. A reading of Cahan's novel therefore makes evident that Bourdieu's model of cultural capital should be revised to take account of how individual subjects do not simply acquire a unitary "disposition" associated with a single "habitus," but instead are structured by multiple, often conflicting, dispositions and social identifications, as well as by multiple habita.[9] Furthermore, *The Rise of David Levinsky* shows that what Bourdieu calls "crudely material reality" (p. 196) ought not be taken for granted as an easily identifiable locus, nor made automatically synonymous, as it tends to be in Bourdieu's account, with either "the objective conditions" of the working classes (p. 381) or "the physical order of bodies" (p. 174). Bourdieu assumes that, in contrast to obviously evaluative aesthetic terms like "tasteful" and "vulgar," the categories of "necessity," "nature," "material constraints" (p. 376) and "material reality" (p. 196) exist outside of or prior to an aesthetic system; "objective necessity" is what it is, and therefore one can easily gesture towards it. (Indeed the working classes, for Bourdieu, cannot but have direct access to necessity. He values the "extraordinary *realism* of the working classes," which he sees as the result of their being forced into unmediated contact with, hence acknowledgement of, the material world [p. 381; Bourdieu's italics]. But we should recall here, for instance, the figural substitutability that *The Wings of the Dove* presumes between Milly Theale's "incurable pain" and the brute poverty on view at Regent's Park.) Crude materiality becomes even more mobile, Levinsky's narrative suggests, when it is used as a "base" from which cultural distinction exhibits its distance.

My reading of *The Rise of David Levinsky* thus follows Bourdieu in tracing the social and political functions of marking distance from material necessity, but by stressing Levinsky's positionings, and repositionings, of materiality, I hope also to clarify how Bourdieu's sociological model might take more advantage than it does of poststructuralist insights (see Introduction, above). While *Distinction* tracks the continual generating of "the different" and "the new" for cultural privileging, Cahan's novel points to what is related but not identical: the generating of ever new locus points for bodily necessity and crude reality, *against which* cultural elevation can define and redefine itself.

Like the wholesale butcher he encounters on the train, Levinsky learns the importance of the raw. He tells us at the book's close that, as "my garment business continued to grow, my consumption of raw material reached gigantic dimensions," and explains that he is able to acquire the raw cloth he needs because "I own considerable stock in the

very mills" which produce it (p. 522). Levinsky accumulates cultural
capital by developing a similar relation with what might be called cultural "raw material." Locating instances of such materiality within himself
– even owning "considerable stock" in it – enables him to establish a
special mastery of materiality. By himself containing both poles of the
relations of distinction that, in Bourdieu's analyses, differentiate classes
and class fractions, Levinsky can best valorize those aspects of himself
distinct from materiality. Levinsky can exhibit one, "materialized"
dimension or moment of his self as recognized, and recognized as separate, by another – thereby elevated – dimension of his self. This structure explains Levinsky's foregrounding, during dinner with the three
gentiles, the discrepancy between his "elaborate discourse" and two
degrading associations with his body: first, the taste of the food in his
mouth and, second, his Talmudic gesticulations (which he earlier refers
to as a physical "deformity" [p. 328]).

After the dinner with the gentiles is through and Levinsky starts to fear
that he has made a "nuisance" of himself, however, he associates with
degrading materiality the same elaborate "discourse" he had until then
been positioning as incommensurable with it. Levinsky decides that his
"talk" itself was inappropriate, both because it took up "too much"
space and because its motive may have been too visibly instrumental
(while speaking, he had exulted in "the success I was apparently scoring"
with gentile businessmen). He feels "wretched." Although the questions
ending the chapter – "Had I talked too much? Had I made a nuisance
of myself?" (p. 330) – again represent familiar immigrant anxieties, they
also produce two interdependent yet incommensurable positions: the
Levinsky whose elaborate speech may indeed have occupied too much
time and space, been too self-interested, too "crudely material" in
Bourdieu's sense; and the later Levinsky, both close and distant enough
from his "discourse" to recognize and regret these characteristics.[10]

The categories I am suggesting that Levinsky's narrative, even in this
one scene, aligns with "the material" may seem inconsistent or not necessarily to correlate with one another: eating, hand gesticulations, excessive talking. My point, however, is that cultural distinction defines itself
here in relation to a term whose referent changes so quickly that it
indeed becomes difficult to follow. Very often what counts as distinction
at one point of this novel will in another instant be positioned as the base
materiality against which a new example of cultural distinction identifies
itself.

DIALECT AND LEVINSKY'S RISE

The butcher incident culminates in Levinsky's placing his own "talk" in the relational position of materiality previously occupied first by the food in his mouth and then by his hand gesticulations. Representations of Yiddish-American speech were frequently included in Cahan's English-language journalism, especially in his coverage of night schools, court-rooms, and tenement houses as a staff reporter for Lincoln Steffens's *New York Commercial Advertiser*, prior to his career as a novelist.[11] That early journalism by Cahan establishes a rigorous distinction between what is reported, the semiliterate talk of recent immigrants, and the reporter, a highly literate master of several languages functioning as a cosmopolitan central consciousness, a "polyglot visitor" to the immigrants' more limited world.

Cahan's first novel, *Yekl* (1896) – the first American book about Jewish immigrant life actually by an immigrant – also upholds a careful distinction between its immigrant characters' use of what the book represents as obtrusively flawed, coarsely instrumental language and another linguistic position, one defined as both recording and evaluating the immigrant language. While Cahan's journalism embodies the latter position in the reporter, however, who serves as a character in his own writing – as interviewer, investigator, or merely recording observer – such a position in *Yekl* exists entirely outside the scene of the story. Not located in a named or even unnamed human figure within the novel's narrative, the evaluative linguistic position is occupied by the impersonal, third-person narrative voice itself – what Cahan in a footnote calls "this narrative" – which continually distinguishes itself from the dialect of the novel's characters.[12] The italicized typeface of the spoken dialect visually corresponds to the terms "this narrative" employs to describe the protagonist Jake's English: "mutilated," "broken and mispronounced," "gibberish" (pp. 2, 17, 19). Even the phonetic transliterations of Jake's own words contain markers of an outside position that knows his speech is "mutilated" or "broken." For example, in the speech-tag that Jake often adds to his comments, "*Dot'sh a kin' a' man I am*" (e.g., p. 5) the three apostrophes are not themselves said or even registered by the speaker. Rather, they silently point to mutilations or absences (usually of end consonants) in the speaker's words. Not Jake, but the anonymous narrative position which has inserted the apostrophes recognizes the fault in pronunciation, as does the implicit reader.

The two sets of characteristics that *Yekl* attempts absolutely to divide between its immigrant protagonist and "this narrative," *The Rise of David Levinsky* will locate as relational moments of the same consciousness. Levinsky personifies a structure of temporality, in which his "present" self occupies a critical perspective on other versions of itself, aligned with the past. Such a configuration is central to autobiographical narratives, but Levinsky's personified structure of temporality never yields two stable positions: "The amusing part of it was that in 1894, for example, I found that in 1893 my judgement of men and things had been immature and puerile. I was convinced that now at last my insight was a thoroughly reliable instrument, only a year later to look back upon my opinions of 1894 with contempt" (p. 350). Although Levinsky can even patronize his own deluded patronizing of former selves, he is never able to achieve a present perspective on his earlier self which would be guaranteed safe from future criticism.[13] As we will see, however, this apparent failure in the present proves structurally necessary to the possibility of Levinsky's continuing to accumulate cultural capital.

The present "now" of Levinsky's moment-of-writing subtly inscribes its own potential vulnerability to future repositioning when, for example, he summarizes his earlier attempts to attain genteel American dress and manners, and concludes, "The difference between taste and vulgar ostentation was coming slowly, but surely, I hope" (p. 261). The sentence's shift to the present tense of "I hope" stands out in a section of the novel that places all the other affective states it describes in the past. On one level, the sudden allusion to Levinsky's "present" moment of writing evidences a certain modesty in the narrative voice: even now, the writer does not wish to claim that he has yet "surely" achieved the difference between taste and vulgar ostentation. Such unwillingness to boast an accomplishment is an important attribute of the "taste" in question here. But the good taste Levinsky displays by not ostentatiously vaunting its arrival still does not entirely explain his insertion of "I hope," which is almost ungrammatical in its juxtaposition of the past imperfect with a present-tense affective state supposed to refer to it, instead of the expected "hope*d*." The hint of error here, especially striking in a passage where Levinsky stresses his efforts to acquire "genteel" American ways, is reinforced by the fact that the elided final "d" is Cahan's most frequent signifier of immigrant dialect (as in Yekl/Jake's "kin' o' man I am"). The ambiguously appropriate status of "I hope," even as he writes it, presents a dimension of the "difference" between taste and vulgar ostentation which exceeds Levinsky's present understanding. I suggest that Levinsky does not fully master the difference between taste and vulgarity, even in the present of his writing, because his underlying strategy can never be to achieve once and for all that difference, or distinction, that constitutes cultural capital. Rather than a static miser's hoard, Levinsky's cultural capital structures itself as something that he must be continuously "striving" for, so that, like his financial capital, it can be in a state of continual accumulation.

Perhaps the most significant shift in Levinsky's relation to English occurs around the "use" he makes of his increasing mastery of American words and phrases (p. 291). The narrating Levinsky describes himself, when he first began his "canvassing activities" outside New York, as "thirstily drinking in" what he calls "business rhetoric": "'What do you think of this number, Mr. So-and-so?' I would say, self-consciously, to a merchant, as I dangled a garment in front of him. 'You can make a run on it. It's the kind of suit that gives the wearer an air of distinction'" (p. 291). Because the narrating Levinsky is now using words to represent the story of his life, he cannot actually copy what he has since those early days noticed about highly placed WASP buyers: their reticence. Only by elaborating his own earlier talkativeness can the narrating Levinsky imply that now he has begun to move toward the "full-blooded Anglo-Saxon" buyer Mr. Eaton's "few words." The narrating Levinsky insists on a difference from that earlier moment of himself when he "was apt to talk too much": "I was too exuberant in praising my own goods . . . I would do so partly for the sheer lust of hearing myself use the jargon of the market, but chiefly, of course, from eagerness to make a sale, from over-insistence . . . Altogether there was more emphasis than dignity in my appeal" (p. 321). Levinsky opposes "emphasis" to "dignity," placing the former in the past and aligning it not only with unmediated "eagerness to make a sale" but with a bodily "sheer lust" for the physical sensation of "hearing myself use the jargon of the market." Evoking such materialized images for his earlier sales pitches, Levinsky now reproduces the conflict that the butcher instantiates between the grossly physical "character of his business" and his "cultured English" and "vocabulary" – entirely within the second pole of that opposition, instances of language.[14]

RECOGNIZING MISRECOGNITION

Levinsky's accession to "the world of refined ways" turns out to be more complicated than it first appears (p. 175):

I sought to dress like a genteel American . . . I remember the passionate efforts I made to learn to tie a four-in-hand cravat, then a recent invention. I was forever watching and striving to imitate the dress and the ways of the well-bred American merchants with whom I was, or trying to be, thrown. All this, I felt, was an essential element in achieving business success; but the ambition to act and look like a gentleman grew in me quite apart from these motives (p. 260).

Levinsky explicitly ascribes his desire to acquire "taste" to his belief that it "was an essential element in achieving business success." He watches and attempts to assume "genteel" "dress and . . . ways" as part of his admitted "trying" to establish financially profitable connections with "well-bred American merchants." Yet by the close of the paragraph Levinsky is also insisting, "but the ambition to act and look like a gentleman grew in me quite apart from these motives." The supplemental "but" is necessary because the "ways" in question (those of "a gentleman") are defined as not motivated solely by pecuniary advantage. One can not say that one has truly acquired "refined ways" so long as the acquisition's motive can still be regarded as vulgarly economic. (Even Levinsky's "passionate efforts" to tie a four-in-hand cravat must therefore be ultimately perceivable as passionate effort for its own aesthetic sake, *l'art pour l'art* "quite apart from" worldly motives.)

The past tense of two important verbs in this last sentence of the paragraph raises a further question, however: "All this, I *felt*, was an essential element in achieving business success; but the ambition to act and look like a gentleman *grew in me* quite apart from these motives." "I *felt*" places Levinsky's mercantile strategizing in the past, thereby suggesting his present distance from such strategizing. But the main verb after the semicolon – "*grew* in me quite apart from these motives" – is in the same simple past tense as the "I felt" that introduces, and distances as past, the mercantile strategizing. Does the past tense of the passage's final clause imply a temporal separation from its own assertion of a disinterested aesthetic sense, just as the parallel grammar of the previous clause does? That is, is the narrating Levinsky here introducing, via use of the past tense, a distancing perspective even on his arrived-at conviction that he has indeed begun to act "quite apart" from basely interested motives? The sentence hints at Levinsky's growing recognition of how any self-distancing from "base" behavior can itself serve, even if unconsciously, self-interested aims.

Several incidents lead Levinsky toward clarifying for himself some of the interrelations among different forms of economic and cultural capital, as well as why those interrelations tend to be obscured or misrecognized. At a resort hotel in the Catskills, he overhears a conversation that leads him to recognize parallels between two different acts involving charity, first the use of a difficult specialized term, "scientific philanthropy," by a recent immigrant showing off his English and, second, the immigrant's actual contribution of sums. Levinsky realizes that both gestures – using a fancy phrase and donating money – represent means by which the immigrant earns cultural "credit" (p. 427). When Levinsky encounters his former night-school teacher, Mr. Bender, he has a still more explicit insight about the sorts of cultural profits that both expertise and disinterestedness can earn. In their conversation, Mr. Bender "dwelt on the civil-service reform of President Cleveland, charging the Republicans with 'offensive partisanship,' a Cleveland phrase then as new as four-in-hand neckties" (p. 313). Identifying them both as "new" cultural phenomena, Levinsky's description links Mr. Bender's very use of the Cleveland phrase "offensive partisanship" with the recent fashion in difficult ties. Both these practices of the former teacher – his pronouncing the impressive phrase and his wearing the new fashion – signify cultural distinction. But Levinsky's phrasing also makes these practices parallel with Mr. Bender's "dwel[ling] on the civil-service reform of President Cleveland."

In perceiving the unconscious self-interestedness even in his teacher's sincere support for civil-service reform, Levinsky implicitly performs an analysis parallel to Bourdieu's. Levinsky recognizes what capital – of abstract merit, of a distance from need, of disinterested honesty – can be accrued by reformers, whose emphasis on *form* asserts a distance from base interest and necessity. Although Mr. Bender is himself "naive" and "spotlessly honest" (p. 314), Levinsky's sentence points out that, at some misrecognized level, the teacher's commitment to civil-service reform is like the literary and artistic commitments Mr. Bender also often invokes: a formal or aesthetic commitment, by definition detached from base selfishness, his commitment to civil-service reform increases the teacher's cultural status.

Their encounter inverts the previous power relation of the two men, leaving "something like obsequiousness" in Bender's voice (p. 313). Although the power shift results in part from Levinsky's now being in a position to offer his former instructor a job, it stems also from Levinsky's recognizing in Bender's cultural practices what Bender himself misrecognizes. The superior intellectual position Levinsky thereby achieves vis-à-vis Bender can be compared with the superior position *Distinction* claims for the sociologist who succeeds in discovering "the social

motivations behind structures that positivism sees as arbitrary and for-
tuitous."[15] The distinction of *Distinction*, one might say, lies in the book's
recognition of social misrecognition – the misrecognized interests and
motivations that are a structural aspect of "disinterested" behavior in
bourgeois culture. Such bourgeois misrecognitions constitute the "material" from which, for over 600 pages, *Distinction*'s own insight distinguishes it. In contrast to Levinsky, however, Bourdieu's study never
situates within itself, and itself within, the matters it explicates.[16]
Levinsky not only recognizes the "offensive partisanship" of Mr. Bender,
up to and including the self-interest which motivates Bender's very use
of that "new" phrase, but Levinsky is self-consciously aware of – he
often is even self-ironic about – the partisan purposes served by his own
misrecognitions.

   Describing his initial "passion" for the works of Darwin and Spencer,
for example, he writes that these works justified his personally useful
vision of the "working man and everyone else who was poor" as "a
misfit, a weakling, a failure . . . ruck." Levinsky adds that

apart from the purely intellectual intoxication they gave me, they flattered my
vanity as one of the "fittest." It was as though all the wonders of learning,
acumen, ingenuity, and assiduity displayed in these works had been intended,
among other purposes, to establish my title as one of the Victors of Existence.
(p. 283)

   Levinsky's allusion to his vanity, the caps he uses to write "my title as
one of the Victors of Existence," and the explanation he goes on to give
of the concrete application that he made to his own employees demonstrate that he now recognizes not only his own prior misrecognitions but
their underlying purpose, of which he was not fully aware at the time.
He now perceives that his excited "intoxication" while reading was just
as linked to personal profit as it was to any freedom of the "purely intellectual." Levinsky's own "acumen" elicits credit from the reader here not
so much for the "ingenuity and assiduity" necessary for a recent immigrant to read the difficult Darwin and Spencer, but for his later reading
of his own reading, the perspective evidenced in his present *interpretation*
(introduced by "it was as though . . .") of the then misrecognized ideological function his reading served for him.[17]

   I do not wish to argue that, because self-consciousness can bring such
cultural credit with it, self-consciousness is ethically or politically wrong.
On the contrary, in many contexts self-consciousness is a necessary condition for ethical or political intervention. Yet I do suggest that we should

try to be as aware as possible of the cultural "elevations" self-consciousness can accrue (here I note, self-consciously of course, the paradoxes in my own statement), especially since we are only beginning to understand the complex interlocking spirals of various possible forms of capital accumulation. Again and again, Levinsky's "meta"-perspective on the economic value of what had been posed as "pure" practices (purely intellectual, spiritual, aesthetic) yields at least a slight distance for him from the economic interestedness involved.[18] At such moments Levinsky both receives the "purely intellectual" credit of a self-conscious viewpoint that exceeds the instrumental and still also receives whatever economic profit is in question.

THE GENUINE ARTICLE

Levinsky's pointing to and describing forms of economic functionalism, especially those forms that are rarely recognized as economic functionalism, produces a position for him slightly detached from it. His detachment from instrumentality can be seen in the most general perspective, however, as made possible by the gap entailed by any given designation of "reality." Whether the real is identified as the instrumental, as use, as labor, or as the body, such an identification cannot but bring with it the *différance* (difference/deferral) inherent in all acts of naming. *The Rise of David Levinsky* demonstrates how the *différance* involved in any designation of the real can be effectively *credited* to the cultural or intellectual account of an individual. (In chapter 5, I will consider the intellectual prestige at stake when individual critical theorists or critical approaches seek to privilege certain categories or terms as "materiality.") The gap necessarily accompanying specifications of materiality can be refigured as a privileged distance from it, as "distinction" in Bourdieu's precise sense of the term. Levinsky's distinction, we might even say, derives from his managing himself to occupy, or indeed to personify, the gap between materiality and any name for it. Levinsky achieves this refiguration through his assumption of the responsibility, at least within the space of his narrative, for elaborating what will count as the really real.

The latter portion of this chapter focuses on the financial profits and the profits of cultural status that Levinsky gains through positioning his own Yiddish past as a locus of reality, as "the genuine article" – a gesture which involves his recurrent re-presentations of that past: "I love to brood over my youth . . . It seems more real to me" (pp. 3–4). It is worth noting first, however, that the fact that representation includes a

temporal space between signifier and signified is thematized from the
start as central to Levinsky's business venture. When he begins his
factory, "the magic word 'credit' loomed in letters of gold before me."
He uses his new checkbook to take advantage of representation's
"magic" gap, and of the "time" that gap makes it possible to produce:
"One might issue a check before one had the amount and thereby gain
a day's time" (p. 204). A similar temporal gap between representation
and what is represented allows Levinsky to engage in "the practice of
pirating designs" from better-established manufacturers. Because of the
necessary interposition of time between a designer's sketch and the
"new cloak or suit" to which it corresponds, Levinsky's black-market
purchases of stolen sketches gives his small factory the opportunity to
beat larger competitors to the market with the very garments that they
themselves had commissioned (p. 345).

It is re-presenting his own "wretched" past, however (his "wretched
boyhood" in the Old Country and the "wretched period" when he had
first arrived in America [pp. 4, 140]), and re-presenting this Yiddish past
as what still, really, constitutes his own "inner identity" that provides
Levinsky with "the most important of all the items that gave me an
advantage over the princes of the trade. That was cheap labor" (p. 271).[19]
He employs "the best ladies' tailors . . . old-fashioned pious people, green
in the country," who also happen to be "the cheapest labor obtainable"
(pp. 323, 271). Decrying those who "were constantly harping on 'class
struggle,' 'class antagonism,' 'class psychology,'" Levinsky insists, "I
would dismiss it all as absurd" (p. 519). But reproducing, as the most
"inner" part of his current identity, his "old self" (who was "born and
reared in the lowest depth of poverty and . . . arrived in America – in
1885 – with four cents in my pocket"), serves a function very like that
which would be served by a factory manager's understanding the "class
psychology" of his workers. It enables Levinsky to acquire a cohesive,
union-proof group of skilled employees: "They felt perfectly at home in
my shop, and would rather be underpaid than be employed in an up-to-
date factory where a tailor was expected to wear a starched collar and
necktie and was made the butt of ridicule if he covered his head every
time he took a drink of water" (p. 270).

Levinsky's ability "to picture . . . the working" of a recent immigrant's
mind multiplies the number of such immigrants who work for him. His
ability to produce this "picture," however, depends on his locating those
workings as also "my own," something that, for example, the less self-
conscious night-school teacher Mr. Bender cannot do: "It did not occur

to him that people born to speak another language were guided by another language logic, so to say, and that in order to reach my under-standing he would have to impart his ideas in terms of my own linguis-tic psychology" (p. 134). That what he calls his "own linguistic psychology" is central in Levinsky's labor relations is emphasized by the fact that most of his employees bear "the Antomir accent" of Levinsky's hometown in Russia. "Gradually an Antomir atmosphere had been established in my shop, and something like a family spirit of which I was proud. We had formed a Levinsky Antomir Benefit Society of which I was an honorary member and which was made up, for the most part, of my own employees" (p. 378). Levinsky's status as "honorary member" of the Antomir Society signifies his own privileged position in the factory. The honorary member encompasses at the same time Levinsky's poor immigrant self, identified with the other, laboring members of the Antomir Society, and the aspects of his current self in excess of that identification.[20]

To manage his labor force Levinsky turns repeatedly to a dimension of himself he identifies as still "precisely the same" as the Levinsky who "arrived in America – in 1885 – with four cents in my pocket" (p. 4). Depicting earlier moments of his immigrant past as what comprises his real, essential self also becomes crucial to Levinsky's marketing strate-gies. The Russian-Jewish Levinsky explains to gentile buyers that he will guarantee to undersell the German-American Jews because they are pri-marily merchants, not mechanics. Because he is himself nothing more, deep down, than a common "cloak-operator," Levinsky argues that he knows ways to economize "that never occurred to the heads of the old houses" (p. 337). When marketing his garments, Levinsky asserts himself to *be* the immigrant laborer he once was. Although he insists to them that "I mean it in a literal sense," however, that self-designation represents only one dimension of Levinsky's self that another, distinct dimension, the American businessman, seeks to exchange with the buyers.

Always, Levinsky's "more real" immigrant identifications become profitable because of how they operate in conjunction with his other set of allegiances: to Americanized standards. Thus, the low "actual wage" Levinsky secretly gives his old-country tailors makes money for his busi-ness because of its relational opposition to the "union wages" paid by all the other New York shops (p. 285). In this connection, the content of the primary repeated example of Jake/Yekl's speech, "*Dot'sh a kin' a' man I am*," becomes significant. The repetition in *Yekl* of this same phrase with the same mutilations and breaks begins to evoke an iterable kind or type.

The "kin'" that Jake's dropped consonants inscribe him within becomes a category composed of deviations from the standard. In the linguistic register, as well, *Yekl* suggests that it contains several different Yiddish dialects, all deviant from the standard: "English was the official language of the academy, where it was broken and mispronounced in as many different ways as there were Yiddish dialects represented in that institution" (p. 17). The "academy"/"institution" referred to here is a dancing school, but the sentence articulates the relation that *Yekl* itself establishes between its narrative voice's "official language" and the "broken" dialects which are "represented *in* that institution." More generally, the cultural capital *Yekl's* narrative accrues – like that accrued by the institution of the ethnic realist novel itself – comes from its special access to, yet important distinction from, the broken bits of the real represented in it. Even the most assimilationist of ethnic narratives, such as Mary Antin's *The Promised Land*, derives cultural capital from its detailedly intimate grasp of the *pre*-assimilated life that it also denigrates as inferior.

The Rise of David Levinsky sets up such a relation with what might be called the ethnic real in Levinsky's figuration of traditional Judaism as "fall[en] to pieces" in America (p. 110). We have already seen how Levinsky profits financially by constructing his factory as a place where certain facets of "the orthodox Jewish faith" (such as covering one's head to take a drink of water, or not allowing work on Saturdays) can be found as isolated shards of "the Old Ghetto way" (p. 233). The novel further suggests, however, that the cultural power of a figure such as Levinsky to preserve any parts of traditional Judaism within the American context depends on the Jewish past being somehow broken into such iterable pieces. Levinsky's claiming the right to designate bits of old-country Jewish culture as "the genuine article" (his phrase for a bowl of traditionally prepared sorrel soup) becomes a characteristic practice, one that elevates his cultural position as well as adds to his financial success.

Each of the specific aspects of traditional Jewish culture that *The Rise of David Levinsky* includes in its narrative figures as an isolated, even defective "piece," whose status as fragment nevertheless both gives it a compelling reality and makes possible its iteration in America. When Levinsky lights a *Yarzeit* (memorial) candle for his mother, for example, he emphasizes the very fragmentedness that is foregrounded in the candle's juxtaposition against the plush Americanized synagogue. The jaggedness of the candle's small flame evokes, Levinsky insists, the uninterrupted "reality" of his "Russian past." The flame's flicker "turned my present life into a dream and my Russian past into reality" (pp. 388–9).

Similarly, when Levinsky attends a Passover seder held in the home of
an Americanized Russian-Jewish family, he participates in the ironic distance of the children toward the ritual ("Anna gave me a merry wink").
At the same time, however, he inhabits what he insists is not "pretended"
in "the scene": "I could almost see the memories of his childhood days
which the scene evoked in the father's mind. I could feel the solemnity
that swelled his heart." In Levinsky's formulation, the authentic Jewish
foods at the seder reproduce, fragmentarily but with a tactile realness,
the history of "our unhappy people," which was also being reproduced
at other seders, all over the world (pp. 494–6).[21]

YIDDISH-SPEAKING WOMEN

On the veranda of a Catskills resort, Levinsky describes himself hearing,
as he listens to the other guests, "a hubbub of broken English, the gibberish being mostly spoken with self-confidence and ease . . . Bad
English replete with literal translations from untranslatable Yiddish
idioms had become [these people's] natural speech" (p. 426). It is crucial
to see that what differentiates the status of the other resort guests from
Levinsky's own narrating position is not the guests' "literal translations
from untranslatable Yiddish idioms" as such. Like the other pieces of
"the old Ghetto way" that *The Rise of David Levinsky* values as "precisely
the same" – the seder ritual, Yarzeit candles, greenhorn tailors who
"work about fourteen hours a day" just as they did in Europe – literal
translations of idiomatic Yiddish phrases occur throughout Levinsky's
own narrative. Levinsky's narrative, however, explicitly identifies *his*
literal translations as "bad English" by putting them in extra quotation
marks. (In such moments, we might say that Levinsky simultaneously
incorporates the linguistic positions represented both by Silas Lapham
and by the realist taste of Silas's "literary" daughter, Penelope.) By contrast, the speech of the hotel guests presents the literal without recognizing the damage thereby done to untranslatable idioms. The hotel guests'
deluded "self-confidence and ease" (as opposed to Levinsky's "great self-
consciousness") means that they are entrapped in the givens of Yiddish
word-choice and syntax without the profit of enough distance to identify the literal translations as "literal," to identify and value the ethnic
real as such.[22]

Levinsky's own narrative, however, does include a few actually quoted
direct translations that are not marked off within extra quotation marks.
The first time Levinsky meets a potential love-interest, Dora, she scolds

her daughter: "Is that the vay to talk to a gentleman? . . . Vere you lea'n up to be such a pig? Not by your mamma!" (p. 229). Reserving to himself the moment of pointing out to Dora the examples of too-literal translations from Yiddish in her speech – such as her placement of the prepositions "up" and "by" – produces erotic pleasure for Levinsky (pp. 229–30, 255): Dora becomes his only full-scale love affair.[23] A closely parallel erotic charge displays itself in Levinsky's experience of the Jewish-immigrant prostitutes in New York. He attributes his fascination with them to the fact that they can be found mixed in with the population. Like "English replete with literal translations from untranslatable Yiddish idioms" (as opposed both to Yiddish and to properly idiomatic English), the prostitutes are "allowed to live in the same tenement-houses with respectable people . . ." (p. 125). He enjoys walking around neighborhoods identifying "women of the approachable class." Collating with his relation to ethnic "pieces," Levinsky's relation to Jewish women is structured by this sense of pleasure and power that he gets from identifying dimensions of them that he can position as a degraded "real," including Dora's literally translated Yiddish prepositions and pronunciations, her sorrel soup, and the accessible sexuality of prostitutes. (We might also include here the "homely rhetoric" that Levinsky informs us "is rather a common talent among Yiddish-speaking women" [p. 300].)

By contrast, Jake/Yekl utterly rejects such materialized dimensions of his wife Gitl (he ultimately divorces her):

[H]e would see . . . Gitl's bandanna kerchief and her prominent gums, or hear an un-American piece of Yiddish pronounced with Gitl's peculiar lisp – that very lisp, which three years ago he used to mimic fondly, but which now grated on his nerves and was apt to make his face twitch with sheer disgust . . . "Ah, may she be killed, the horrid greenhorn." (p. 44)

Gitl's lisp, which evokes both her body and her resistantly Yiddish-sounding language, disgusts Jake. But the twitching face that indicates his inability to form a structured relation with Gitl's lisp is in itself an uncontrollable "physical defect" signaling to readers that Jake himself constitutes that novel's primary alignment with ethnic materiality. Unlike the moment in *The Wings of the Dove* when Densher's identificatory "wince" mimes Milly's physical suffering but he then immediately regains control, Jake can assert no control over his own twitching face. Never achieving the leverage over his own ethnic responses that would allow him to appreciate Gitl's ethnic realness (both to take pleasure in it, that is, and to gain value from it), Jake finds himself collapsed back into the Yekl that the book's title emphasizes he has never really "risen" from. By contrast to Levinsky's valuing of Dora as "the genuine article," Jake's uncontrollable horror at Gitl's "uncouth and un-American" character-istics (she refuses, for example, to surrender the wig Orthodox Judaism requires for married women and will change nothing in "the baggy shapelessness of the Povodye garment" in which she arrives from Russia) marks his own failure to become a distinct American agent (pp. 34, 36).

Within the novel *Yekl*, the intellectual Bernstein, Jake's shopmate and lodger, stands for the Levinsky-like relation to Gitl that Jake never real-izes. While the greenhorn Jake ironically finds untenable the juxtaposi-tion of "he . . . Jake the Yankee, with this bonnetless, wigged, dowdyish little greenhorn by his side" (p. 23), Bernstein establishes a relation with her parallel to the identificatory, yet bi-positional, one of reading. In an emblematic moment allying his interest in various levels of language with his appreciation of Gitl's old ghetto ways, Bernstein keeps "his index finger on the passage he had been reading, and his eyes on Gitl's plumpish cheek, bathed in the roseate light" (p. 53). In *Yekl*, it is Bernstein who assumes the position of praising Gitl's "sour soup," which he values as a reproduced piece of an earlier moment: "It's a long time since I tasted such a borscht" (p. 46).

While Bernstein eventually marries Gitl, however, David Levinsky never does establish a domestic relationship with any one. As Levinsky's rise progresses, with each of his successive encounters with women not resulting in marriage, his loneliness takes on the "pungency of acute physical discomfort," becoming an increasingly prominent dimension of his self (p. 377). His feelings of loneliness – experienced as "intervals [of] a steady gnawing pain" (p. 311) – especially mark the final section of the book, titled "Episodes of a Lonely Life," where Levinsky describes how he reached "the height of my business success." Levinsky's question of what his success means without any loved ones to share it, his recurring question of "who I worked for," comes in this final section to obsess him more and more (p. 525).

I wish to conclude by suggesting that rather than Levinsky's painful loneliness functioning as an allegory for the Jewish people's alienation in America (this is the most typical claim in the criticism of Cahan's novel, just as it is a convention in criticism of Jewish-American fiction),[24] his repeated inability to set up a domestic scene ultimately works more efficiently to accrue cultural capital for him than would any of the mar-riages he contemplates. Levinsky's repeated question of "who I worked for" insistently reminds the reader of his continued separation from any actual, specifiable motivation. The pronoun "who" serves to personify the "void of significance" that Levinsky begins the book by telling us "is coupled with" his business success. "Who" is a personal pronoun, but as an interrogative (rather than a nominative or objective) pronoun it is a purely formal term; unlike other pronouns (including deictics such as "this" and "that"), it does not point even contingently to a segment of the phenomenal world. Levinsky's deciding that his has been and will be a "lonely life" locates the empty "who" his question keeps repeating as a permanent internal dimension of him: indeed, the syntax of his question suggests that he works *for* that empty "who." Levinsky's very life (rather than simply a wife) thereby becomes the materiality against which an empty-by-definition internal term becomes marked. The phrase "lonely life" juxtaposes an ostentatiously materialized term (Levinsky's money-making "life" itself) and an ostentatiously non-materialized one ("*who* I worked for").[25] The "ache" of regret that Merton Densher hangs onto as *The Wings of the Dove* ends will allow Densher indefinitely to prolong those aspects of his relation with Milly that raised his cultural status. Here, however, Levinsky's entire American "rise" becomes, like the wholesale butcher who epitomizes his discovery of the country, the site of a disjunction between materiality and what, next to it, can thereby be most tellingly distinguished from it.

CHAPTER FOUR

What Nona knows

Some lived in it and never felt it but he knew it all was nada y pues nada y nada y pues nada. Our nada who art in nada nada be thy name thy kingdom nada thy will be nada in nada as it is in nada.
                    Ernest Hemingway, "A Clean, Well-Lighted Place"

"Oh, but I mean a convent where nobody believes in anything."
                    Nona, in Edith Wharton's *Twilight Sleep*

"You are all a lost generation."
                    Gertrude Stein, as cited by Ernest Hemingway

Edith Wharton's scandalized disapproval of the flapper makes for part of a widely held notion that she disdained modernist cultural forms, whether they were instantiated in twenties jazz culture or in the literary modernism that rose to prominence during the post-War portion of her own career.[1] Wharton was indeed harsh both towards what she saw as the self-indulgent narcissism of the "new" New Woman and towards the "turgid welter of pornography" that, in her view, comprised much of the literature celebrated by the "youngs."[2] The overlap in her views of modern women and of modernist literature is shown by her response when asked in 1928 whether she had yet read Virginia Woolf's *Orlando*. No, Wharton said. The photographs of Woolf in publicity for the book "made me quite ill. I can't believe that where there is exhibitionism of that order there can be any real creative gift."[3] References to being nauseated or worse by the period's self-vaunting young women, especially those who claimed public recognition as artists or intellectuals, occur regularly in Wharton's letters and incidental writings of the period. Writing to a friend, for example, about having read a new "'jazz' book" by Stella Benson, "the young English novelist whom all the 'youngs' in England consider their best," Wharton proclaims "it makes me want to crawl away and die."[4]

The disgust went both ways. Wharton (who always insisted on being named in public as *Mrs*. Wharton, despite her own divorce) was one of the iconic figures whom the intellectuals and artists included in Ann Douglas's *Terrible Honesty: Mongrel Manhattan in the 1920s* saw themselves as rebelling against. Carl Van Vechten, whom Douglas identifies as "PR man extraordinaire" for New York City's modernist scene, employed her as a touchstone for all that was stodgy and repressed in old New York and in the traditional novel alike.[5] Nella Larsen made similar rhetorical use of her.[6] Yet, as is perhaps hinted by Wharton's recurrent imagery of nauseated sickness, she did keep trying, maybe not to swallow, but somehow to incorporate or assimilate "jazz" culture and its most emblematic figure, the flapper. Stella Benson's "jazz" novel *The Poor Man* (1922) may have made Wharton want to crawl away and die, but with a vexed admiration she also called it "brilliant & fatiguing."[7] More notably, intellectual or artistic flappers figure with increasing complexity in Wharton's novels of the mid 1920s, including *The Glimpses of the Moon* (1922), *The Mother's Recompense* (1925), and, the book that I will focus on here, *Twilight Sleep* (1927).

Although it has been strangely overlooked by Wharton criticism – perhaps because most critics still treat her as a pre- or at the least a resolutely antimodernist writer – *Twilight Sleep* represents Wharton's most powerful attempt to take the flapper seriously as a thinking, feeling, and, I will contend, "realist" sensibility. Nona Manford, the novel's flapper protagonist, belongs "to the generation of bewildered disenchanted young people who had grown up since the Great War."[8] Like Fitzgerald's and Hemingway's better-known youths of the period, Nona and her set (as an older character remarks) "jazz all day and drink all night – or vice versa" (p. 43). Having enjoyed "her full share of the perpetual modern agitations," Nona knows "most of the new ways of being rotten" (pp. 109, 206). "Oh, what we girls don't know, mother!" (p. 190). I wish to suggest that Wharton's book ultimately accords to Nona a unique intellectual status, although one that is hard to think of as elevated because it is so oppressively heavy as literally to prostrate her.

Within *Twilight Sleep*, Nona becomes the physical, but even more the cognitive and emotional, bearer of what might be thought of as a "jazz knowledge." The knowledge that Nona carries in both body and mind is, first, an intimate, insider's grasp of elements that Wharton found most disturbing about jazz-age American culture: its solipsistic pursuit of pleasure and "self-expression," its (ostensible) celebration of unrestrained female sexuality, its forays into race-mixing, and its fashionable nihilism ("nothing lasts for our lot," Nona remarks [p. 143]). Yet, at the same time, what the flapper Nona comes to know is deeper, scarier, more catastrophic than all of these.

ONE OF THE TRENCH WATCHERS

Twilight Sleep is the novel of Wharton's where bottom-line "reality" is most explicitly up for grabs. The title itself evokes an in-between state where it is difficult to tell reality from dream or from illusion. With an almost allegorical clarity, the book anatomizes competing forces and figures that each strive for the cultural authority (borrowing a phrase from Amy Kaplan) "both to possess and to dispense access to the real."[9] Among the conflicting versions of reality advanced by figures in the novel, who range from Progressive reformers to New Thought mystics to Nona's hard-headed attorney father, the catastrophic real with which Nona ultimately establishes an understanding (understanding in the sense of both comprehension and arrangement) is the same real that the novel itself despairingly corroborates. Put most broadly, that real is the inherently self-destructive inner nature of civilization and law themselves. Wharton may have criticized aspects of them throughout her career, but she had always believed that the ideals that "history and conduct and civilization" were supposed to incarnate – ideals of intellectual and aesthetic achievement, as well as of underlying order and stability – were what "made the world livable."[10] Wharton has Nona confront the same real, however, that she felt herself to be facing in the 1920s – a real where irrational self-destructiveness seems not only outside but also to inhere *within* "conduct and civilization."

In the fiction for which she is best known today, that set among the social elite of nineteenth-century and turn-of-the-century New York, Wharton depicts as most substantive, as most undeniably and effectively *there*, the stabilizing weight of social usage. Nancy Bentley has recently analyzed the intricate and inescapable structures of convention that this fiction explores as the "tribal discipline" of manners. Wharton's portrayal of manners reveals how "the operations of everyday social life" constitute "subtle internal forces that members of a social caste exert upon each other in their efforts to keep up standards of taste or brilliance, which in turn are the regulating boundaries that determine class power." In Wharton's work, "manners become the keys to the secrets of social control and cohesion." Like the contemporary ethnographers and anthropologists with whom Bentley associates her, moreover, Wharton gains for her authorial voice "a special analytic expertise" by revealing the underlying mechanisms, including the violent mechanisms, that social control depends on. Such violent mechanisms include, for instance, old New York's "sacrificial" rituals, which help to maintain communal stability through the expulsion of disruptive figures such as Ellen Olenska.[11] In *Twilight Sleep*, however, Wharton's only novel focused entirely on 1920s America, Nona faces a social order that is not violent only to maintain or protect itself. The real that *Twilight Sleep* depicts is of the social order's perverse violence *against* itself, against all that it supposedly holds dear.

Towards the end of *Twilight Sleep*, Wharton makes the novel's sole reference to World War I:

Nona herself felt more and more like one of the trench watchers pictured in the war-time papers. There she sat in the darkness on her narrow perch, her eyes glued to the observation-slit which looked out over seeming emptiness . . . (p. 237)

I will return shortly to the significance of Nona's evoking the war and its trenches. In its most immediate context, however, the passage refers metaphorically to Nona's difficult position as the only character in the book, including her father himself, who can even begin to direct her gaze towards the dangerous terrain created by her father's incestuous passion for his daughter-in-law Lita. As New York's most prominent attorney, Dexter Manford's "power" is both "professional and social" (p. 60). A significant relay point between the city's wealthiest families and its juridical establishment (including the police), Dexter represents their combined authority. Personally instantiating lawful control, he embodies "a calm sense of mastery – mastery over himself and others" (p. 52).[12] But the father-lawyer's professional, social, and paternal mastery all turn out, not simply to conceal, but in fact to be permeated by, even organized around, his violent and self-destructive desire for his symbolic daughter.[13] Wharton describes this incestuous desire, which runs counter to the founding prohibition of family and society alike, as operating in "fundamental indifference" to all but its "own comfort and convenience" (p. 232). Dexter's desire for Lita is not even quite conscious to himself until its sudden consummation in the book's final chapters, yet it "obscurely" guides all of his decisions both in his office and at home (p. 235). Even Dexter doesn't understand why, for example, he irrationally commits some of his wife's fortune to pay off the debts of a profligate young Italian, but this has the indirect effect of keeping the glamorous and potentially distracting Michaelangelo out of New York and away from Lita. "It was as if he were engrossed in some deep and secret purpose, and resolved to clear away whatever threatened to block his obstinate advance" (p. 235).

The several members of Dexter's family and extended family who balance their own stability on his "far-reaching" authority have, at intervals, a new and disturbing "sense of moving among incomprehensible and overpowering forces" (pp. 71, 158). Dexter's family includes not only his biological daughter, Nona, and his wife Pauline, but also the son from his wife's previous marriage, Jim Wyant, for whom Dexter has taken on the paternal role – as he therefore has for Lita, to whom Jim is married. The family over which Dexter watches and wards extends even to his wife's alcoholic aristocrat of an ex-husband, Arthur Wyant, who carries a "profound impression" of Dexter's masterful strength and turns to him whenever he needs help or guidance (p. 217). Among these familial dependents, only Nona Manford begins to apprehend that the patriarchal position Dexter embodies has been (adapting a phrase from Juliet Flower MacCannell) "divested of its symbolic, law-giving, life-preserving function."[14] Only Nona turns her direct gaze toward the "blurred and uncertain" void (p. 134) that Dexter Manford's incestuous drive produces in the very place previously filled, in the prewar world of Wharton's earlier work, by the rules, conventions, and manners of civilization itself.

Wharton's image, cited above, of Nona as "one of the trench watchers pictured in the war-time papers," looking through an observation-slit "over seeming emptiness," connects the domestic terrain Nona sees with the effects and implications of World War I. Like the apocalyptic landscapes that recur so inescapably in the writing of postwar modernists, the emptiness over which Nona looks is not neutral but instead traumatically threatening. The "seeming emptiness" of Nona's battlefield thus differs significantly from the all-but personified absence that David Levinsky's vacant "who" represents. David Levinsky's conjugal intimacy with the empty "who" for whom he "works" may make him feel alienated from his own material success, but at the same time it helps to distinguish him from basely material concerns. Nona, however, is like the wise waiter given privileged insight by fellow lost-generationer Hemingway in "A Clean, Well-Lighted Place" (cited in my first epigraph, above). Nona not only lives in and feels emptiness, but, like Hemingway's waiter, she goes farther than most in recognizing that it *all* "was nada y pues nada." As is perhaps suggested, however, by the closeness of nada and Nona, or by the "no" within Nona, Wharton's character cannot escape even temporarily into a refuge like that of the waiter's clean, well-lighted café.

Wharton's description of Nona's "glued eyes" echoes a motif of her wartime journalism, letters, and fiction: that of witnesses (wounded soldiers, refugees, medical personnel) returned from the front with "fixed eyes" forever stuck on a "vision of the horror" that "one dare not picture."[15] So too, Nona cannot avert her gaze from a catastrophe so horrific that it defies representation ("one dare not picture" it). Unlike those literally returned from the battlefield, however, she always remains on "the front," even or especially at home. For her, the extremely clean, all too well-lighted paternal estate is itself trenched with danger. At Cedarledge, the family's country house on the Hudson, Dexter and Lita start taking off together for longer and longer stretches of time, leaving Nona and her mother to share awkward dinners, full of forced conversation and sudden silences. Sensing an impending disaster that she cannot yet name, Nona ponders her realization that the "daisy bank at home" cannot be firmly separated from the confusing "Flanders mud," where brutal violence may erupt at any moment and "a man [can be] led out to be shot" by his own officers merely for dozing while on watch (p. 237).

For Wharton, the Great War had changed the face not only of Europe but also of her native city: "The catastrophe of 1914 had 'cut all likeness from the name' of my old New York," she writes in her autobiography. For Wharton's New York, the catastrophe meant the obliteration of everyday life's very "frame-work." "What had seemed unalterable rules of conduct became of a sudden observances as quaintly arbitrary as the domestic rites of the Pharaohs."[16] The war's traumatic "violation of the laws regulating the relations between civilized peoples" – those laws that had, for better and worse, subtended the world Wharton knew and wrote about – was signaled initially by the "perfidy" that underlay Germany's attack on Belgium. It was then savagely evidenced in the fighting itself, years of

fathomless mud, rat-haunted trenches . . . men dying in the barbed wire between the lines or crawling out to save a comrade and being shattered to death on their return.

Still more hideous, for Wharton, was the "dancing and flirting and money-making on the great red mounds of dead" that continued through the war on both sides of the Atlantic, in New York as in Paris, often by those older than the barely adult soldiers who were fighting and dying.[17]

Although she was a passionate advocate for the Allies and against the Germans, when Wharton did refer to the national and international politics behind the war, especially those behind its seemingly interminable duration, she often sounded like the Ezra Pound of "Hugh Selwyn Mauberly," blaming "old men's lies" for the obscene waste of "young blood and high blood,/fair cheeks and fine bodies." She spoke of "young intelligences" victimized by "centuries of sinister diplomacy" and alluded to the men "in high places" on both sides who were guilty of "evil ambitions and connivances" (pp. 192–3).[18] She shared the shock of one of her fictional characters at the possibility "that some senile old beast of a diplomatist should agree, after a good dinner, that all we love best must be offered up."[19]

In a superb unpublished dissertation on Edith Wharton, Jennie Kassanoff corraborates that, for Wharton, "the Great War dismantled the binaristic logic of 'war front' versus 'home front.'" Although she does not treat *Twilight Sleep*, Kassanoff confirms a consistently strong link for Wharton between the war and the theme of incest tracing a remarkable series of images in Wharton's non-fiction writing about France under war, in her novels that focus on the war itself, and in *The Mother's Recompense* (1925), a novel set in Europe and New York during the early 1920s. For Kassanoff, the image that Wharton came most "to associate with wartime and post-war civilization was that of a roofless house." In literally blowing the roof off of supposedly safe domestic spaces, "the war had stripped the family bare . . . exposing the taboos and transgressions housed within its borders."[20] Alan Price, who has performed the most detailed extant research on Wharton during the war, similarly observes that, during and after the war, Wharton's "fictional production dealt repeatedly with the taboo of incest." The incest, he points out, was sometimes between a father and biological daughter, as in the Beatrice Palmato fragment, but "more frequently it involved an intergenerational advance by a much older male guardian toward a female ward, as was the case between Charity and Lawyer Royall in *Summer*" (p. 173).[21] I would add that, although Wharton describes her incest novel *Summer*, composed in war-torn Paris during 1916, as "as remote as possible in setting and subject from the scenes about me," she notes in the same paragraph that it was written "while the rest of my being was steeped in the tragic realities of the war" (*Backward Glance*, p. 356).[22] If the war affected Wharton "less as an international military conflict than as a systematic attack on the ancestral home," as Kassanoff claims,[23] then Wharton found fathers and other male "guardians" inside the home to be as implicated in its violation as any shells falling from outside.

I have been referring to Dexter's incestuous desire as violent primarily because, in traducing the family and social order's most fundamental law, it creates battlefield-like "havoc" across all of the terrain covered by the novel (p. 176). Indeed, the secret sex that Dexter and Lita finally commence causes the climactic but unintended shooting of Nona by Arthur Wyant, her mother's weak and alcoholic ex-husband, who is the novel's other father figure. *Twilight Sleep* continually associates the patriarch's carnal desire with the carnage of war. As Nona intuits from the start, however, Dexter's desire also figures as violent for its own underlying impulse towards death. This most "deep and secret purpose" (again, secret even from himself) that Nona senses in her father closely resembles the fundamental death drive that Freud describes in *Beyond the Pleasure Principle*, published seven years before *Twilight Sleep* in 1920.

The organism that Freud posits in *Beyond the Pleasure Principle* wishes above all to relieve itself of tension by returning to an earlier state, that of being inanimate. The organism's various "component instincts," including even instincts of "self-assertion and of mastery" (traits strongly associated with *Twilight Sleep*'s "resolute and purposeful" lawyer-father) thus turn out to have as their ultimate function "to assure that the organism shall follow its own path to death."[24] Although Freud initially attempts to separate those instincts that function in the service of death from "erotic" or "life" instincts, the more that he writes about the death drive, as Dennis Foster points out, the more that "love and death twist together."[25] So too, throughout Wharton's novel Dexter strategizes actively and elaborately (albeit for the most part unconsciously) to consummate his passion for Lita. Yet at the core of this same motivation is his longing to enter the "great pool of silence," the "reservoir" of tranquility that her image mysteriously evokes for him (p. 72). Although he finds her intensely exciting, Dexter's sense that a woman like Lita could "flood one's soul with peace," his imagination of "let[ting] himself sink" into her "spring sweetness as a man might sink on a woman's breast," represent at once a fantasized return to infancy and a desire to drown (p. 219). The morning after Dexter and Lita first have sex, her father tellingly strikes Nona as having achieved a final state of inanimation: he looks "strangely different" – "rather like his own memorial bust in bronze. She shivered a little . . ." (p. 280).

Twilight Sleep connects the threatening emptiness between battlefield trenches – "no man's land," as it came to be called – with the loss at home of the structuring "frame-work" provided by "what had seemed unalterable rules of conduct."[26] These rules had been anchored by (again quoting MacCannell) "the symbolic, law-giving, life-preserving function" presumed to reside in the father.[27] In the novel's world, the "Great War" and its battlefields can be openly mentioned, even pictured in old newspapers (pp. 12, 237). But it is the gutting from within of the very "laws regulating the relations between civilized people" – a gutting that is effected by the same paternal authority "in high places" supposed to represent and guarantee lawful conduct – that becomes most devastating. Unlike the horrors of the Great War itself, the postwar lawyer-father's "ambitions and connivances" (here I am returning to the phrase that Wharton used to describe betrayals by political and financial leaders during wartime) to commit incest with a daughter are approached only with indirectness and ambiguity, even by Wharton's authorial voice.

Described at several key moments with language that suggestively connotes the ominous, Dexter's physical presence itself accrues a portentous aura of frightening transgression, as he startles female family members by appearing unexpectedly, usually in intimate female spaces within the home. This is how Wharton depicts Pauline's entry into the darkened sitting room of Kitty Landish, a female relative who has previously been a sort of guardian to Lita:

The void into which Pauline advanced gave prominence to the figure of a man who stood with his back to her, looking through the window . . . The visitor, duskily blocked against a sullen March sky, was at first not recognizable; but half way toward him Pauline exclaimed: "Dexter!" He turned, and his surprise met hers. (p. 133)

The passage's imagery evokes the obtrusively prominent but barely recognizable quality of Dexter's incestuous desire. Pauline at first sees not her husband but a "visitor," whose "duskily blocked" presence, obstructing the window, helps to give Pauline the unsettling sense of advancing into a "void." Dexter is there, as he tells his wife with an oddly "defiant jauntiness," to get information about Lita, but then she notices that "his face grew blurred and uncertain" (p. 134).

On the one occasion in the novel when the incestuous possibility comes closest to direct articulation, that possibility is immediately, almost hysterically, repressed. After a strange conversation with her husband about midway through the novel, Pauline experiences a "cold brush," "the mere flit of a doubt – no more" that Dexter may have shown "an exaggerated interest" in his daughter-in-law: but she quickly "felt its preposterousness and banished it in disgust and fear" (p. 236). Similarly Dexter himself, driving in a car with Lita, restrains his "impulse to lay a hand over hers" and then, very briefly, has "the sense of having just grazed something dark and lurid, which had threatened to submerge them" (p. 215). Here the darkly lurid "something" remains unspecified. Even in the book's last chapter, just after the climactic night-time scene when Nona has walked in on Dexter and Lita in the latter's bedroom and been accidentally shot, Nona finds herself suddenly awakened, "started up out of nothingness," only to find a "shadowy bulk" beside her bed; it is her father, who had felt, suggestively, "a vague craving to be alone with her." He mumbles a few fragmentary phrases and finally, having "groped for her forehead" to kiss it, leaves Nona alone "in the darkness" (pp. 312–13). Nona's conclusion proves accurate: Everything surrounding her shooting – that is, her father's relentless desire for his daughter-in-law, and the trauma that desire has meant for his family, for the social order, and for the "law" as such – will continue to remain "out of sight and under ground" for all of the characters except herself (p. 307). Throughout the novel, however, the unmentionable status of Dexter's death-linked desire only contributes to its continued positioning as the book's largest, most formidable reality.

From relatively near the beginning of *Twilight Sleep*, the reader starts to realize that Dexter's desire is operating within the book's universe as a level of reality more irresolvable, and more forcefully determining of the trajectory of events, than any other. Like some massive but unseen body, the real of Dexter's desire exerts an indefeasible gravitational pull. In ways that *Twilight Sleep* enables its readers to grasp but that even Dexter himself does not consciously see, his incestuous desire directs characters' movements within houses and from one house to another; it underlies discussions and anxieties that seem to involve entirely other topics; it leads to the stopping, restarting, and then stopping again of an official investigation into "the Mahatma," who is an influential spiritual leader relied on by Dexter's wife Pauline.

Consider a conversation held in Pauline's own boudoir early in the book. Dexter asks his wife to "give me time . . . time . . ." with Lita to try to rescue her from the allure of seeking Hollywood movie stardom (p. 175; ellipses in original). But then, "he stopped abruptly, as if the 'me' had slipped out by mistake," and corrects himself "with a touch of forensic emphasis": "We must all stand shoulder to shoulder to put up this fight for her." Although it is not explicitly spelled out for us, Dexter's abrupt stop and then hasty self-correction from "me" to "we" provide a clear signal of something both selfish and unspeakable in his desire to "rescue" Lita from Hollywood. Yet the reality of Dexter's desire still remains opaque to Pauline who, though she senses a frightening force in Dexter's words, cannot identify its valence. When he leaves her boudoir, Pauline looks slowly around the room: "It was as if she were taking stock of the havoc wrought by an earthquake; but nothing about her showed any sign of disorder except the armchair her husband had pushed back, the rug his movement had displaced" (p. 176). A moment such as this one purposefully confers on the novel's readers the intellectual privilege occasioned by dramatic irony. Albeit with discomfort and pity, *we*, unlike Pauline, do recognize the real shape of the seismic force that she only confusedly senses and then promptly tries to forget ("Sternly she addressed herself to relaxation").

Insofar as, throughout *Twilight Sleep*, the reader is led to recognize various uncomfortable realities that all but one of the novel's characters – Nona – either do not or will not acknowledge, the book positions its readers as more "realist" than the characters and indeed than the entire upper-class American culture that *Twilight Sleep* portrays. The phrase "twilight sleep" literally denotes a compound popular among upper-class women of the 1920s for anesthetizing the pain of childbirth.[28] Wharton's novel expands "twilight sleep"'s meaning to refer to whatever helps one to evade encountering a disturbing reality, whether it be the reality of labor and delivery, the tragic likelihood that a minor character's cancer will recur, awkward conflicts between the religious beliefs of different characters, or even the fact that human beings defecate (more on the latter below). Forms of "twilight sleep" that recur throughout the novel include, for instance, drugs, drinking, and dancing, athletics, society hostessing, and Pauline's sequential devotions to a series of New Thought "healers" who promise to keep her young, to remove "frustration" from her life or wrinkles from the corners of her eyes, or to prove to her the non-existence of suffering.

Wharton sets up scene after scene so that her readers both see a disturbing reality – such as the inevitability of aging – and see through whatever mode of twilight sleep characters employ in attempting to dodge contact with it. Wharton thus rhetorically positions readers so as to feel themselves participants in the movement for "terrible honesty" that Ann Douglas shows to be intellectual and literary modernism's most privileged trope. It is when Wharton invites us, however, to recognize that appeals to "reality" can themselves serve as twilight sleep, covering over a devastating real that is too disruptive for direct representation, that her readers experience the frisson of sharing in the most terrible honesty of all.

Below, I will concentrate on the flapper's intellectual status as conscious bearer of catastrophic knowledge – an ambivalently onerous form of distinction that contrasts with the reader's simpler intellectual privilege. The next section, however, explores further the realer-than-thou experience that *Twilight Sleep* proffers to its readers.

HANDLES OF REALITY

[T]he reality of the child's reproach to his father, "Can't you see that I am burning?", implying the father's fundamental guilt – is more terrifying than so-called external reality itself. He escapes into so-called reality to be able to continue to sleep, to maintain his blindness, to elude awakening into the real of his desire. We can rephrase here the old "hippie" motto of the 1960s: reality is for those who cannot support the dream. "Reality" is a fantasy-construction which enables us to mask the Real of our desire. (Slavoj Žižek, analyzing Freud's "Dream of the Burning Child"[29])

That dishevelled spectre had become Pauline Manford again, in command of herself and the situation, as soon as she could seize on its immediate, its practical sides, could grasp those handles of reality to which she always clung. (*Twilight Sleep*, p. 307)

Wharton's novel sets up an opposition similar to that which Slovenian theorist Slavoj Žižek has identified in Freud's writing between a "real" of terrifying desire and more assimilable "realities." In *Twilight Sleep*, realities serve as "handles" (Wharton's term) that characters reach for in attempting to evade an unbearable real. Dexter's incestuous drive may be always disguised, always concealed underneath or behind something else, but the novel also depicts it paradoxically as, at the same time, an obstinately present real that requires characters' strategic, if unconscious, efforts *not* to see it. The most complex of the strategies employed for *not* recognizing Dexter's catastrophic desire involves characters appealing to what we might call red-herring realities, which they try to give solid value to by setting them over against "artificial activities."

Consider, for instance, the following sequence that Wharton narrates from the perspective of Dexter himself. While he and his wife are hosting a boring, superficial society dinner, Dexter takes refuge in a daydream of escaping his New York life for the ownership of a Midwestern farm, where he would use "his brains, muscles, the whole of him, body and soul, to do real things, bring about real results in the world" instead of his usual round of "exertions that led to nothing, nothing, nothing . . ." (p. 71; ellipses in text). Yet this vision of escaping high society's empty artificiality for a productive world of immediacy and practicality, of "real things . . . real results," is itself a cover for the real of Dexter's desire. His vision of life on a farm turns next to imagining that, after a long tramp with a passel of "healthy, blustery" offspring – "boys and girls (girls too, more little Nonas)" – he and they return to "a woman who looked so absurdly young to be their mother; so – ". The Marchesa, sitting next to Dexter, suddenly breaks in:

You're looking at Jim's wife? . . . No wonder! *Très en beauté* our Lita! . . . But a little difficult to talk to? Little too silent? No? Ah, not to *you*, perhaps – her dear father! Father-in-law, I mean – (p. 72)

Although he *thought* he was envisioning an escape from his current artificial existence to a world of "real things" out in the rural Midwest, Dexter has in fact been staring at Lita. With his waking fantasy coming to rest on the vision of himself married to a woman who is "so absurdly young . . .", Dexter's vision of a more authentic farm existence has allowed him to approach his actual, unacceptable desire, which has nothing to do with the Midwest. (The Marchesa's pointed addition of "father-in-*law*" to her initial designation of Dexter as Lita's "father" emphasizes that his proper position in relation to her is intimately bound up with the law that he himself is supposed to personify.)

Wharton so constructs this scene that we readers, unlike Dexter, discern the bi-level mechanism by which the "father-in-law" rejects dinner-party chitchat to envision a burly authenticity that is itself factitious. We become especially skilled analysts as we recognize that Dexter's vision of working a farm is some sort of screen, which has the sole function of allowing him indirectly to enjoy his *real* fantasy while he still continues not to acknowledge that it even exists. Pushing behind the opposition that Dexter establishes between "artificial" New York society and the "real things" of rural existence (a rather clichéd opposition even in the 1920s, we might conclude with intellectual satisfaction), the reader is led to glimpse the "shadowy bulk" of the father's incestuous desire (p. 312).

The reader is likewise provided with a sensation of doubled access to the *real* real when interpreting Pauline's relatively demystified grasp of what Wharton's earlier *The House of Mirth* calls the "machinery" of wealthy living. For most of the rich, "that machinery is so carefully concealed that one scene flows into another without perceptible agency."[30]

But when Pauline looks, for example, at a beautifully landscaped country estate, she never stops seeing that

each tree, shrub, water-course, herbaceous border, meant not only itself, but the surveying of grades, transporting of soil, tunnelling for drainage, conducting of water . . . [H]er eyes could not linger on any particular beauty without its dissolving into soil, manure, nursery-men's catalogues, and bills . . . (p. 214)

Here Pauline seems to achieve a moment of canonically realist insight. Not unlike Howells's Reverend Sewell or Basil March, who each learn to look *through* the picturesque to underlying poverty, Pauline is able to read specific elements of landscaped beauty for the un-pretty materiality that inheres in them. (Of course, she still elides the actual laborers who dig the drainage tunnels and transport the soil.) The reader of the novel, however, has already gleaned from implicit textual hints that Dexter has (again unconsciously) organized this family sojourn in the country so as to give himself unfettered access to Lita without her husband's presence. Pauline has seen or heard most of the same hints available to the reader, but has failed to apprehend their meaning. Thus, Pauline's vision here may indeed penetrate beneath an aesthetic surface to the unbeautiful realities of money and manure that help to make it up. But this classic act of realist penetration misses the larger, more determining reality of Dexter's "duskily blocked" desire (p. 133). Unlike Pauline herself, the reader perceives that the unacknowledged real of her husband's incestuous desire has at that very moment positioned Pauline on the same landscape whose nitty-gritty construction provides her with a "handle of reality" to grasp in defense.

As I have been employing some terms from psychoanalytic discourse, let me here interject a word about the place of Freud in my reading of Wharton's novel. Although it is difficult to discover how much or which of his writing she read, Wharton often made a point of deriding Freud's ideas and, even more, Freud's cultural influence. Her 1927 novel includes fifteen-minute psychoanalytic sessions as one among the many modes used by fashionable New Yorkers for achieving a "twilight sleep" that evades disturbing experience or knowledge. She also sometimes rejected psychoanalysis for seemingly opposite reasons, however. Writing to Bernard Berenson in 1922 about a depressed young Frenchwoman whose mind and spirit she admired (Philomène de Lévis-Mirepoix, who later wrote for publication as Claude Sylve), Wharton insisted "Above all, please ask Mary not to befuddle her with Freudianism & all its jargon. She'd take to it like a duck to – sewerage. And what she wants is to develop the *conscious*, and not grub after the sub-conscious."[31]

Reading over Wharton's *œuvre*, especially that of the late teens and twenties, with its repeated portrayals of incestuous desires, unconscious motivations, repressed ghosts that keep returning, internally punishing superegos, and so on, one might choose to be obnoxiously Freudian and speculate that Wharton's hostility towards psychoanalysis was an example of what Freud himself called *disavowal*, the pushing away of what comes too close to one's own truth. But I think that it makes more sense to argue, with Ann Douglas, that "evidence of direct transmission" between Freud and American modernists (among whom Douglas, like most other critics, unfortunately fails to include Wharton) would in any case be a less powerful explanation for overlapping themes and observations than the shared "mindset and mood" out of which such insights came.[32] If, as historians of psychoanalysis suggest, the First World War played a significant role in Freud's coming to theorize the death drive's ineradicable place in civilization and its discontents, so too the war turned Wharton's focus towards the painful centrality of "sewerage" in human experience and human relations. Like Freud, she explored the consequences of seeking always to rush sewerage underground, out of sight and smell.

It is not merely by caprice that I extend the unconscious-as-sewerage metaphor that Wharton uses in her letter to Berenson. In *Twilight Sleep* Wharton keeps drawing her readers' attention to Pauline's attachment to ever-more modern plumbing and gleaming bathrooms, "all ablaze with white tiling and silvered taps and tubes" (p. 177). Wharton portrays Pauline's investment in the latest sanitary attainments as continuous with her commitment to Progressive reform, which, as Dale Bauer points out, is a major target of the novel's satire. *Twilight Sleep*'s gleaming pipes and technocratic reformers alike signify what the novel portrays as the peculiarly American belief that whatever is undesirable, disgusting, or destructive can be, and should be, "disinfected and whitewashed."[33] "Ah, this marvellous American plumbing! I believe you all treat yourselves to a new set of bathrooms every year," a visitor from Italy exclaims (p. 155).[34]

Pauline belongs to numerous Progressivist committees and groups whose common link strikes Nona as a determination "to force certain persons to do things that those persons preferred not to do" (p. 12). For instance, Pauline helps to fund a "League" that, in the words of its promoter Mrs. Swoffer, stands "against the dreadful old practice of telling children they were naughty" because "how could there be bad men if there were no bad children? And how could there be bad children if children were never allowed to know that such a thing as badness existed?" (p. 118). The satiric point Wharton invites her readers to share here is that "badness" is not a cultural or linguistic construction that might be eliminated if people could only be made to clean up their representational practices, if they would only, for example, stop making incorrect word choices (like "naughty") or letting children play with objects that evoke weapons. "Badness" has a fundamental, inescapable reality. Perhaps referencing the ineffectual League of Nations, which Woodrow Wilson posed as the climactic fulfillment of his Progressivist beliefs and which was supposed to bring an end to war, Mrs. Swoffer's "League" aspires to "get up a gigantic world-wide movement to boycott the manufacturers and sellers of all military toys, tin soldiers, cannon, toy rifles, water-pistols and so on . . . [S]everal governments had joined the movement already: the Philippines, Mrs. Swoffer thought, and possibly Montenegro" (p. 118). But aggression, violence, suffering, "sewerage" – these all help constitute what Nona tries to convince her mother is the "plain human tangle" (p. 276).

In Nona's assessment, her mother's "whole life (if one chose to look at it from a certain angle) had been a long uninterrupted struggle against the encroachment of every form of pain" (p. 260). To conceive pain as an "encroachment," however, as Pauline does, is to locate pain and all that brings pain as external, outside of oneself and one's intimate sphere. If Pauline insists that "dreadful" words such as "naughty" should be excluded from language (to protect children from "badness" itself), so too she buys "a new and singularly complete system of burglar alarm for Cedarledge" in order to keep all bad people outside of her home (p. 154).

Ironically, Pauline's assumption that badness and suffering derive from outside and hence can at least theoretically be avoided or even eliminated parallels what has been the dominant way of reading and writing about Edith Wharton, in her own day as well as more recently, which is as a critic or satirist of "society." Recent feminist criticism of Wharton's work has certainly developed this assumption (Wharton as social or cultural critic) more powerfully, interestingly, and usefully than have previous critical approaches. Yet, with few exceptions, most feminist readings of Wharton's work finally follow Pauline Manford in seeing badness solely as something that encroaches from the exterior, from a broken social sphere, onto the self.

For instance, Dale Bauer's incisive reading of *Twilight Sleep*, which is one of the very few extended discussions of the novel that I have found, locates the "source" of the pain and suffering in the book as "ideological." It should at bottom be attributed to "a culture of masculinist and racist hegemony," the latter unfortunately representing a "cultural privilege which Wharton all too often supported."[35] Speaking more generally, Gilbert and Gubar praise Wharton for having "forced herself, and her readers, to face the social facts that made her women (and their men) what they were."[36] I agree, of course, that Wharton's work does mordantly expose how "masculinist" "social facts" – "facts" including social and institutional arrangements, as well as cultural attitudes – deform individuals and relationships. Yet, as *Twilight Sleep* makes especially clear, she also attends to the place held by another order of "fact," another real. This latter order may not be strictly social – it resides at the limit of what is symbolizable within socially recognizable discourses – yet it nonetheless helps to make "her women (and their men) what they" are. Wharton's own maddeningly uneven, contradictory attitudes towards feminist concepts, which many critics have noticed, the "fact" of her nasty racism (which the editors of the currently authoritative edition of her letters made a conscious effort to downplay),[37] as well as her citing, on the first page of her autobiography, "the arch-enemy sorrow" as an almost constant life companion – these all begin to hint that in reading Wharton one may encounter realities of irrational aggression, of internal pains and losses, in short realities of "badness" (using Mrs. Swoffer's word) not always traceable back to the blamable social world.[38]

Without doubt, Dexter's incestuous desire for Lita, as well as the trauma that it causes for others, cannot be understood as separate from his privileged sociocultural status as a ruling-class white man. At the same time, however, *Twilight Sleep* depicts Dexter's desire as a seismic force that, operating with "a fundamental indifference" to "all the world" (p. 232), creates "havoc" within the social and psychic systems that the novel portrays. His implacable drive towards sex with his daughter-in-law renders the face of the lawyer-father (who is supposed to anchor those same social and psychic systems) "blurred and uncertain" (p. 134). Wharton positions Dexter's incestuous desire as a real more fundamental, but less discursively assimilable, than those "handles of reality" that usually pass for the real.[39]

Even after Dexter and Lita are discovered in bed and Nona is shot, for instance, the loyal family butler (whose name "Powder" fits his role as a supplier of cover stories, an agent of twilight sleep) explains the commotion by contriving a narrative of burglars who got past the alarm. He establishes "positive proof" for his explanation by "discovering" (purposefully planting, it is implied) muddy footprints on the pantry floor

(p. 303). "Within twenty-four hours the Cedarledge burglary was an established fact, and suburban millionaires were doubling the number of their night watchmen" (p. 305): the "established fact" of the burglary can serve to emblematize what Žižek means by "external reality" and Wharton by "handles of reality." The burglary intrusion provides a coherent scenario, buttressed by empirical evidence, but which in fact is a form of "twilight sleep" that covers over (for everyone but Nona and the novel's readers) the *real* real of internal violence and desire.

Of all the handles of reality revealed within the novel as forms of twilight sleep, as defenses against confronting the law's own unlawful, self-imploding desires, white panic about racial and cultural otherness is the most troubling to a critic who (like myself) wishes to admire Wharton. The racist fear and disgust displayed by most of Wharton's white characters, including both Nona and *Twilight Sleep*'s own authorial voice, might lead one to argue that, in the late 1920s, Edith Wharton felt racial and cultural others to constitute the most profound menace facing the heirs of her "old New York." Such figures as the "thick-lipped oily Mahatma," a "Hindu sage" with a large following among the city's wealthy women, and the Jewish movie producer Klawhammer, whose hair is "deceptively blonde" but also, like the Mahatma, has telltale "thick lips," as well as a name that confirms his grasping and predatory destructiveness, are depicted in the novel as epicenters of corruption (pp. 272, 79). Their popularity is made to symptomize a sickening crisis in upper-class white America. Moreover, *Twilight Sleep*'s authorial voice treats jazz music, jazz dancing, and nightclubbing in Harlem, all of which implicitly or explicitly evoke the influence of New York's urban black culture, with disdain and repugnance. In addition, within the sexually-laden context of the novel, "jazz" – which the text often uses as a verb (as in "jazz all day and drink all night – or vice versa" [p. 43]) – may also carry some of its original four-letter connotations as a slang word for intercourse.[40] Given all this, one might be led to argue that the intrafamilial "havoc" wrought by Dexter Manford's incestuous desire should be viewed as a displacement of what both Wharton and her novel take to be the more essential, more frightening catastrophe: a social sphere increasingly corrupted by racial and cultural heterogeneity, including the possibility of interracial "jazzing."[41]

Such a reading of *Twilight Sleep* would have the virtue of seeming to ground the text's realism in an historical specificity that also possesses urgent relevance today. Yet although Wharton was indeed quite heavily invested, throughout the 1920s and earlier, in maintaining the purity and superiority of Christian Euro-American whiteness,[42] *Twilight Sleep* itself nonetheless insists that the disaster most cataclysmically destructive of society as such is the white lawyer-father's incestuous drive. Although this cannot be taken to minimize the ugly weight of Edith Wharton's own racism, she constructs her novel so as to show that racist distress can itself serve as a graspable "handle of reality," and thus as a sort of last-ditch mode of twilight sleep. Let me be clear: I would not argue that Edith Wharton's racial hostilities and fears, which scholars are only just beginning to document and explore, were less central or "real" for her than the horrors World War I seemed to lay bare, horrors of irrational self-destructiveness inhering within white Euro-American "history and conduct and civilization." Trying to judge one or the other of these fears as in some basic sense more "primary" for Wharton or her corpus of writing would be pointless. In fact, they were often inseparable, as is shown, for example, in the anxiety about "race suicide" that she shared with many of her elite white contemporaries – the worry, that is, that whites were not keeping up with the rapid reproduction rates of non-white "races".[43] Indeed, if one were to step back far enough from *Twilight Sleep*'s details, one might even choose to locate its treatment of incest and racial alterity within the paradigms of "nativist modernism" that Walter Benn Michaels has recently proposed as "typical of American writing in the '20s."[44] Michaels contends that the incest thematics of Faulkner's *The Sound and the Fury* (1929), for instance, derive from a nativist obsession with racial purity: insofar as incest keeps everything within the family, it can serve as radical protection against intrusions by the foreign or other.[45]

Reading *Twilight Sleep* as an example of nativist modernism, or as a novel that instances Wharton's anxiety about race suicide, would not be wrong – these elements do help to constitute the novel's field of meaning, for her as well as, undoubtedly, many of her 1920s readers. Yet to arrive at the perceived menace of foreign immigration, or of a newly prominent and vastly increased African–American presence in Northeastern cities, as the underlying social reality that motivates *Twilight Sleep*'s scarifying aura of catastrophe would be to overlook crucial textual dynamics within the book itself. These textual dynamics are significant, in particular, to the novel's conferral of unique realist prestige on the flapper Nona.

In subtle but clear ways, *Twilight Sleep* asks its readers to view the "law giving, life-preserving" father's incestuous drive as the most relentless and devastating reality in the novel's world.[46] Importantly, the menace of interracial sex in the book, though frightening, is attached to specific individuals and social locations which, the novel at least tries to imagine, it is still possible to marginalize, to keep outside or away. The law can investigate and, if necessary, shut down the "thick-lipped oily Mahatma"'s weekend retreats for wealthy women. Though she is always difficult to manage, Lita can be sent with Jim on an extended European tour, away from the taboo-breaking mixed-race New York "set" with which she spends her evenings. But the lawyer-father's incestuous drive is, so to speak, less handle-able. With a "fundamental indifference" to all but its own fulfillment (p. 232), it inheres as an ever-present possibility, a "hidden influence" (p. 239) that is "incomprehensible and overpowering . . . impenetrable" (p. 158), within even the seemingly most protected sanctums of law and civilization, including the lily-white familial retreat at Cedarledge.

It is worth mentioning that the novel's older characters and authorial voice all complain with easy openness about the new prominence of racial others in American life, which contrasts markedly with the indirect yet portentuous language that, as I have already mentioned, the novel uses when referring to Dexter's incestuous desire. Amounting to a linguistic aversion well beyond any need Wharton may have felt to participate in the coy decorum surrounding discussions of sex in the 1920s American novel, these avoidant but heavily freighted references contribute to the positioning of Dexter's incestuous drive as *Twilight Sleep*'s most inescapable and formidable level of reality. I want to emphasize that it is not illicit sex as such, only incest, that calls forth portentously evasive phrasing in the novel. Like Pauline, who has developed a certain "wifely philosophy" about the likelihood that husbands will occasionally stray, Nona has no trouble accepting that her father is probably having an affair with the suggestively named Mrs. Toy, a married woman close to his own age. And the novel itself easily describes Dexter surreptitiously kissing the latter, "a rich armful," and later undressing her with his eyes at a party, criticizing the garishness of her outfit and remembering how much better he liked her without "any" clothes at all (pp. 231, 248). Yet while Nona regards it as "perfectly normal" that Dexter should find himself involved while on vacation "with a stupid woman he would forget as soon as he got back to town," she can only barely approach, even in her own mind, the possibility that her father is sexually drawn to his daughter-in-law. The mere thought of it is a "horrible morbid thing" (p. 239). Similar language arises when Dexter, driving in a car with Lita, restrains his "impulse to lay a hand over hers" and then, very briefly, has "the sense of having just grazed something dark and lurid, which had threatened to submerge them." Although racial mixing may occasion anxiety and even abhorrence in the novel, this evasive language of darkly lurid primal threats never attaches to it. For instance, speaking in what is for him a relatively normal register, Arthur Wyant calls movie producer Klawhammer a "dirty Jew . . . the kind we used to horsewhip," but then acknowledges with a defeated equanimity, "Well, I don't under-stand the new code." Similarly, the authorial voice enjoys making mean but uncomplicated fun of "the octoroon pianist" Jossie Keiller's attempt to strike a "provocative pose" despite her "sausage arms and bolster legs" (p. 79).

As I will demonstrate shortly, moreover, Wharton depicts Nona making what might almost be thought of as last-ditch grasps for racial panic, which is uncomfortable but bearable for her, in an effort to cover over the much more destabilizing disruption represented by her father's unswerving desire. Again, I do not claim that the white patriarch's inces-tuous drive is always more scarily primal than perceived racial threats either for Wharton or for her writing.[47] Nonetheless, *Twilight Sleep*'s – and ultimately Nona's – resolute positioning of Dexter's desire as the book's most terrifying and most structuring reality helps explain why Nona's final "knowing" of Dexter's destructive desire will yield her a special form of realist distinction. Nona's knowing, which is compounded of insight, containment, trauma, and, implicitly, creativity, distinguishes her with the same ambivalent status that the twentieth century has tended to give to expressive witnesses of overwhelming catastrophe, those burdened with what psychiatrist Stevan Weine has called "the wit-nessing imagination" (p. 168). Cathy Caruth's description of "traumatic witnessing" also helps to suggest the special, and painfully difficult, form of realist prestige that Wharton embodies in Nona. For Caruth, such witnessing "involves intense personal suffering, but it also involves the recognition of realities that most of us have not begun to face." Further elaborating the uniquely burdensome version of what I would still call "realist distinction" carried by those who witness "unthinkable realities," Caruth argues that what they "face and quite often try to transmit to us" carries unique "force and truth."[48]

Two brief scenes illustrate how the novel establishes that the threat of racial otherness, even of interracial sexuality, carries less real force (and hence less realness) than what the book renders as a deeper cataclysm originating inside the culturally central white family and its institutionally sanctioned bonds. Returning home after a late-night search for Lita has brought Nona into contact with the "octoroon pianist" Jossie Keiler and the Jewish producer Klawhammer, Nona discovers her father smoking comfortably in the library (p. 80). After he assures her of Lita's safety, she drops "a kiss on his thinning hair" and runs "up to her room humming Miss Jossie Keiler's jazz tune," thinking "perhaps after all it wasn't such a rotten world." So long as her father remains distinct from the "rotten world" comprised by jazz and racial mixing, he can anchor the possibility of Nona's enjoying it. He is the phallic guarantor of order whose stable meaning grounds Nona's jazz forays.

Several chapters later, however, Nona sits with Stan Heuston in a Harlem nightclub called The Housetop (the house-stop?). Enjoying a show in which "black dancers tossed and capered," she momentarily glances up at the balcony and sees Lita with "that awful Keiler woman" (p. 147). Disgusted at her sister-in-law's conduct (watching black dancers is one thing; doing so as a member of a racially mixed party is quite another), Nona resolves to climb up to the balcony and intervene. Witnessing the "ugly and disquieting realities" of Lita's ostentatious social contacts with racial others makes Nona angry (p. 147), yet it also gives her a clear course of action. "Ugly and disquieting realities" of racial mixing nonetheless offer Nona a hold, a grip around which to organize herself. Suddenly, however, Nona interrupts her disapproving climb and sits down again. She has seen something that paralyzes her:

For a moment or two she did not speak, nor look at Heuston. She had seen the massive outline of a familiar figure rising from a seat near the front and planting itself there for a slow gaze about the audience. (p. 149)

The "familiar figure rising" is, of course, her father, whose familial body turns, in its rise, not toward the stage but towards the audience, as he scans for Lita. Finding him in the nightclub causes a category confusion – "I didn't know he patronized this kind of show," Heuston says – yet one that might be resolvable if only Nona's mother and aunt have accompanied him (p. 148). Nona, however, immediately and uncannily knows better: "She could not take her eyes from her father. How queer he looked – how different! . . . tired, inexpressibly tired, as if with some profound inner fatigue which made him straighten himself a little too rigidly, and throw back his head with a masterful young-mannish air" (p. 149). The "massive outline" from which Nona cannot take her eyes constitutes the real of her father's desire. Terms such as "rising," "massive," "rigidly," "masterful" and "straighten himself" may seem to connote phallic presence. But here the father's phallus is revealed as "strained" with desire, and not towards the racialized, sexualized "ripe fruits" ("black figs flung about") on the stage but backwards, towards a daughter (p. 147). Nona feels at the scene's end as if she had been "enclosed . . . in a crystal globe" that now has been "splintered to atoms," leaving her "stammering and exposed" (p. 150).

Nona has a more difficult relationship than do the novel's readers to the seismically convulsive real of her father's incestuous drive. Readers can derive a charge of superior and daring discernment – the frisson of the 1920s "terrible honesty" – by identifying the gravitational pull of that drive's "shadowy bulk," which, as Wharton allows us to make out, directs characters' thoughts and actions without the characters themselves being aware of it. By contrast to the novel's readers, however, Nona is not able to look and then, having seen, look away. As is emphasized by the image of her in a Flanders trench ever vulnerable to attack, Nona's eyes must remain unceasingly "glued to the observation-slit." As "the modern girl," Nona's youthful status is stressed throughout the novel, but she comes paradoxically to "feel like the oldest person in the world, and yet with the longest life ahead of me" (p. 238). Nona ends the book literally prostrate, alone in bed, waiting to recover from a bullet wound. Yet, as I will argue in conclusion, Wharton grants her the same sort of female realist "disposition" that she came to claim for herself during and after the war, one that derives from involuntarily knowing traumatic reality, "the hard drubbing of life," yet containing it – and even creating from it.[49]

When her mother commences a platitudinous warning to Nona, "Of course, if you take sorrow and suffering for granted" – Nona's interruption displays certain aspects of her intellectual superiority: "I don't, mother; but, apparently, Somebody does, judging from their diffusion and persistency, as the natural history books say" (p. 276). Neither Nona's quick-witted appropriation of diction from evolutionary biology, however, nor the hardboiled and ironic metaphysics she shows here lies at the center of the particular intellectual prestige that Wharton grants her. Rather, Nona's "certain angle" on the father-lawyer's incestuous desire is linked with her status as daughter of the imploded patriarchy, a female member of the "generation of bewildered, disenchanted young people who had grown up since the Great War" (p. 12). As daughter, Nona is denied any "privilege of distance" from *Twilight Sleep*'s traumatic real. She is not herself the direct object of her father's desire, but she is doubled throughout the book with the "daughter-in-law" who is. "Nearly of an age," she and Lita are often "together all day long" and then go to cabarets where they dance "away the nights" (pp. 14, 17, 236). When Dexter Manford encounters them together, he treats "both in the same way, as a man treats two indulged and amusing daughters" (p. 236).

Where Lita (of whom Wharton says, "all her expression was in her body") and Dexter end up actually sleeping together, however, Wharton calls Nona a "little Iphigenia" (pp. 75, 45). In Euripides's treatment of her story, Iphigenia only just evades her father Agammemnon's sacrificial knife in the very moment when, eyes closed, he has lifted his hand to plunge it in; a hind is substituted in her stead. Iphigenia is then placed on the island Taurus, though, where she is forced to oversee the sacrifices of captured Greeks, who are her own people, in "deeds of blood, too horrid to be told" (in Robert Potter's translation). Nona is not herself seduced by Dexter, but the Iphigenia comparison suggests that, just narrowly eluding that fate, she is instead cast as the central witness of what the novel represents as "too horrid to be told."

Nona's parents' generation of liberal New Yorkers, which Wharton depicts as most prominently comprised of Progressives and professionals, refuse the seemingly helpless passivity, as well as the pain, inherent in witnessing horrors. Optimistic and confident after the war, they strike Nona as determined to "think . . . away" sorrow and evil "as superannuated bogies, survivals of some obsolete European superstition unworthy of enlightened Americans, to whom plumbing and dentistry had given higher standards." Yet, Nona asserts from early on, "somebody in every family had to remember now and then that such things as wickedness, suffering and death had not yet been banished . . ." (p. 45). With her mother "mailed in massage and optimism," only Nona's gaze remains attuned to "the powers of darkness" (p. 46).

Wharton's choice of the phrase "powers of darkness" in this context is telling. The passage is one of several where the novel might appear to speak in a generalized tone about the fact that badness still exists and bad things still happen. But although "powers of darkness" may sound even less concrete than the phrases "wickedness, suffering, and death" or "sorrow and evil" that appear near it, "powers of darkness" repeats the title of a volume of stories that Wharton conceived "at some unspecified time in the postwar years."[50] *Powers of Darkness* never materialized as a collection, but Wharton purposefully preserved in her literary estate the plot outline of, and a fragment from, what seems to have been the only story, "Beatrice Palmato," that she ever began working on for the volume. The outline and fragment center on the incest between the title character and her father, a rich banker. [51]

The fragment, which Wharton labeled "unpublishable," is pornographicly explicit in detailing the orgasmic pleasure of the first time that Beatrice and her father actually consummate intercourse, an event that occurs shortly after her marriage although, as the plot outline indicates, the two have been having sexual encounters since Beatrice was twelve. Put next to the ecstatic fragment, the plot outline makes clear, however, that even if the consummation of the real of "unpublishable" desire may yield *jouissance* for the daughter as well as the father, the father's incestuous desire has also all along constituted a devastating "hidden power" in the Palmatos' familial and social context. This "hidden power" has been the source of unmeasurable catastrophe. (The outline's phrase "hidden power" chiastically echoes "Powers of Darkness," the title of the planned volume, which also appears in *Twilight Sleep*, as well as "hidden influence," a phrase that the latter uses to describe how Nona first perceives Dexter's incestuous desire [p. 239].) Beatrice's eldest sister, Isa, committed suicide at age seventeen, shortly after returning from the convent school where she had lived for several years. Her suicide is implicitly a result of some incestuous advance by Mr. Palmato, although whether to Isa ("I-saw"?) herself or to her younger sister is uncertain. In addition, after Mr. Palmato has commenced his incest with Beatrice, Beatrice's mother suddenly "grows quite mad. She tries to kill her husband, has to be shut up, and dies in an insane asylum a few months later."[52] Years later, after her lover-father's death, Beatrice one day happens upon her own husband hugging their six year-old daughter and screams with rage and fear, snatching the little girl away from him. Beatrice thereupon drops the girl, flies upstairs, and shoots herself.

In the urban "jazz" setting that Wharton gives to *Twilight Sleep*, "powers of darkness" does serve obliquely to evoke the hovering threat posed by racial others. I would insist, however, that the intertextual link with the "Beatrice Palmato" fragment forged by the phrase is even more significant. Although maybe without conscious intention (but also perhaps as a private reference), Wharton's using "powers of darkness" early in the novel to encapsulate what awareness must be borne specifically by Nona helps to focus the book's rhetorical mentions of "wickedness, sorrow and death" or "evil and sorrow" as, in some more specific and fundamental sense, references to the father's incestuous, and violently damaging, drive. Keeping this intertextual link in mind, I suggest that a first way to understand Nona's achievement is as a sister, an Isa or "I-saw" who doesn't die. The "Beatrice Palmato" outline tells of three women, comprising mothers, sisters, and daughters, each of whom is driven to death by an unbearable recognition of patriarchal abuse. By contrast, *Twilight Sleep*'s Nona is a sister who witnesses, but who remains alive and present. Nona's witnessing helps to carry or contain the father's incestuous violence, as well as, finally, to wrench creative power from it.

NONA'S HANDS

Nona ends the novel in her own bed, recovering from a bullet shot into her arm that also grazed her lung. We have not been made privy to the nighttime scene during which she received her wound, only to that scene's aftermath, and thus we can only surmise its details. Roughly, a drunken Arthur Wyant has discovered Dexter Manford in a compromising position with his son's wife and has fired at least two shots. Somehow Nona, who may have heard the nighttime commotion in Lita's room and rushed in, or may simply have been on guard for a crisis, receives the only shot that actually hits anyone. The lack of direct representation (or even explanation) accorded to this climactic intersection of fathers, daughters, sex, and a gun – how does Nona get shot? – contributes to a sense of it as the book's central vortex, a black hole that has been pulling everything towards itself.

In anticipating this scene that will itself go unrepresented, Wharton describes Pauline in bed before the shooting. Her language prepares the reader for a close encounter with a reality – a real – that is other from the "handles of reality" that Pauline grips everyday with such mastery. Pauline first hears the "queer" and "unnatural" sounds of a car that seems to head directly for the house itself, rather than towards the garage: "It was uncanny, hearing that invisible motor" (p. 258). Pauline falls asleep, but later she sits "up suddenly in bed. It was as if an invisible hand had touched a spring in her spinal column, and set her upright in the darkness before she was aware of any reason for it" (p. 296). As in Wharton's ghost stories, which this language recalls, Pauline is affected by an "invisible" agency with an "uncanny" power to disturb, an agency that permeates everyday realities but whose own location and status is not quite fathomable. The reader already knows better, but Pauline immediately tries to convince herself that Dexter must have forgotten to set the burglar alarm, thus allowing entrance to an anonymous intruder.

Excellently prepared to defend against encroachments by any external cause, she dons the "emergency garb" that "always lay at her bedside in case of nocturnal alarms" and sounds the "general summons for Powder, the footmen, the gardeners and chauffeurs." Thinking it "just as well to rouse the neighborhood," she also pushes the button that connects to the local fire department (for whom she has recently bought a new fire engine) (p. 297).

Wharton describes Pauline's run down the hallway towards Lita's room in terms that evoke a subject moving, in a dream, towards some repressed real:

On the deeply carpeted floors her footfall made no sound, and she had the sense of skimming over the ground inaudibly, like something ghostly, disembodied, which had no power to break the hush and make itself heard . . . Halfway down the passage she was startled to see the door of Lita's bedroom open. Sounds at last – sounds low, confused, and terrified – issued from it. What kind of sounds? Pauline could not tell; they were rushing together in a vortex in her brain. She heard herself scream "Help!" with the strangled voice of a nightmare. (p. 298; ellipses in text)

Pauline enters and finds "all the lights were on – the room was a glare" (p. 299). She sees her husband ("powerless and motionless," his "face a ruin"), Arthur Wyant ("shrinking, motionless"), Lita ("huddled on the couch . . . like a festal garment flung off by its wearer"), and the wounded Nona. As she bends to her daughter, Nona's blood spatters across the "silvery folds" of Pauline's "rest-gown, destroying it forever as a symbol of safety and repose" (p. 299). Pauline grabs hold of a handle of reality, however, thus turning her attention away from what the tableau lays bare, by grabbing, as it were, Nona's broken arm. "My broken arm saved her," Nona thinks a few weeks later, as she realizes, "with a sort of ironical admiration," that everything else that became visible in the scene "was now as if it had never existed for Pauline, who was more than ever resolutely two-dimensional" (p. 307).

By contrast to Pauline, although prostrate and in pain Nona had remained conscious throughout as a witness both to the real that her mother could not face and to her mother's continuing strategy of rendering all "badness" as external. When the Cedarledge fire brigade had shown up at the end of the chapter, "arriving double quick in answer to their benefactress's summons," Nona had managed a "wan smile" at her mother's assumption that, no matter what the crisis, a well-equipped fire company could make everything safe and clean (p. 301). Nona's "wan smile" may recall the wry smiles and rueful laughs at seemingly intransigent social problems that, as I argued in chapter 2, marked the realist distinction of such W. D. Howells characters as the Reverend Sewell and Basil March. As with the qualified laughs and smiles of those protagonists, Nona's wan smile marks not only her clear-eyed recognition of difficult realities but also her ability to maintain a sense of irony in relation to them.

Sewell and March, however, never get shot. Their irony provides at least enough distance to protect their persons. The troublingly complex realities that Howells's middle and late protagonists distinguish themselves by recognizing are located in a social realm external to their selves and families.[53] Thus, Howells's male bearers of realist prestige always have a variety of options for temporary respite from disturbing realities. They can, as Basil March puts it, "go to the theater and forget them."[54] When Nona goes to a cabaret, by contrast, the "massive outline" of Dexter's "familiar figure" uncannily rises before her from just in front of the stage. As a daughter, she cannot escape her own location upon the terrain shaped by the real of the father's incestuous drive, even though it may not (although it always may) be her that he specifically desires. Nona's finishing the book "confined to her room" by her wounded arm, grazed lung, and ensuing fever thus underlines what might, by comparison with March and Sewell, strike one as her feminized entrapment within the realities she witnesses (p. 302). Even Merton Densher reserves the personal mobility, at the close of *The Wings of the Dove*, that allows him to go out and leave behind the wounded body – the "maimed child," wrapped in blankets in a "sacred corner" – by which he images his pained regret at having allowed Milly's final letter to burn.[55] By contrast, Nona cannot get up from and return to a wounded body because that body is her own.

Here it should be remembered, however, that the literary realist Edith Wharton did all of her own writing in bed, spending the morning hours propped up by pillows, pen in hand. Contrary to the Victorian, as well as male modernist, cliché of the bed-ridden female, neuresthenetic and unproductive, for Edith Wharton intellectual achievement and a woman lying in bed were not antagonistic terms. *Twilight Sleep*'s final scene of Nona in bed hints that the latter's prostration before the real may be yielding her a distinct cognitive and emotional power, as well as the possibility for artistic creativity. One last time in the novel, Nona is startled by the unexpected appearance of her father. Although on the level of plot he is probably actually there, the circumstances again suggest a dream state where one encounters some difficult but unavoidable truth.

Having been asleep, Nona "started up out of nothingness to find her father at her side" (p. 311). The two have not spoken privately since the incident in Lita's room. He will be leaving with Pauline that night for the Rockies, and then to Japan, Ceylon, and India, on a recuperative trip that Pauline has, characteristically, scheduled down to the last detail. Dexter appears not to know what to say, however. "Nona was aware of the presence at her side only as a shadowy bulk" (p. 312). Obliquely evoking to herself the incestuous drive that has brought them to this point, she thinks that "Perhaps he had been led to her side, almost in spite of himself, by a craving to be alone with her just once before they parted." After trying and failing to speak, Dexter bends "down over her" and presses "his forehead against the coverlet of her bed." She tells him not to speak – "Don't. There's nothing to say" – and runs her hand through his "thin hair": "She felt a tremor of his shoulders as they pressed against her, and the tremor ran through her body and seemed to loosen the fibres of her heart." On the one hand, this "tremor" of Nona's father suggests the invasiveness and violation of an incestuous advance. As he presses against her in bed, his tremor seems almost to push itself "through her body" as it "loosen[s] the fibres of her heart." Yet Nona's loosened heart fibres quickly reconfigure into an image that yields her at least the possibility of a mediating, symbolizing control over her father's continuing desire and the indissoluble trauma that desire represents. Having "groped for her forehead" to kiss it again, Dexter Manford leaves the room: Nona "closed her eyes and lay in the darkness, her heart folded like two hands around the thought of him" (pp. 312–13).

This last image is remarkable. Nona's heart, her emotional center, asserts the shaping, holding agency of hands. The power that the image suggests is, first, to symbolize through "thought" – perhaps (because of the hands) even to write – her father and, second, to hold, or hold in, the chaotic forces that he has become associated with. Wharton's metaphorically invoking Nona's hands as the agents of this symbolizing and holding power is especially suggestive because of the significance that fathers' hands have in her writings about incestuous daughter–father relations. Beatrice Palmato and her father privately refer to the father's penis as "his third hand." Several critics have noted that the name *Palma*to, which is reiterated numerous times in the unpublished incest outline, resonates with the description of what Wharton's autobiography claims as her very first memory, a walk that she took with her own father. Wharton remembers how one of her hands "lay in the large safe hollow of her father's bare hand; her tall handsome father, who was so warm-blooded that in the coldest weather he always went out without gloves."[56] Whether or not Wharton was herself an incest victim, as Barbara White has used the resonance between this passage and the Palmato fragment (as well as other clues) to argue, the first name of *Twilight Sleep*'s incestuous father, Dexter Manford, also connotes both right-handedness and sure-handedness.

Moreover, the way that Wharton signals the actual moment when Dexter and Lita first start having sex is to write, at the end of a charged scene between the two, "he put his hand over hers. Let the whole world crash after this . . ." (p. 256; ellipses in text). Thus when Nona's heart is folded "like two hands around the thought of him," the metaphoric motion both recalls the power of Dexter's incestuous drive and reclaims some of his hand's phallic force for Nona herself.

That power is still, however, of a profoundly ambivalent sort. The fact that all the other members of Nona's family, including her father, plan to disperse to Egypt, Europe, the Canadian Rockies, and Maine even before she recovers from her bullet wound emphasizes that Nona is left alone with the task of holding, containing the traumatic emptiness that Dexter's desire has produced in the place of the law. The image of Nona's "heart folded like two hands" around the thought of her father also implies that this is not a thought she will ever be able to move past, to distance herself from. Even as her "hands" contain the traumatic thought of her father, they also seem to use it to retain their shape, even to remain upright, thus leaving permanently open the threat of a dissolving collapse.

For the male figures focused on in earlier chapters of this study – including Howells's middle–late protagonists, James's Merton Densher, and Cahan's David Levinsky – developing specifically "realist" modes of cultural distinction ultimately involved valorizing (with whatever apparent ambivalence and rueful melancholy) the separation implied by the word "distinction." By contrast, the darkness in which Nona lays as her father leaves, which echoes the inescapable "powers of darkness" that he represents, seems to have become a necessary part of her interior sense of identity, in the same way that her name would not be possible without "no." Nona's distinction here derives from her hard-won ability to, as it were, include traumatic emptiness within her own daily, domestic "fold."

At the end of the war Wharton had two close American women friends, Mary Berenson and Lizzie Cameron, who were paralyzed by depression. Wharton took what today seems a harsh, and perhaps even misogynist, line towards her friends, judging them as clinging to "childish sickness" in narcissistic attempts to escape from life and its "mailed fist."[57] "When I see women behaving as poor Lizzie has for the last months I wonder when our sex is coming out of its kindergarten," she wrote in a barbed letter to Mary Berenson, when the latter was herself only just returning to "normal activities" after depression. She had earlier described Mary Berenson herself as "a spoilt child."[58] Making a similar kindergarten reference, Wharton asserted in *French Ways and Their Meaning*, published during the same year, that "the average American woman" is not "*grown up*."[59] She wrote to another friend about Cameron that

Lizzie is behaving like a mad-woman – sometimes I feel like saying simply, "like a woman"! – I can't understand it, at over 50. I should think the hard drubbing of life wd. by that time have had its effect.[60]

When combined with her reference to life's "mailed fist," Wharton's image of life providing a "hard drubbing" suggests physical beating by a male ("mailed") figure. Life, in this set of images, is a violent father.

For an American woman to grow up means not only for her to recognize the inescapable reality of this pain-bringing father but to accept his real presence inside her own most domestic, intimate spaces. "My sorrows are real and substantial," Wharton wrote in another letter from the war's final year, "and I lunch and dine with them daily."[61] Towards the middle of *Twilight Sleep*, as Nona becomes ever-more acutely aware of the complex crisis building in her family, she glances down at "her slim young hands – so helpless and inexperienced looking. All these tangled cross-threads of life, inextricably and fatally interwoven; how were a girl's hands to unravel them?" (p. 184). I suggest that when Nona's heart "is folded like two hands" around the thought of her father, the flapper has graduated from kindergarten.

CHAPTER FIVE

From reality, to materiality, to the real (and back again): the dynamics of distinction on the recent critical scene

> It is a work of art, first of all, and we think of fine art; though the material will strike many gentilities as coarse and common.
>
> William Dean Howells, Review of Hamlin Garland's
> *Main-Travelled Roads* (1890)[1]

> For many intellectuals, such a politics [as that informing cultural studies] has always been and still is difficult to imagine, let alone accept, because of its necessary engagement with aggressively indifferent attitudes toward the life of the mind and the protocols of knowledge; because it appeals to the body in ways which cannot always be trusted; and because it trades on pleasures which a training in political rationality encourages us to devalue.
>
> Andrew Ross, "New Intellectuals"[2] (concluding section of
> *No Respect: Intellectuals and Popular Culture*, 1989)

In 1990, the University of Illinois sponsored a conference on cultural studies. As several speakers pointed out, the conference's sheer magnitude, if nothing else, served to announce cultural studies' impressive new status in the US literary academy.[3] That status magnified further over the next several years, as scholarly journals, book series, and additional conferences identified themselves with a cultural studies approach, as did a growing number of graduate student and faculty adherents within literature departments. During the 1990 Illinois conference, audience members paid close attention to a keynote address by Stuart Hall, long-time director of Birmingham's Centre for Contemporary Cultural Studies. Founded in 1963 by a group of scholars and activists, the Birmingham Centre had offered an intellectual center and home base for cultural studies during leaner years, before its US popularity, and as a result Hall spoke as something of a founding father.

Hall's address dwelt above all on the "dirtiness" of cultural studies as an intellectual mode. This dirtiness, he stressed, is a result of cultural studies' turn "from the clean air of meaning and textuality and theory to the something nasty down below." Hall emphasized that intellectuals taking a cultural studies approach should continue to recognize that a "delay, a displacement," as articulated by poststructuralist theorists, "is *always* implied in the concept of culture." He suggested, however, that his listeners should regard poststructuralist accounts of language and textuality as "a point beyond which cultural studies must now always necessarily locate itself." Cultural studies intellectuals should not lose sight of key poststructuralist insights, but they should move "beyond" them to develop more local, on-the-ground, and explicitly political inquiries.[4]

Commenting upon and, at least implicitly, also promoting cultural studies' rise to prominence on the US critical scene, Hall makes here what might be called a "realer than thou" move, as does Andrew Ross in the 1989 passage on "new intellectuals" quoted in my second epigraph, above. Both Hall and Ross, that is, claim for cultural studies practitioners a closer engagement with some "down below," nitty-gritty reality that usually eludes intellectual discourse. This down-below reality, they assert, causes squeamishness on the part of traditional liberal academics. Claims such as these made on behalf of cultural studies follow in form the claim made one hundred years earlier by William Dean Howells regarding Hamlin Garland's "coarse" "material" and the distraught response to it that Howells predicted "many gentilities" would undoubtedly have (see the first epigraph). Then, as now, remarks about getting in touch with nitty-gritty materiality have as part of their purpose subtly to elevate one group of literary intellectuals over another. The superior literary intellectuals are distinguished by their orientation towards hard, non-pretty realities.

Ross and Hall are each careful, however, to stress a theoretically sophisticated awareness that all culture, no matter how "dirty," is bound up with discourse and textuality, so that even the grittiest real can never be accessed without, as Hall puts it, "a delay, a displacement." Such mediation, Hall reminds his listeners, "is *always* implied in the concept of culture." For Ross, cultural studies work involves a continual "critique of essentialist notions" of gender, sexuality, and race, even as such work focuses on the "effects of these categories upon real, persecuted bodies." For both Ross and Hall, the assertion that cultural studies allows a more immediate, more serious access to nitty-gritty realities ("real, persecuted bodies") appears with an accompanying insistence that potentially distancing "discursive or representational categories" will, no matter what, always form part of those realities.

Significantly, however, scholars identified with deconstructive theory had made a parallel two-sided claim about a dirty reality down below. Deconstruction is the main predecessor whose academic prestige in the United States cultural studies sought to supplant: the editors of the 1990 Illinois conference proceedings, for example, allude pejoratively to deconstruction as "'pure' and implacably ahistorical theory." Yet deconstruction had claimed that *it* could point to a corrupting, disfiguring "sheer materiality" – that of language – which previous approaches had glossed over. That underlying linguistic real was also, in Paul de Man's words, "impossible to isolate," and thus could never be touched directly.[5]

I do not wish to argue for any direct genealogical descent from literary-realist modes of claiming intellectual distinction around the turn of the last century to these more recent bids for intellectual authority on the academic–critical scene. Even in their US incarnations both deconstruction and cultural studies have in large part been shaped by European influences. Previous chapters of this book do suggest, however, that double-edged "realer-than-thou" moves such as those made by both deconstruction and cultural studies (comprising claims both of unique intimacy with, and of a signifying distance from, some hard reality) nonetheless have a rich history in American literary culture. Listening for resonances with the dynamics of intellectual prestige in American literary realism can help us, I believe, to better grasp some ins and outs of similar dynamics in recently prominent competitions for critical prestige. Above all, we can better recognize that claims to be more genuinely in touch than others with intransigent material reality continue to play central roles in literary-critical debates. The centrality of such claims extends well beyond debates involving, say, heavily historicized or explicitly marxist approaches to literature, whose critical authority one would expect to see ascribed to their supposed grounding in the real world.

Attempts to stake out realer-than-thou, more-material-than-thou, and even dirtier-than-thou ground currently characterize a wide variety of professional approaches to literary studies. Guided by diverse, often conflicting critical and political agendas, recent approaches to literature nonetheless assert their own intellectual distinction and authority through claims to have an intimate, even a defining, relation to some bottomline material reality. In his preface to *The Awkward Age*, Henry James identified his own primary (at least in the sense of initial) task as a writer as locating "the real things, the hard, the cruel and even the tender things, the true elements of any tension and the true facts of any crisis." Such "real things," James continued, must "for the critic's use, be translated into terms." The "critic" – for James a category that here included realist novelists such as himself – then works with a situation constructed "in the distinguished name of . . . for the right employment of" these terms that represent "the real things."[6] Although it may be impossible for the critic to directly seize the underlying "real things" or "true elements" in question, nonetheless certain "terms" are "distinguished" because they offer the best access available. The Jamesian "critic" distinguishes *himself* by identifying and building upon these terms. Almost as if adapting the paradigm that James articulates in this preface, a significant variety of recent critical approaches make a point of locating what shall count as the *realest* real underlying and informing literature itself; they thereby achieve their own privileged relationship with materiality. In fact even the New Criticism, today frequently reviled for its supposedly rarefied dismissal of the real world and its real concerns as "extrinsic" to literature and its literariness, did so only as part of a claim to provide a more accurate take on reality itself. As Evan Carton and Gerald Graff have recently put it, for the New Critics "the special linguistic density that makes literature uniquely literary ultimately makes it more 'real' than what usually passes for descriptions of reality."[7]

I focus in this concluding chapter on five critics: Lionel Trilling, John Guillory, Paul de Man, Joan Copjec, and Judith Butler. My choice of these five writers is to some extent personal, insofar as I have found the work of each particularly acute and illuminating – each has helped to shape my own critical priorities and methods and has influenced the present project. These five appeal for other reasons as well, however, in the context of a discussion about "realist prestige" and our recent critical scene. First, de Man, Copjec, and Butler exemplify and engage with various American manifestations of poststructuralism. Although in the US today "poststructuralism" tends to refer to a large, only loosely definable grouping of critical perspectives, "poststructuralist" approaches have in common, if nothing else, the reputation of having broken with realist claims to provide readers with any sort of access to reality. Because they are taken to lie beyond realist assumptions and goals, the success of poststructuralist theory and criticism offers fruitful terrain for exploring what I see as the continued predominance – at least among those ever-competitive members of the US middle classes who belong to the literary academy – of realist strategies for acquiring intellectual distinction. Paul de Man was the best known and most widely influential practitioner of deconstruction identified with the US literary academy.

Joan Copjec, whose latest work polemically insists on its allegiance to the insights of Jacques Lacan, serves as a compelling metonym for the continuing Lacanian presence on the American critical scene. Judith Butler's open reliance on and continuing dialogue with the work of Lacan, Foucault, and Derrida puts poststructuralism at the center of today's brilliant effloresence of queer studies in the US, a movement in which Butler's work is by far the most often cited.

By contrast, although John Guillory's writing displays erudite and incisive reading in poststructuralist theory, not to mention marxism and a number of other intellectual traditions, his *Cultural Capital: the Problem of Literary Canon Formation* identifies itself as drawing most upon the sociology of Pierre Bourdieu.[8] Indeed, it is fair to say that in *Cultural Capital* and elsewhere Guillory has done more than any other American scholar to bring Bourdieu's insights to the United States' literary-critical scene. Because paradigms and questions derived from Bourdieu also play a central role in the present book, trying to analyze what I see as Guillory's participation in realer-than-thou modes of bidding for intellectual status seems, among other things, a way to begin reflecting, at least indirectly, upon my own strategies of distinction. (It is not false modesty to confess I was certain that readers would find a discussion of Guillory more interesting than they would any directly self-reflexive consideration of my own attempts at advantageous positioning in an intellectual field.)

I turn first to Lionel Trilling, however. Arguably "the most influential literary critic in America" during the 1950s, Trilling constructed his own intellectual authority through defining and redefining the notion of reality one must possess in order to perform valid literary criticism. Of course, one figure cannot serve to bridge the large historical gap between the question of intellectual prestige in turn-of-the-century realist literature and that same question brought to the "are we being material enough yet?" paradigms of 1980s and 1990s critical writing. But I do not believe that attempting to trace specific networks of intellectual descent (a project that would quickly take me back in time as well as to Europe, and then very likely mushroom into Causabon-like meaninglessness) is necessary to find analytically suggestive resonances between turn-of-the-century "realist dispositions" and critical theory's more recent material claims. Rather, Trilling, whose most important essay is titled "Reality in America," provides a framework for understanding certain gestures that recur in literary studies' current contests for distinction.[9]

Despite such assertions as Robert Boyers's that, "though he was

ambivalent about everything . . . Trilling felt he knew with some certainty what was real and what was not," in fact Trilling strategically oscil-
lated in how he located what was real, at least what was most real about
literature.[10] Trilling's shifting assertions about the nature of literature's
reality helped both in developing and in sustaining his own critical distinction. Further, the specific form of Trilling's shifting anticipates a
striking feature of more recent joustings for critical prestige. Like
Trilling, recent critical or theoretical perspectives frequently employ
both of what might otherwise seem like two disjunctive techniques for
asserting their own superior purchase on materiality. A given poststructuralist perspective, for example, will suggest on the one hand that the
real materiality of literature is more complexly *relational*, and hence less
accessible to a positivist gaze, than is assumed even by competing poststructuralist viewpoints that themselves purport to work from a thoroughly relational model. On the other hand, the first perspective will at
the same time also suggest that literature's materiality is more literally in
front of our eyes than the too-eager sophistication of other poststructuralist perspectives has been able to perceive.

Published in 1950 as "one of the first serious paperbacks," *The Liberal
Imagination* sold over 100,000 copies and "made Trilling a household
name among American intellectuals."[11] *The Liberal Imagination*'s first and
most widely read chapter, "Reality in America," has garnered a tremen-
dous amount of critical commentary. I wish only to point out how explicitly that essay ties the rearticulation of what should count as literature's
"real" to the dynamics of critical prestige and influence. The essay
champions Henry James over Theodore Dreiser. As others have noted,
Trilling's praise of James and denigration of Dreiser is also a way of valorizing Trilling's own critical perspective over and against what he took
to be the dominant one of the 1930s and 40s: the marxian viewpoint represented for him by Vernon Parrington.

Trilling begins the essay by decrying the critical prestige still accorded
to Parrington, which he connects to a widespread but mistaken sense
that Parrington's criticism is more in touch with "the actual" than are
other critical approaches:

It is possible to say of V. L. Parrington that with his *Main Currents in American
Thought* he has had an influence on our conception of American culture which
is not equaled by that of any other writer of the last two decades. His ideas are
now the accepted ones wherever the college course in American literature is
given by a teacher who conceives himself to be opposed to the genteel and the
academic and in alliance with the vigorous and the actual. (p. 15)

Importantly, Trilling has no quarrel with a given critical approach accruing prestige and influence because of that approach's alliance with "the
actual." His argument against Parrington's influence fully accepts, even
embraces, the notion that critical status should and does derive from an
approach's intimacy with material reality. Indeed, Trilling goes so far as
to praise Parrington for possessing "what we like to think of as the saving
salt of the American mind, the lively sense of the practical, workaday
world, of the welter of ordinary undistinguished things and people, of
the tangible, quirky, unrefined elements of life" (p. 15). But, as it turns
out, in Parrington's lively sense of the "unrefined elements" of
American life he overlooks the quite quirky, quite tangible and, most
important, the primal character of complication itself. For Trilling, to
miss the primacy of complication – of ambiguity, variousness, difficulty
– is to fail to grasp the very nature of America's everyday actuality.

If, as Trilling argues, Parrington regards reality as "always reliable,
always the same, always easily to be known," this simple positivist notion
of the real leads the critic foolishly to dismiss Nathaniel Hawthorne
because, as Trilling mockingly cites him, Parrington finds Hawthorne to
be "scarcely aware of the 'substantial world of Puritan reality that
Samuel Sewall knew'" (pp. 16, 19). Elaborating his own sense of a non-
positivist real, one grounded in irresolvable psychic and socio-historical
complexity, Trilling contends that we should value those writers – as well
as the ways of reading those writers – who give "the fullest and most
precise account" of it. Rather than accepting at face value the opposition that Hawthorne himself often invokes between aesthetic or "airy"
categories such as spirit or fancy and "earthy," material categories such
as the physical body, Trilling effectively redefines earthiness so that it
encompasses the opposition itself.[12] "Shadows are also part of reality,"
Trilling insists. Hence, no matter how lost in the ether the narrowly
literal-minded may take Hawthorne's writing to be, Trilling can argue,
"The fact is that Hawthorne was dealing beautifully with realities, with
substantial things" (p. 20).[13] What is important here is that Trilling both
explains his taste for Hawthorne and demonstrates his own critical
acumen by pointing us toward the *real* earthiness in Hawthorne's work,
a substantial actuality that is in itself constituted by epistemological
difficulty and which a critic such as Parrington, for all his talk about
hard realities, cannot locate.[14] Further, Trilling emphasizes the aesthetic
rewards available to readers who grasp where the *real* real lies in
Hawthorne's writing: "Hawthorne was dealing *beautifully* with realities . . ."

In 1940, when the first version of "Reality in America" was published in *Partisan Review*, as well as in 1950, when it was reprinted as *The Liberal Imagination*'s first chapter, Trilling's primary aim was to distinguish his own complexly sophisticated grasp of reality from the "limited . . . conception of reality" that led Parrington – as well as the critics, teachers, and students that Trilling saw as under Parrington's influence – to egregious errors in literary taste, symptomized by the preference for Dreiser above Hawthorne and James.[15] By 1955, when Trilling published his next collection of critical essays, *The Opposing Self*, his perception of the critical climate had changed. Parringtonism (in David Shumway's useful term) was no longer a dominating perspective. In no small part thanks to the efforts of Trilling and other members of his circle of New York intellectuals, educated readers were coming to pride themselves on having learned to appreciate not only Henry James's intricacies but also the dark modernism of *The Waste Land* and of Kafka. As Trilling puts it in what one recent critic has aptly named *The Opposing Self*'s central chapter, "William Dean Howells and the Roots of Modern Taste," contemporary taste is characterized by a preference for "what James calls the rare and strange" and by an assumption that "evil is of the very essence of reality." As a result, "the awareness of evil" has come to confer "a certain kind of spiritual status and prestige upon the person who exercises it" (p. 87). As Trilling sees it, in other words, the highbrow reading public has learned to conceptualize the inescapable realities of human experience differently, and hence it now distributes prestige to literary intellectuals in a new manner. Cultural capital currently attaches, we might almost say, to the type of realist viewpoint embodied in Wharton's Nona Manford. Unlike in *Twilight Sleep* itself, the highbrow public at large has now come to privilege (to confer "spiritual status and prestige" on) those who are oriented towards ineffable powers of darkness as the epitome of reality.

Despite his own influential praise of Henry James's "imagination of disaster" in *The Liberal Imagination* (p. 67), however, Trilling now finds contemporary taste lacking for its failure to appreciate "the literality of matter, the peculiar authenticity and authority of the merely denotative."[16] As he puts it in a revealing footnote, "Students have a trick of speaking of money in Dostoevski's novels as 'symbolic,' as if no one ever needed, or spent, or gambled, or squandered the stuff – and as if to think of it as an actuality were subliterary" (p. 82). Now, rather than Parrington's assumption that reality is "easily to be known," even undergraduates conceive of the real that literature points one toward as something "hidden and ambiguous" (p. 87).

But if even undergraduates now commonly read for a dark, complex, non-positivist real, this mode of reading can no longer by itself offer one a high degree of critical distinction. In pointing out that his students' desire to show off their high-culture sophistication makes them miss what he calls the plain "literality of matter" – the "stuff" – to be found in their own pockets, Trilling again invokes an overlooked "reality" in literature (p. 82). It is a reality to be found "down-below" (to allude to Stuart Hall's description of the reality that cultural studies strives toward) where, in this case, it has been dismissed as the *sub*literary. Trilling, of course, is not calling for literary criticism to return to Parrington's simplistic positivism. He still will most often, when responding to students' and other commentators' treatments of reality, take the position that, "it's more complicated than that." Nonetheless, here and elsewhere, Trilling quietly but strategically redesigns his own critical distinction through constructing himself as the one who, among a group of pompous sophisticates, retains a grasp on literature's connection to the "literality" of "stuff." At such moments, Trilling repeats the *form* of his Parrington critique's key component, but changes its content. Trilling had earlier distinguished himself from Parringtonism – and, more broadly, from all those interwar commentators who assumed that realism in American literary culture requires first an ability to smell "the odors of the shop" – by insisting that American "actuality" was complex and marked by epistemological difficulty (*Liberal Imagination*, p. 24). Now, in his later essay on Howells, Trilling again points to an overlooked real, which distinguishes him from the widespread "modern taste" that his undergraduates most immediately represent but that, Trilling implies, also permeates many more advanced readers in America as well.[17] The only shift is in how Trilling characterizes that real.

Both in 1950 and in 1955 Trilling seeks to establish a realer-than-thou critical position, first in relation to "proletarian" criticism and then later in relation to the eager sophistication of modern taste. His gestures at these two moments follow inverse but ultimately complementary paths. It is worth emphasizing that the two inverse assertions Trilling makes in these critical moments parallel the two different modes of realist taste elaborated by Howells. As chapter 1 discusses, in the early to middle portion of his literary career Howells strives to establish that a cultivated taste for representations of commonplace vernacular realities can help to demonstrate a reader's aesthetic discernment, especially in comparison to readers whose cultural-capital portfolios are otherwise roughly similar. Later in his career, portraying protagonists such as Basil March and the Reverend Sewell, Howells emphasizes the cultural prestige available to those intellectuals who develop an affinity for the painfully irresolvable contradictions, the recalcitrant ironies presented by America's social problems. Similarly (albeit in reverse order), at one moment in his critical development, Trilling insists that real reality, comprised by "variousness, possibility, complexity, and difficulty," is not as unproblematically available as others appear to think. On the other hand, however, Trilling also says: I perceive that the realest reality is so *literal* that others, in their formulaic attempts at sophistication, look right past it. Can't you see, one can imagine him exclaiming, that the real nitty-gritty at issue in this passage of Dostoevski is as close as the money you use to buy the cafeteria lunches over which you natter about existential angst? Throughout Trilling's career, this hey!-reality-is-right-in-front-of-your-eyes move does play a less prominent role in his criticism than does the reality-is-too-complicated-for-your-simplistic-epistemology move, but at key moments he employs the former to supplement the latter. And, at every juncture Trilling insists that to better grasp the nature of literature's constitutive reality, however he at that moment defines it, is also to have better taste.

These same two claims – one, literature's reality is not as empirically accessible as you simple-mindedly assume; two, literature's reality is more literal, more directly in front of your eyes, than your eager sophistication lets you recognize – together form the molds shaping a diverse range of subsequent critical position-taking. Poststructuralist perspectives are particularly interesting in this regard because they tend to find ways of making both species of material claims simultaneously, or even of compacting the two into one. By exploring poststructuralist adaptations of realist prestige, I hope in what follows both to demonstrate the continued centrality of American realist paradigms to American literary culture and also to contribute to contemporary discussions (by John Guillory and Jane Gallop, for instance) about the cachet that poststructuralist approaches gained among academic literary critics in the United States during the 1970s and 1980s.[18]

Paul de Man might seem to epitomize the abandonment of the "public intellectual" role that is lamented by so many commentators, a role of which Lionel Trilling is often considered America's last great exemplar. De Man's writing is notoriously inaccessible for readers not versed in the terminology of European-descended critical theory.

Moreover, de Man's writing seemed to grow ever more densely special-ized as his career progressed, so that even the title of one of his most important later essays, "Hypogram and Inscription," might well seem cryptic and off-putting not only to non-academic readers but to many academics as well. Of course it is easy to see how this very inaccessibil-ity might contribute to de Man's critical prestige by separating the few elite readers who could understand his writing from the many who could not.

Yet the first paragraph of "Hypogram and Inscription" devotes itself to arguing that what admittedly appears as an "arcane" theoretical debate actually possesses crucial pertinence from a "public perspective." The theoretical debate whose public profile de Man wishes to heighten is that between "semioticians and grammarians" on the one hand and, on the other hand, "theoreticians of rhetoric" – that is, in other words, between structuralist literary theory and de Man's version of decon-structive literary theory.[19] Why should a larger public care? As de Man's essay proceeds, it becomes clear that his claim on the "public," or at least on the public he refers to as "literary journalists and literary critics," depends on his framing the "abstruse" debate between deconstruction and structuralism as one about the materiality of literature, about what dimension of it can be considered most undeniably real.

In *Cultural Capital,* John Guillory has recently addressed the relation between Paul de Man's critical prestige and the "specifically American institutional" contexts in which it developed (p. 238). Guillory locates the prestige of de Manian deconstruction within the sociohistorical juncture in which literature departments in US universities have lately found themselves, especially as that juncture is shaped by dramatic changes in United States and global capitalism. Although I find much of Guillory's argument persuasive, I believe it also helps us better understand de Manian prestige to recognize its affinities with a specific institution that Guillory does not mention: American literary realism. (In fact, I will go on to argue below that, *especially* in the form of its attack on de Man's status, Guillory's own argument interestingly reverberates with the same literary tradition of realer-than-thou one-upmanship that I have focused on.)

De Man chooses to demonstrate the difference between a structural-ist and a deconstructive approach to literature through considering the "scientist" Michael Riffaterre's reading of Victor Hugo's poem, "Ecrit sur une fenêtre flamande." He begins with a pointed allusion to the broad success, "now widely acknowledged here and abroad," of

Riffaterre's "didactic model for the teaching of literature" (p. 28). Whether this supposedly widespread acceptance of Riffaterre's model for teaching literature ever really existed to the extent that de Man suggests is not important for my purposes. More significant is how de Man's opening description of Riffaterre's wide influence in literature classrooms echoes Trilling's assertion, at the beginning of "Reality in America," that V. L. Parrington's "ideas are now the accepted ones wherever the college course in American literature is given by a teacher who conceives himself to be opposed to the genteel and the academic and in alliance with the vigorous and the actual." Like Trilling, de Man from the start explicitly frames his own claim to offer a better grasp on literature's reality within the question of critical and professional status. Also worth noting here is de Man's declaration that Riffaterre's orientation toward the phenomenality of the reading experience "makes him an 'American' as opposed to a 'French' critic" (p. 33). Trilling calls Parrington's positivist notion of the real an unfortunate aspect of "the American mind." For de Man, despite the fact that both he and Riffaterre were born in Europe and mostly focus on European texts, it is still "American" conceptions of reality that remain at stake.

Of course Riffaterre does not, for de Man, represent the same naïve positivism that Trilling attacked in Parrington. As a structuralist, Riffaterre easily assumes that signs do not refer directly to the outside world but instead take their meaning from a larger linguistic system, a system composed, moreover, not of positive values but of relations among signs. De Man's challenge, in "Hypogram and Inscription," will nonetheless be to make Riffaterre into his Parrington, a critic whose literary judgment is faulty because it rests on a mistaken belief that reality is solid, stable and self-evident.

To achieve this transformation of a non-reference based, structuralist perspective, de Man focuses on the status of the sign itself in Riffaterre's discussions of poetry. Riffaterre's reader-oriented method claims that poems have no referential link to the outside world. Instead, individual poems derive from a single minimal kernel, such as a clichéd sentence or stereotype, which functions as the poem's "matrix," appearing and reappearing in different modes and forms throughout the poem.[20] Because of his disregard for any external "meaning" that a poem might have and his exclusive focus on the effects of the poem's linguistic operations, Riffaterre can legitimately be considered as the most pure of formalists. Yet, de Man insists, that does not mean that Riffaterre avoids the error of regarding reality as a "determined, stable principle" (p. 39).

Riffaterre's approach may dispense with referentiality and even with normative notions of reality, but his approach still does assume the phenomenal existence of a poem's signifying elements themselves, their availability to sense perception. "All formalist theories of poetry sooner or later have to confront a similar problem: their adequation to the phenomenally realized aspects of their topic" – their grounding themselves, that is, in whatever elements they believe actually constitute a poem's "form" – "makes them highly effective as a descriptive discipline, but at the cost of understanding" (p. 30).

Trilling's critique of Parrington offered a larger challenge to the authority of various critics and critical perspectives purporting to ground themselves in "the odors of the shop." De Man repeats Trilling's move but with an additional turn of the screw: he finds that same limited idea of reality as defined by what impinges on the physical senses to underlie even the most aggressively antireferential structuralist criticism. De Man points out that, for Riffaterre, a formal element "can be lexical, grammatical, syntactical, figural or intratextual, but whatever the linguistic mode may be, its actuality is always determined by its phenomenality" (p. 34). For instance, de Man finds Riffaterre reproving a fellow theorist (Ricardou) who, attempting to employ a method similar to Riffaterre's own search for a poem's formal matrix, discovers the anagram "gold" in Poe's phrase "right hol*d*ing." Because the "g" in "right" remains unpronounced in English, Riffaterre considers that particular "g" as "not accessible to the senses" and hence as possessing "no phenomenal reality," at least not for the purposes of analyzing poetic form (p. 34). Riffaterre, in short, might pay no attention to any supposedly free-standing external reality, but he still takes as the bedrock of his readings what de Man calls the "phenomenal substance of the sign" (p. 34). Riffaterre dismisses an unpronounced letter as not "actualized," just as, for Trilling's Parrington, if something was "not literal . . . not, as it were, a public document" then it "did not seem quite real" (*Liberal Imagination*, p. 16). For de Man, Riffaterre is reductive in assuming that a sign itself is (I again adapt from Trilling's description of Parrington's reality) "irreducible" (p. 16).

"What," de Man asks, "has Riffaterre omitted?" (p. 44). Parrington, in Trilling's representation of him, was "at a loss" when confronted with "realities" constituted by difficulty or complexity. What, for de Man, shall count as "Riffaterre's blind spot," the point where de Man can claim a purchase on the really real superior to that not only of Riffaterre's structuralist formalism but, by implication, to other "formalist" approaches to literature (p. 41)? De Man, of course, is no more inter-ested than Riffaterre in claiming access to any extra-linguistic "real world" of tables, chairs, people, etc. Still, he insists, building up antici-pation almost as a detective story does, there are "certain dimensions" of texts that are "beyond the reach of a theoretical model that they put in jeopardy" (p. 43). The threatening real that Riffaterre's structuralist formalism cannot reach – that Riffaterre, de Man says, even seeks to evade – is signification's "materiality" – "materiality," crucially, as "dis-tinct from phenomenality" (p. 51).

For de Man, "phenomenality" correlates with a notion of mere per-ception, that which appears as immediately available for processing by the senses, while "materiality" is bottomline irrefutable reality. In refer-ring to the "materiality" of language, and differentiating it from lan-guage's availability to sense perception or even cognition, de Man means to evoke what he elsewhere describes as the "random positioning" of indeterminably meaningful marks, which makes language possible in the first place. It is only after language arbitrarily posits meaningfulness for some of these random marks but not for others, de Man insists, that signification itself can at least contingently operate. This initial positing of a field where meaning can occur outlines, as it were, the elements of a face, where previously there existed only random traces. De Man adapts the rhetorical term prosopopoeia (the giving of face) to describe this initial act of positing, of arbitrarily designating shapes, forms and patterns that shall count as at least potentially meaningful elements (letters and words, for instance, and not the patterns one might find within the texture of the paper on which the letters are written, or in the woodgrain or the dust on the desk where the paper lies). De Man calls prosopopoeia the "master trope" because the giving of face, the posit-ing of a potentially meaningful field, must precede the operation of any figural tropes, linguistic structures or other systems by which language makes meaning (p. 48).

De Man's notion of "materiality" attempts to capture a moment even before prosopopoeia's initial positing of form as such, when the indeter-minably meaningful mark cannot yet be regarded either as a sign or as not a sign. These indeterminably meaningful marks, with the "arbitrary and aleatory character" of their positioning, are the necessary condition for language to occur.[21] They constitute "the materiality of signification," yet they do not, by themselves, either signify or not signify meaning. Why, however, did de Man's appeal to this version of language's (and litera-ture's) underlying materiality prove so gripping to a large cohort of

American literary theorists, and accrue so much talismanic prestige among an even larger group of literary academics who were not theorists?

One key reason for the prestige, I suggest, is that de Man's "materiality" succeeds in combining into one two inverse modes of pointing to an overlooked "reality." These two inverse gestures – one, reality is more complex, even indescribably so, than "they" naively believe; two, reality is right in front of their over-sophisticated eyes – appear as disparate and, to an extent, even incompatible moments in Trilling's own criticism. By contrast, the "materiality" revealed by de Man's critical gaze succeeds in making both of these claims at one and the same time. The indeterminably significant marks from which signs are constituted *are* literally right in front of us any time we read or listen to a word – without them there would be nothing to read or listen to at all. That is why de Man can accuse Riffaterre of, in his eager search for the "matrix" of Hugo's poem, looking right past the poem's "most literal" dimension: "The actual title, however, is 'Ecrit sur la vitre d'une fenêtre flamande,' the 'here' and the 'now' of the poem which elicits no comment from Riffaterre and remains to be accounted for" (p. 48). Riffaterre's formalism overlooks the most basic thing about the poem: "That it was written cannot be denied" (p. 51). That the poem is "written" will end up, for de Man, making it the opposite of transparently readable. Nonetheless, by pointing out that Riffaterre somehow fails to observe this first, most commonsense feature of the work, de Man implicitly stakes his own claim to the prestige Americans like to accord to the more down-to-earth, less fanciful, of two intellectual perspectives.

Yet the other face of de Man's reminder to us that Hugo's poem is undeniably constituted by the "materiality of an inscription" is the assertion of de Man's orientation towards an underlying real more complexly difficult, more epistemologically challenging, than any other supposedly fundamental elements of texts pointed to by alternative critical approaches. The "materiality of an inscription" may well be the first, most undeniable thing to say about Hugo's poem, but that same materiality also turns out to be inaccessible and indeed indescribable: "Inscription is neither a figure, nor a sign, nor a cognition, nor a desire, nor a hypogram, nor a matrix" (p. 51). The "uncontrollable power of the letter as inscription" (p. 37) is language's most absolute necessity – without it there could be no language at all – yet it resists, even undoes, description. As Cynthia Chase explains de Man's thinking,

The materiality of an inscription must be distinguished from the phenomenal, sensory existence of a particular piece of writing. By *inscription* is meant marks or traces that indeed exist and occur, not in a perceptible space, but to a perceiver in the process of reading, of rendering intelligible, a diffusion of marks or traces. Such marks cannot be known to *signify* and cannot be said to be *perceived*, since their form, their shape, their phenomenal status . . . can only be postulated for them.[22]

Inscription as such is "senseless." Our senses can only perceive the sen-*sible*. Sheer inscription, the random positioning of indeterminably significant marks, remains uninterpretable until it has been posited into some sort of structured field, where some elements are taken for meaningful (for signs) and others are not. As de Man famously puts it in *Allegories of Reading*, "it seems to be impossible to isolate the moment in which the fiction stands free of any signification . . . Yet without this moment, never allowed to exist as such, no such thing as a text is conceivable."[23]

De Man's own writing, and the critical approach that he promoted, could not "isolate" as such the sheer linguistic materiality whose constitutive necessity he insisted on. He could not capture it and put it on display. But de Man did, implicitly and explicitly, offer to provide a closer and better perspective on "sheer materiality" than that of other critics. His stance might be compared to that of some future guide to the sub-atomic realm, who claims that he can achieve for *his* customers a closer proximity (although they still won't be able to directly see or touch it) than any competitor guides can to the destructive nuclear force residing within the atoms all around us.

John Guillory's *Cultural Capital* has a lengthy chapter on Paul de Man. *Cultural Capital* explores how, during the past few centuries, the institutional teaching of literature has differentially distributed skills, knowledges, and tastes in such a way as to help reproduce both educational institutions themselves and larger structures of social hierarchy. The book's chapter on de Man, "Literature after Theory: the Lesson of Paul de Man," represents Guillory's most sustained attention to a single figure. De Man, Guillory argues, possesses a "symptomatic significance" insofar as he and his work ultimately became equated, both in the media and in literary academia's own "professional imaginary," with the status of "theory" as such (p. 178).

I will not try here to offer a thorough summary of Guillory's trenchant and careful analysis of the remarkable status achieved by de Man and by de Manian deconstruction within the literary-critical profession. Instead, I will focus on showing how Guillory's mostly deflationary argument about de Man's prestige itself calls upon the same two varieties of realer-than-thou one-upmanship that we have already found in both Trilling and de Man. Like Trilling on Parrington, and also like de Man on Riffaterre, Guillory begins his critique with the problem of de Man's wide influence on literature teachers, taking as his chapter's subtitle the title of *Yale French Studies*' 1984 memorial issue, *The Lesson of Paul de Man*. The issue included a series of testimonial essays from literature professors about de Man and his influence, offering substantial evidence for the belief, as Guillory puts it, that de Man "seed[ed] the profession with his disciples" (p. 178).

Guillory is particularly interested in how de Man's "disciples," even after his death, continue to seize upon his notion of linguistic materiality. They claim to find there, as Guillory reports it, a powerful tool for oppositional politics (p. 236). After offering his own paraphrase of how de Man construes the materiality of signification, Guillory asks his readers, "Shall we now say that the thematic of chance and necessity has led de Man to a version of *materialism*? For that is, indeed . . . how his theory of language has been interpreted by the disciples themselves" (p. 228). The answer to Guillory's question about whether "we" can judge de Man to have achieved a genuinely *material* theoretical insight will, of course, be no. First, Guillory argues, in focusing on inscribed marks that are made to serve as signifiers, de Man restricts his notion of materiality to the limited sphere of the "simply *physical*." In speaking "casually and ubiquitously of the materiality of the signifier," de Manian deconstruction finds only, Guillory insists, a "'materiality'" that "is nothing more than the 'matter' of vulgar materialism, a literalization whose consequence will concern us presently" (p. 229).

Here, Guillory moves to Parrington-ize de Man. In the 1950s, the anti-communist Trilling in effect made Parrington a target of the New York Intellectuals' critique of the "vulgar materialism" that they associated with Stalinism and the proletarian aesthetic. Forty years later, it is, iron-ically, the marxian critic Guillory – a critic much more directly inter-ested, for instance, in the conditions and organization of labor than is either Trilling or de Man – who wields the charge of vulgar materialism against a critical theorist usually regarded as, if anything, too abstract. I would contend that the ready availability of this charge in late twenti-eth-century literary criticism – the charge of subscribing to an overly reductive materialism, of understanding the real as merely physical matter – indicates that, at least in American literary culture, the charge has less to do with the specifics of any political debate than with the dynamics of distinction and status. The accusation, after all, is one of *vulgarity*.

One might argue against Guillory here that his equation of de Man's materiality with the "simply physical" pays insufficient heed to de Man's insistence that he means a materiality "distinct from phenomenality," distinct from that which already exists in a perceptual space. As if in response to just such an argument, however – an argument that de Manian deconstruction reveals the signifier's constitutive indeterminacy and not its vulgarly physical matter – Guillory turns to the *predictability* of de Manian literary readings. This predictability itself allows Guillory to depict de Manian deconstruction as too positivistic, which makes it inadequate to multivalent reality. For assessing what exactly deconstructive readings of literature make visible to us, "It scarcely matters . . . whether the name of the conclusion is 'indeterminacy,' not if the same conclusion (or knowledge) is always produced by adhering in the practice of reading to what is already known about the nature of language itself" (p. 232). The sheer linguistic indeterminacy located by de Manian reading is supposed to undo the possibility of a stable world upon which perception, cognition, or meaning could ever ground themselves. But Guillory's formulation of what such readings actually find – "what is already known about the nature of language itself" – implicitly aligns them with the most unsophisticated of naturalizing perspectives. Like Parrington's history of American literature, which Trilling finds inadequate to its topic because of its own pat "assumptions about the nature of reality," de Manian reading, in Guillory's characterization, acts as if it knows perfectly well, thank you, about the "nature" of language. De Man, in what seems a virtually absolute contrast with Parrington, may thematize an unstable and never directly knowable linguistic materiality, but "the very *logic* of rhetorical reading" (p. 232; Guillory's emphasis), its always inevitable trajectory towards the same linguistic materiality, replicates Parrington's sense of reality as (again borrowing Trilling's words) "always reliable, always the same, always easily to be known."

If the answer is thus predictably negative to Guillory's query regarding whether "we shall now say" that de Man has developed "a version of *materialism*" (Guillory's emphasis), then what would a truly materialist account look like for Guillory, a materialist account, for instance, of the professional prestige accrued by de Man himself? More specifically, what materiality does Guillory offer in replacement for the vulgar simplification that he finds in de Man's concept of linguistic materiality? Unconsciously repeating de Man's tactic of building detective-story suspense about what exactly "Riffaterre's blind spot" might be overlooking, Guillory moves through an accelerating series of questions and hints towards what he calls "the real question, the invisible question": the question of the "real nature of [the] conditions" for which de Man's critical prestige serves only as a "symptom" (p. 180).

The answer Guillory elaborates centers on "the adjustment of critical practice to new socioinstitutional conditions of literary pedagogy" (p. 181). For Guillory, the political purchase that de Man's disciples believe one can gain through recognizing signification's underlying materiality, as well as de Manian deconstruction's much-bruited intellectual "rigor," can best be understood as the desperate, unconscious attempt by one faction within the critical establishment to regain some of the culturally privileged status that the profession of literary study as such has lost over the past few decades. Although misrecognized even by deconstruction's practitioners, deconstruction responds to the decreasing cultural capital that American society, and most immediately American research universities themselves, assign to literary study. Deconstruction represents an attempt launched from within the literary critical profession to compensate for "the diminished significance of the literary curriculum in the context of the university's perceived social function, the perceived demand for the knowledges it disseminates" (p. 261).

"Practices" that occur in relation to "socioinstitutional conditions": *these*, for Guillory, constitute the ineluctably grounding real of any critical analysis. They are his "rather different explanatory context" (p. 230), that irreducible level of material explanation to which, he says, a "trick of ideological optics" (p. 242) blinds both deconstruction's detractors and its defenders. Designating his own irreducible level of analysis allows Guillory to make the realist promise that "at this point we may go on to contextualize the entire de Manian thematic by turning it inside out, as it were, by correlating the terms which are internal to its discourse with the terms defining the conditions of its institutional practice" (p. 257).

Just as indeterminably significant marks served de Man as both a more resistantly complex *and* as a more it's-right-there-in-front-of-you! reality than Riffaterre's formalism could even gesture towards, so too Guillory's notion of the *relation* between practices and socioinstitutional conditions lends itself to these same two varieties of (what we should at this point call) more-materialist-than-thou claims. On the one hand, changes in the social demand for the different sorts of knowledges the university offers "ultimately" derive, Guillory insists, from shifts in the functioning and global organization of production itself. Intellectual labor in the US has become increasingly dominated by "technobureau-cratic" modes of work, which no longer require the privileged mastery of that "refined bourgeois language," "'literary' English," which it was once the task of literary education to differentially distribute and with-hold (pp. 261–2). Thus, the "world . . . of relations" that, Guillory insists, should be understood as "circumscribing and conditioning" the intellec-tual prestige accorded to de Man consists, in the last analysis, of "nothing less than the total socio-economic order" (p. 255). Chapter 2, above, discusses Henry James's notion, developed in his preface to *Roderick Hudson*, of a relational "whole matter" underlying art itself: "Really, universally, relations stop nowhere . . ." Guillory's concept of "historical materialism" is similar in its emphasis on a fundamental matrix that is *relational* all the way down: for historical materialism, "it may be said that the world is the totality of relations, not things" (p. 229).

The multiple levels of relations and mediations comprising Guillory's "total socio-economic order" might in theory be accessible to direct, systematic knowledge. But the scale and sheer complexity of these rela-tions has the effect of rendering a full grasp of them as something always to be deferred. Guillory's multiple "relations" can be pointed at – for instance, by Guillory's neologistic compound words, such as "socioinsti-tutional" (p. 181), "psycho-pedagogy" (p. 190), and "technobureaucratic" (p. 261), all of which syntactically suggest the mutual overdetermination of entities usually thought about separately. But comprehensive mastery over "the totality of relations" can never be achieved. Guillory's book signals the necessity of deferring any such mastery by phrases like "in the meanwhile we can say that . . ." (p. 181). The sheer difficulty (in prac-tice insurmountable) of fully grasping "the totality of relations" that Guillory presents as real materiality cannot help but imply that the mate-riality Guillory brings to our attention makes the same claim as de Man's "materiality of signification." That is, like de Man, Guillory claims to orient us toward a materiality more inaccessible, more resistant to cog-nitive assimilation, than can even be imagined by those simplistic souls for whom bottom-line reality resides in "the world of things" (as it does for de Man himself, according to Guillory).

In addition to framing it as defying our full comprehension (in this case by virtue of its unimaginable complexity), however, Guillory also suggests that his category of bottom-line materiality – practices in relation to institutions – has been overlooked by other analysts because it has been hidden in plain view. If we wish to understand deconstruction's intellectual prestige, Guillory insists, we must turn to "the everyday life of the professors of literature" (p. 245). For Guillory, this attention to the quotidian circumstances of professors' lives, to the "very specific context of contemporary literary pedagogy," in its "historical time and place," is the necessary, elemental step in conceiving "the relation of [deconstructive] discourse to its institutional conditions" (pp. 245–6, 233). Lionel Trilling rebukes sophomorically sophisticated readers for assuming that "money" in Dostoevski has nothing to do with what's in their own pockets but must be "symbolic, as if no one ever needed, or spent, or gambled or squandered the stuff – and as if to think of it as an actuality were subliterary" (*The Opposing Self*, p. 82). Similarly, Guillory criticizes most discussions of "the 'politics of deconstruction'" for approaching the question only allegorically, so that deconstruction becomes "either the allegory of the evasion of the political, according to its detractors, or the allegory of its secret subversiveness, according to its defenders" (p. 245). Hey professors, we can imagine Guillory saying, pay some attention to the actual institutional politics that helps determine, say, the size of the graduate program in which you will debate deconstruction. Guillory's criticism of those who discuss deconstruction's significance on an allegorical level instead of on the institutionally "specifying" level of his own analysis ("specifying" and "specific" occur very frequently in this portion of Guillory's argument) here takes the form of a commonsense "realist" privileging of the empirically quotidian over symbols and allegories. Of course neither Trilling (who attacks the "American mind" for being overly-literal in its understanding of reality) nor Guillory (who stresses the primacy of "relations, not things") consistently equates empirical immediacy with material reality as such. My point is that, like Trilling, both Guillory and de Man display the superiority of their own intellectual purchase on materiality through tactically shifting assertions about where we should even begin looking for it.

WHAT MATTERS

"What about the materiality of the body, *Judy*?" On the first page of her 1993 *Bodies that Matter: On the Discursive Limits of Sex*, Judith Butler relates that she "repeatedly" received this question following upon the remarkable prominence achieved by her earlier *Gender Trouble: Feminism and the Subversion of Identity* (1990).[24] (On this book's rapidly accrued status: Eve Sedgwick reports that no one could "help being awed" as Butler's work was "appealed to in paper after paper" at the seminal 1991 Gay and Lesbian Studies conference at Rutgers.[25] Shortly thereafter an unprecedented graduate student "fanzine" devoted to Butler appeared.) This oft-repeated question to her about the materiality of the body had, as Butler experienced it, a "certain patronizing quality." She took the question, including its aggressive insistence on the diminutive nickname "Judy," as "an effort to dislodge me from the more formal 'Judith' and to recall me to a bodily life that could not be theorized away" (p. ix). Yet at roughly the same moment as she was being charged with having overlooked the everyday facticity of basic biology, Butler was also criticized in a forceful (and twice reprinted) essay by Joan Copjec for having failed to achieve a radical enough "desubstantialization of sex" – that is, for having treated sex too much as a positive substance – because of her failure to attend to the Real as theorized by Lacan's later work.[26]

Two very different attempts to "dislodge" *Gender Trouble* took the tack of asserting that *Gender Trouble* had overlooked the really real, that which, if one wishes to perform valid cultural analysis, must be recognized as a level of utter intransigence. Those questioners who criticized Butler by appealing to commonsense biology might be seen as having adopted the "don't you see that *real* reality is right in front of you?" tactic discussed above (manifested here almost as an accusation that Butler has ignored the obviousness of her own body). By contrast, Copjec's invocation of a Lacanian order of the Real seeks, if I can use the phrase once again, to "Parrington-ize" Butler, to position her as a positivistic naïf. For Copjec, Butler fails to deal with that negativity which marks the radical limit of symbolization: castration, the terrifyingly empty lack that traverses the human subject. "Sex," for Copjec, derives from, can even be said to "coincide with," language's inability ever to gain a purchase on castration, on the subject's contentless division from itself. For Copjec, "sex is . . . the failure of signification" (p. 204). "Sex," that is, does not itself have an unstable meaning. Rather, "sex" is what ensures "the impossibility of completing meaning." The crucial point then, for Copjec, "is that sex is the structural incompleteness of language, not that sex is itself incomplete" (p. 206). In disregarding this definition of sex as coinciding with language's "radical impasse," *Gender Trouble*, according to Copjec, "for all its talk about sex, eliminates sex itself" (p. 211).

Because Butler does not grapple with the negative real "cutting up" subjects and language both, she remains a mere "discourse analyst," dismissable insofar as she recognizes *only* the symbolic order, only the "official" system of positions, relations, and signification that characterizes the social. Even here, in this recondite and seemingly removed 1990s feminist theory context, Trilling's indictment of Parrington's inability to face any reality "that was not, as it were, a public document" still echoes in Copjec's indictment of Butler for blindness to any order other than the symbolic.

Bodies That Matter has relatively little trouble providing a response to that criticism of *Gender Trouble* which appeals to biological facticity over and against fancy theory ("What about the materiality of the body, *Judy?*"). A by now substantial amount of deconstructive writing about the body, including *Gender Trouble* itself, offers a set of powerful arguments on the problems involved in appealing to a prediscursive body. (First of all, the appeal constitutes in discourse the very body supposed to be prior to discourse.) I will therefore focus primarily on Butler's response to the Lacanian critique articulated by Copjec, a critique which also attempts, albeit from a different point of view, to "dislodge" *Gender Trouble* for not being real enough.

Butler's confrontation with the Lacanian REALer-than-thou charge represents an *intra*-poststructuralist struggle over how to conceive materiality. Although she does not respond to Copjec directly, I take Butler's extended chapter "Arguing with the Real," where she concentrates on Slavoj Žižek's recently influential interpretation of Lacanian theory, to serve as, among other things, such a response. Žižek is a mentor to Copjec: the central paragraph of *Read My Desire*'s acknowledgments begins by thanking him for helping her to develop a "specifically . . . Lacanian" critical approach. Žižek and Copjec are both prominent members of the critical cohort that James M. Mellard has recently dubbed New Lacanians, who tend to emphasize "Lacan's late notions of drive, *jouissance*, and the real" (other prominent examples cited by Mellard include Juliet Flower MacCannell and Elizabeth Cowie). As Mellard explains of this "cadre," Žižek's "readings of Lacan have influenced the others perhaps as greatly as Lacan himself has."[27]

Before turning, however, to Butler's argument with Žižek's Lacanian real, it's worth dwelling for a moment on Copjec's own invocation of this real as her trump card against Foucault, in what she blatantly portrays as a competition for intellectual prestige on the contemporary critical scene. Copjec's overriding aim in *Read My Desire* is to counter "Foucault's ascendancy over Lacan in the academy" (p. 19).[28] Her acknowledgments, where she alludes to "the good times, when psychoanalysis was the 'hot' discourse," indicate from before her argument even begins that the conflict announced in her subtitle – "Lacan against the Historicists" – refers not only to disagreements of theory but also to the question of comparative critical prestige. Throughout her text, Copjec remains openly concerned with critical prestige, which she seems to conceive of as a zero-sum economy. More prestige given to one critical approach means that much less given to another.

For our inquiry into realism's continuing role within even poststructuralism's internecine dynamics of intellectual prestige, what stands out in Copjec's attempt to undercut the perceived ascendancy of Foucault (whose "historicism . . . pervades much of the thinking of our time" [p. 12]) is not her focus on how Foucault conceives "the very *matter* of the social" (p. 5; my emphasis).[29] We have already seen that different poststructuralist approaches tend to compete over materiality and where to look for it. The critics that we have looked at so far, however, characteristically assert both a more literal *and* a more relational notion of materiality, usually giving a heavier emphasis to the latter and aligning it with complexity and empirical inaccessibility. By contrast, Copjec's Lacanian account makes any relationality at all, relationality as such, into a falsification of the Real. For Copjec, the Real's *literality* itself, paradoxically, is what makes it impossible to grasp, since relational signifiers constitute the only tools with which we might even attempt such grasping.

That is, Copjec does not say, as Guillory does regarding de Manian deconstruction, that Foucault's notion of materiality isn't really as *relational* as it claims to be. (Recall, Guillory accuses de Man's "materiality of language" of accessing only "the world of *things,* not *relations*" [Guillory, *Cultural Capital,* p. 229].) Nor does Copjec try to argue, as does de Man himself about Riffaterre, that the problem with Foucault's relational system is that it includes only phenomenally stable elements. (De Man charges Riffaterre's "formalism" with taking for granted the "phenomenal substance of the sign" and thereby overlooking its inherent indeterminacy [de Man, "Hypogram and Inscription," p. 34].) Rather, Copjec readily concedes that the "minimal unit" of Foucault's investigations "is never simply an isolable point, whether this be a person or a position, but always a relation." Yet, she asserts, even Foucault's notion of unstable points linked in a "network of uneven relations" makes reality too simplistically coherent, too easily knowable, and too stable (p. 5).

As Copjec will later insist when criticizing Butler's analysis of sexual identity (which she pejoratively dubs "historicist/ deconstructionist"), even the trademark poststructuralist claim that any identity will always be "incomplete, unstable" still fails to acknowledge the "terrifying real" of empty negation that internally divides – or castrates – all identities, ensuring the impossibility of any relations among them, however uneven or unstable (p. 120). Thus Foucault's points linked in "uneven relations" with one another still constitute a "historicist . . . *reduction* of society to its indwelling network of relations of power and knowledge" (Copjec, p. 6; my italics). However nuanced and complex it may be, Foucault's relationality implicitly assumes the "positivity of the social" (p. 4) and thus denies the Real of castration. Despite the bottom-line unpredictability of their valences, Foucault's uneven relations make the social seem "real-tight" (Copjec's term) which, for her, belies the negative Real itself (p. 14).

Copjec does concede that, insofar as desire is for "the object *a*," which (we wrongly suppose) would cancel the castrating emptiness that splits us, desire does reference the negative Real, even though by definition that Real cannot ever be articulated. Desire is produced as a striving for an indeterminate "something else or something more." It stems "from the feeling of our having been duped by language, cheated of something," blocked from some "essential thing" that would complete us, which we construe as the object *a*. As human subjects constituted by castration, however, we never *can* achieve completion. Hence desire, for Copjec, can never have any actual content. Desire "is for nothing – because language can deliver to us" no positive ground, nothing that could make us whole (pp. 55–6). Nonetheless, because desire at least indicates the lack that it strives, always unsuccessfully, to fill, desire at least alludes to the empty negativity of the real. Desire points to the real and its inevitable failure of structure and meaning. This is why, as Copjec explains, "Lacan insists that we must take desire literally . . . to avoid the pitfall of historicist thinking" (p. 14). Thus, Copjec's book title, "Read My Desire," itself offers the literary realist promise to orient readers towards the *real* real.

On the one hand, "Read My Desire," with its allusion to the aggressive "what you hear, right now, is just exactly what you get" idiom of *Read my lips!* advertises an easy-to-grasp real if readers will only drop their obtusely elaborate interpretative strategies. (The populist appeal of that idiom, *Read my lips!*, is that it deflates any pretensions of complexity in interpreting what one hears.) On the other hand, however, Copjec's title also carries the resonances of George Bush's "Read my lips: No new taxes" vow from the 1988 presidential campaign, which over the next few years (the period when most of the chapters of Copjec's book were first published) became a joky model among journalists and others for the evasiveness that can be present even in seemingly self-evident statements. Moreover, Copjec's substituting "desire" for "lips" frustrates our expectation of the idiom and thus gives the title an oxymoronic structure: if you want the real then just go ahead and *look* at my desire because it's right here in front of you – but wait!, Copjec's title then makes one realize, I have no idea how to look at *desire*. Indeed desire's implication of unsymbolizable lack, as Copjec will proceed to insist in the book itself, bears no relation to signifiers or to signification, so the injunction to "read" desire can never be anything *but* oxymoronic. Its unsymbolizability is also why the Lacanian Real, according to Copjec, *"cannot be deconstructed*, since deconstruction is an operation that can be applied only to culture, to the signifier, and has no purchase on this other realm" (p. 210; Copjec's emphasis). Copjec's "desire," like the other poststructuralist versions of the *real* real that I have discussed, defines itself as both more literal and, paradoxically, less accessible, even to the supposedly inescapable corrosions of deconstruction, than other candidates.

What Butler, however, aptly identifies as the "rhetorical difficulty of circumscribing within symbolic discourse . . . what is and is not symbolizable" (*Bodies That Matter*, p. 190) leads Copjec to a sort of quasi-theological rhetoric regarding this Real. For Copjec, that which belongs to the realm of the Real "has neither an essence nor a signification. It cannot be communicated or exchanged . . ." (*Read My Desire*, p. 119). As Butler demonstrates, Žižek's *The Sublime Object of Ideology*, whose large influence upon her work Copjec acknowledges, insists even more pervasively on the structural impossibility of managing to signify castration's "negativity [which is] more fundamental than any social antagonism" (*Bodies That Matter*, p. 194).

For Copjec, Žižek and the New Lacanians, at issue in how to conceive negativity is the question of whether non-representable lack is dispersed anywhere and everywhere in language, as they take deconstruction to suppose, or whether lack plays the specific role of, as castration, constituting the human subject and enforcing that subject's insuperable division *from* any linguistic system. Yet, Butler points out, as part of Žižek's polemic against what he takes to be deconstruction's misconstrual of materiality (as random contingency), he keeps referring to castration with what Butler aptly calls "materializing" terms: in Žižek's writing castration becomes a "hard kernel," a "substance," and, especially, "the rock of the real" and "the rock of castration," two phrases that Butler finds "intoned . . . throughout the text" (pp. 197–8). Žižek's recurrent allusions to an unsymbolizable "rock" call to mind, for Butler, the Old Testament and ultimately suggest to her that Žižek's "'rock' is the unnamable Yahweh, the principle of monotheism" (p. 200). This evocation of Yahweh serves as an indirect attempt to elevate Žižek, Butler argues, as he who "receives the word from the rock, and brings it down the mountain to us" (p. 200). Žižek's insisting on castration as the one, immovable real constitutes his bid to claim Moses's status as "bearer and spokesman for the Law" (p. 206).

Of primary importance for Butler in challenging Žižek's Mosaic prestige as privileged deliverer of the Real rock – which, Žižek preaches, shall remain "invariant" "for all time" (p. 189) – is her sense that in so reifying castration Žižek also reifies (or, to borrow a term from Amanda Anderson, "thingafies") a rigid account of sexuality and sexual difference. Butler asks, "does the formulation of the real in terms of the threat of castration establish the oedipally induced sexual differential at a prediscursive level?" (p. 195). She then goes on to demonstrate how Žižek's "fixing" castration as *the* prediscursive, preideological "bedrock" effectively "ontologizes subordination" for women and non-heterosexuals (p. 206). In addition to challenging Žižek's attempt to be the Moses of critical theory, Butler is also turning round upon him the same charge of reducing reality to a positive substance that Copjec had directed against Butler's own *Gender Trouble* when she accused it of not recognizing sex's radical negativity. Despite castration's supposed alignment with utter lack, Butler shows how Žižek's rhetoric and the structure of his argument insinuate a "real [that] postures as a self-identical principle" (p. 202). Žižek's insistence on castration as the "rock of the real" leaves him with a reality that, at bottom, yet again resembles Parrington's: "always reliable, always the same, always easily to be known."

But Butler's critique of Žižek's "real" does not stop at accusing him of treating it as a stable and solid substance. Following the same pattern of two-sided critique that I have been tracing throughout this chapter, Butler also adopts a straightforward, even somewhat empiricist-feeling "just pay attention to what's plainly there" approach that accuses Žižek of cavalierly overlooking what should be difficult to miss: the "historical specificity" proper even to radical negativity and its effects on subjectivity, the "historically textured" nature even of "unthinkable losses" such as those associated with concentration camps and with the Gulag (p. 202). Butler's appeal to historical "specificity" and historical "texture" over and against what she, at this moment of her argument, casts as Žižek's too "formal" notion of the real implicitly aligns her with the commonsense gesture towards a felt reality beyond (or prior to) fancy theory. Between her lines, we can almost make out a version of the same abstraction-debunking question that she describes herself receiving about the body: "what about the materiality of history, *Slavoj*?"

What does it mean that we find versions of the same two realer-than-thou claims informing a variety of recent "high theory" discussions of materiality? The critics that I have discussed each claim to offer a more relational or otherwise complex, unfixable material reality at the same time as they assertively call attention to a less mediated, more straightforward, above all more literal "real."[30] The contributions that these critics have made to the important, indeed imperative project of trying to articulate relations between literature and material reality all remain powerful and useful. It is only to our critical advantage for materiality to continue receiving analyses that are as varied and subtle as possible. Nonetheless, the recurrent pattern of similarly structured "my real is more genuinely material than your real" one-upmanship that I have described here does create a certain effect of wheelspinning. While it is perhaps inevitable that critical interventions will carry with them a certain claim to be more right about something than others have been, any assumption that one can be "right" about materiality seems to run counter to some of recent critical theory's own most crucial insights.

I wish to conclude by briefly returning to Butler's account of *materialization*, discussed earlier in my preface, as well as to the close of Wharton's *Twilight Sleep*. The notion of materialization as Butler develops it offers an intriguing framework for continuing to explore and debate materiality while also, perhaps, avoiding some of the repetitive realer-than-thou gestures pointed to above. By "materialization," Butler means the set of processes by which various discourses each "materialize a set of effects" and thereby produce what will appear as unconstructed, prediscursive *matter* (p. 187). My own emphasis throughout this book on the shifting categories that come to count as bottomline irrefutable reality in both literary realism and critical theory has correlated with Butler's argument that "matter" is instituted through iterating textual systems. Like Butler, I have been less interested in trying to talk about materiality as such than in tracing how, and with what effects, that which is "considered to be most real, most pressing, most undeniable" gets textually defined and positioned (Butler, *Bodies That Matter*, p. ix).

Butler's belief that materialization and its effects are always highly gendered and sexualized but not in any "singular and deterministic way" motivates her argument against Žižek's reification of a particular castration schema as having an invariant ontological primacy and unchanging form. More generally, Judith Butler's insistence that the relation between "materialization" and gender is ultimately a flexible one enables her work's liberatory and optimistic dimension, its emphasis on possibilities for "radical rearticulation of the symbolic horizon . . ." (p. 23). Butler's insight that the "highly gendered" character of materialization does not prevent the possibility for "radical rearticulations" is crucial. It suggests that meaningful changes may occur in the arrangements of gender, power, and status even within a persistent context of realer-than-thou or more-material-than-thou claims.

Returning now to Wharton's remarkable achievement in *Twilight Sleep*, I had suggested at the end of the previous chapter that (employing a phrase from one of Wharton's letters) the flapper Nona has "graduated from kindergarten." She has learned to include the devastating and traumatic emptiness associated with her lawyer-father's incestuous drive within, as it were, her own daily, domestic "fold." The very last line of the novel, however, consists of an aggressive joke that Nona makes. Her mother Pauline has popped into Nona's sick room one final time to suggest (quite amazingly, given what has been transpiring with her own husband) that Nona will only be happy when married. Staring "with hard unwavering eyes," Nona exclaims that she would "a thousand times rather" join a convent. Then, in the book's closing words, she clarifies for her shocked mother: "But I mean a convent where nobody believes in anything" (p. 315).

Nona's ironic image perhaps broaches the sort of "radical rearticulation" that Butler will later imagine. In the 1920s context of *Twilight Sleep*, Nona's convent might suggest, first, a group of women institutionally united by their willingness to face the loss of all that had counted as "frame-work" ("frame-work" is the word Wharton's autobiography used to capture all that seemed obliterated after World War I). Nona's imagined convent might even intimate something like a community of modernist women who share the same realist intellectual disposition that Wharton uses Nona to develop. Not a female version of the male modernist's "clean, well-lighted place" where darkness is kept outside, we might rather think of Nona's convent as a habitable space where "powers of darkness," including the father's incestuous desire, could be faced internally.[31] Such might be faced, moreover, not merely as traumatic event but also as "thought" ("her heart folded like two hands around the *thought* of him") – as, that is, matter for intellectual or literary exploration. Here, exploring the real could, at least in imagination, be undertaken without quite the same terrifying isolation implied by the single observation-slit that Nona had earlier felt her "eyes glued to" (p. 237).

Finally, in Nona's "convent where nobody believes in anything," we might choose as well to see an anticipatory image for one recent positive "rearticulation" of, at least, the literary-academic horizon: that is, the rise to critical prominence and professional influence of those feminist and queer approaches to gender and sexuality that Judith Butler herself (among, of course, many others) might be taken to represent. Recent feminist and queer theory is sometimes accused of being hermetic, too set off by theoretical density from the hurly-burly of immediate political struggle. Nonetheless, it has achieved significant critical authority. That authority derives from the "realist distinction" attached to its shared project of dissolving patriarchal beliefs about that which has been taken as the most "deep down and dogged" (in Wharton's words) dimensions of "the plain human tangle."[32]

Notes

1 Hamlin Garland, *Main-Travelled Roads* (Lincoln: University of Nebraska Press, 1995), p. 19; Henry James, *The American Scene* (Bloomington: Indiana University Press, 1968), pp. ix–x.
2 Nancy Bentley, *The Ethnography of Manners: Hawthorne, James, Wharton* (Cambridge University Press, 1995), p. 2.
3 Such changes included the nation's explosive increases in industrialization, urbanization, immigration, corporate expansion, labor strife, and consumerism. Oversimplifying the historicist criticism referred to above, all of which I have found informative and stimulating: Nancy Bentley's *The Ethnography of Manners* demonstrates connections between the realist "novel of manners" and ethnography. June Howard emphasizes naturalism's structural similarities with Progressive reform efforts. See June Howard, *Form and History in American Literary Naturalism* (Chapel Hill: University of North Carolina Press, 1985). Seltzer's *Henry James and the Art of Power* aligns realism with other investigative and disciplinary discourses of the period, such as that of urban policing. His *Bodies and Machines* discovers intricately powerful resonances between realist literature and, for instance, managerial programs such as that of Edward Taylor. See Mark Seltzer, *Bodies and Machines* (New York: Routledge, 1992) and *Henry James and the Art of Power* (Ithaca: Cornell University Press, 1984). For another perspective on Taylor's relation to the period's "narrative productions", see Martha Banta, *Taylored Lives: Narrative Productions in the Age of Taylor, Veblen, and Ford* (University of Chicago Press, 1993). Eric Sundquist's entry on "Realism and Regionalism" in *The Columbia Literary History of the United States* associates literary realism with "the rising spectator culture promoted by newspapers, magazines, advertising, photographs, and later motion pictures." See Eric Sundquist, "Realism and Regionalism," in *Columbia Literary History of the United States*, ed. Emory Elliott (New York: Columbia University Press, 1988), p. 503. I should note, however, that in recent works Brook Thomas and Susan Mizruchi do devote particular – and extremely cogent – attention to delineating the specificity of literary realism even as they also put it into close relation with legal (Thomas), as well as theological and social-scientific (Mizruchi) discourses

of the period. See Susan L. Mizruchi, *The Science of Sacrifice: American Literature and Modern Social Theory* (Princeton University Press, 1998) and Brook Thomas, *American Literary Realism and the Failed Promise of Contract* (Berkeley: University of California Press, 1997).

4 Garland wrote the 1922 preface from which I have quoted for a special edition of *Main-Travelled Roads*, issued by Harpers to coincide with the attention surrounding his prestigious Pulitzer Prize of that year (*Main-Travelled Roads* had first been published in 1890 by Arena Publications). Although Garland's most recent novels at the time he won his Pulitzer had leaned toward adventure and romance genres, he was also engaged in writing a series of autobiographical volumes that stressed his earlier involvement with Howells and the realist movement. Moreover, as Bill Brown has argued, the Pulitzer itself, officially awarded to Garland for the second of these autobiographical volumes (*A Daughter of the Middle Border*), seems to have honored Garland primarily as the grittier-than-Howells realist to whom Sinclair Lewis would pay homage in his own 1930 Nobel speech. See Bill Brown, "The Popular, the Populist, and the Populace – Locating Hamlin Garland in the Politics of Culture," *Arizona Quarterly* 50, no. 3 (1994), p. 107. The two-and-a-half-page 1922 preface, thus, is quite useful insofar as it efficiently indicates key contours shaping the public presentation of one, at that time particularly prominent, "realist disposition."

5 See, however, the chapters on Mark Twain in Warwick Wadlington's *The Confidence Game in American Literature* (Princeton University Press, 1975). Drawing upon Kenneth Burke's notion of "hierarchical motive," Wadlington devotes subtle attention to the rhetoric of Twain's realism in order to tease out dynamics of authority and "courtly" status. He discovers, for instance, that running through many of Twain's works is a "mixed and timed hierarchical arrangement of perspectives . . . whose value is in their rapid mobilization by the author" (p. 195); this insight resonates with my own reading of Abraham Cahan's *The Rise of David Levinsky* in chapter 3, below. See also Wadlington's analysis of the "honor-shame code" operative in Faulkner's work: Warwick Wadlington, *Reading Faulknerian Tragedy* (Ithaca and London: Cornell University Press, 1987), pp. 50–64.

6 The "participant observer" position that Carolyn Porter analyzes in Emerson, James, Adams, and Faulkner has some analogies with the two-sided relationship to the "really real" that I explore. Where she sees a "plight," however, I emphasize the opportunity for acquiring forms of cultural distinction. See Carolyn Porter, *Seeing and Being: the Plight of the Participant Observer in Emerson, James, Adams, and Faulkner* (Middletown, CT: Wesleyan University Press, 1981). On the phenomenon of participant-observers who went "down-and-out" in order to write about lower-class activities and living spaces, see Mark Pittenger, "A World of Difference: Constructing the Underclass in Progressive America," *American Quarterly* 49, no. 1 (1997).

7 Here, I would echo a remark made by Brook Thomas: "My point is not that there is an ahistorical category of the literary. On the contrary, what today

we call the literary has a specific history" (Thomas, *American Literary Realism and the Failed Promise of Contract*, p. 11).

8 See, for example, Amy Kaplan, *The Social Construction of American Realism* (University of Chicago Press, 1988), and June Howard, *Form and History in American Literary Naturalism*, pp. 70–141. By contrast to literary historians interested in the rise of the new middle classes, who have tended not to focus on differences *within* what Richard Brodhead calls the "postbellum elite," historians have provided several quite discipline-specific studies that together help to capture (to cite an exemplary literary historian) some of the "friction between the cultural vocabularies, as it were, within which new-middle-class authority would be phrased." See Christopher P. Wilson, *White Collar Fictions: Class and Social Representation in American Literature, 1885–1925* (Athens: University of Georgia Press, 1992), p. 255. Examples include Don S. Kirschner, *The Paradox of Professionalism: Reform and Public Service in Urban America, 1900–1940* (New York: Greenwood Press, 1986) and Dorothy Ross, *The Origins of American Social Science: Ideas in Context* (Cambridge University Press, 1991).

9 See, for instance, Richard H. Brodhead, *The School of Hawthorne* (New York: Oxford University Press, 1986), chapters 4–8. Also see Richard H. Brodhead, *Cultures of Letters: Scenes of Reading and Writing in Nineteenth-Century America* (University of Chicago Press, 1993), chapters 4–6; and Nancy Glazener, *Reading for Realism: the History of a US Literary Institution, 1850–1910* (Durham, NC: Duke University Press, 1997), pp. 11–50.

10 I use the word "intellectual" somewhat anachronistically here. Ross Posnock's discussion provides a very useful thumbnail history of the term (which emerged during the Dreyfus conflict in France) and of its importation into American discourse by William James. See Ross Posnock, *Color and Culture: Black Writers and the Making of the Modern Intellectual* (Cambridge, MA: Harvard University Press, 1998), pp. 11–23.

11 Jonathan Freedman's *Professions of Taste* is authoritative on how the category of taste operated within late nineteenth-century Anglo-American aesthetic (and aestheticist) culture. My discussion of taste and late nineteenth-century American literature differs in emphasis from that of Freedman, however, insofar as I pursue the implications of developing and seeking to accord cultural privilege to an educated taste for the plain, the rough, or even the ugly. My discussion of "realist taste" and philistinism in chapter 1 develops this point further. See Jonathan Freedman, *Professions of Taste: Henry James, British Aestheticism and Commodity Culture* (Stanford University Press, 1990).

12 Part of my motivation for making this sort of suggestion is that investigations of poststructuralism's rise in the United States literary academy often point to the allure of European theory as such and to how social movements such as feminism and anticolonialism brought to the fore concepts such as margin and center. The New Criticism's emphasis on close reading is also sometimes invoked as having prepared the ground for the taking up of post-structuralism in US universities. But poststructuralism's possible links with

earlier moments in American literary history itself, such as the period of American literary realism, remain too rarely examined.

13 Pierre Bourdieu notes that, in his usage of the term, "disposition" is always a "relationally defined position." Pierre Bourdieu, *Distinction: a Social Critique of the Judgment of Taste*, trans. Richard Nice (Cambridge, MA: Harvard University Press, 1984), p. 246. Further page references to Bourdieu's *Distinction* will appear within the text.

14 Abraham Cahan, *The Rise of David Levinsky* (New York: Harper & Row, 1960), p. 291.

15 I engage with Bourdieu in this project rather than with Bourdieu's American predecessor Thorstein Veblen. Veblen's works analyzing cultural status are contemporary with American literary realist writing and, reviewing his *Theory of the Leisure Class*, William Dean Howells in fact argued that the book's insights represented "an opportunity for American fiction." William Dean Howells, "An Opportunity for American Fiction," review of Thorstein Veblen's *The Theory of the Leisure Class*, *Literature*, 20 May, 1899 and 3 June, 1899. Nonetheless, Veblen's observations addressing intellectual prestige or status focus on the traditional "higher" branches of learning, including "knowledge of the dead languages and the occult sciences; of correct spelling; of syntax and prosody," as well as on the systems of practice and meaning surrounding institutions such as colleges and universities. See Thorstein Veblen, *The Theory of the Leisure Class: an Economic Study of Institutions. 1899* (New York: New American Library, 1953), p. 47. For my project's purpose of trying to understand new forms of "realist" intellectual status, Bourdieu's consistent emphasis in *Distinction* on relations between materiality and cultural prestige is more directly useful.

16 John Guillory, "Bourdieu's Refusal," *Modern Language Quarterly* 58, no. 4 (1997).

17 Bourdieu insists that a taste accrues cultural status (distinction) to its possessor most effectively when the taste appears as an embodied characteristic, not one that can be put on or taken off at will. One might think, for instance, of the genuine physical discomfort that Wharton's Lily Bart feels in "dingy" surroundings, even when she is alone.

18 Edith Wharton, *The House of Mirth* (New York: Penguin, 1985), p. 185.

19 Ibid., pp. 232, 26–7.

20 Michael North, *The Dialect of Modernism: Race, Language, and Twentieth-Century Literature* (New York: Oxford University Press, 1994), p. 23. Also see Bourdieu, *Distinction*, p. 255.

21 While summing up his argument in the last paragraph of *Distinction*'s "Introduction," for instance, Bourdieu mentions "the denial of lower, coarse, vulgar, venal, servile – *in a word, natural* – enjoyment" (ibid., p. 7, my emphasis). Note the easy presumption in the set-off phrase that, once Bourdieu says "in a word, natural," readers will recognize just what the preceding string of adjectives adds up to, as well as how to differentiate "natural" or bodily enjoyments from "cultivated" pleasures. Even such

oft-repeated phrases for describing bourgeois strategies of distinction as "the stylization of life" or "the primacy of form over function" or "manner over matter" imply that it is easy for the sociological analyst and his or her readers to identify where "stylization" stops and "life" itself begins or, in the latter phrases, how to draw a line between, respectively, "form" and "function" or "manner" and "matter." Ironically, Bourdieu's naturalization of the real makes his hostility toward artificial distance from it self-contradictory. To specify the location of "reality" is to make possible another empirically existing, free-standing location that would count as "next to reality," and yet another that would be "further from reality." While to naturalize reality, therefore, does not always mean culturally to privilege "distance" from it, it does give such distance an empirical status. This, paradoxically, confers on hierarchical relations of distinction the very same "natural" status as Bourdieu assumes for material reality. For helpful discussions of Bourdieu, see *Modern Language Quarterly*'s December 1997 special issue (58, no. 4), which is entirely devoted to considerations of his work by literary and cultural critics, as well as the more interdisciplinary Craig Calhoun, Edward LiPuma, and Moishe Postone, ed., *Bourdieu: Critical Perspectives* (University of Chicago Press, 1993). See also Evan Watkins, "Reproduction, Reading, and Resistance," *American Literary History* 2, no. 3 (1990), pp. 550–5; and Elizabeth Wilson, "Picasso and Pâté De Foie Gras: Pierre Bourdieu's Sociology of Culture," *Diacritics* 18 (1988), pp. 47–58.

22 Judith P. Butler, *Bodies That Matter: On the Discursive Limits of "Sex"* (New York: Routledge, 1993), p. 187.

23 Ibid., p. ix.

24 For an extremely deft analysis of Bourdieu's own hostile, but perhaps not so distant as he makes it out to be, relationship with poststructuralism, especially as manifested in the work of Derrida, see Jonathan Loesberg, "Bourdieu's Derrida's Kant: the Aesthetics of Refusing Aesthetics," *Modern Language Quarterly* 58, no. 4 (1997).

25 Joseph Litvak, *Strange Gourmets: Sophistication, Theory, and the Novel* (Durham, NC: Duke University Press, 1997), p. 7.

26 The Chinese Cultural Revolution and Pol Pot's regime in Cambodia suggest that attempts to eliminate the very category of intellectual prestige can be – and perhaps inevitably *are* – horrific.

27 Thanks to David McWhirter for suggesting the phrase in quotation marks.

28 Not only are categories of prestige and distinction probably unavoidable in human society, but "distinction" can be used toward politically progressive ends. Ross Posnock argues, for example, that W.E.B. Du Bois used the "impeccable black intellectual and personal distinction" that he claimed for himself – which some have taken as evidence of Du Bois's commitment to an invidious elitism – against white society's system of racial distinctions. Du Bois's own claims to distinction appropriate "a weapon of racist control and classification" – that is, investment in hierarchies of cultural and racial value – to forward democratizing, antiracist aims (Posnock, *Color and Culture*, p. 111).

29 Michael Davitt Bell, *The Problem of American Realism: Studies in the Cultural History of a Literary Idea* (University of Chicago Press, 1993), pp. 6, 22.
30 On the transition from a culture that privileged ideals of "manliness" to one that privileged "masculinity," see Gail Bederman, *Manliness and Civilization: a Cultural History of Gender and Race in the United States, 1880–1917* (University of Chicago Press, 1995). For discussions of Howells and James that tend to identify manhood in their work more with the set of terms circulating around civilized manliness than with those of rough or "primitive" masculinity, see Alfred Habegger, *Gender, Fantasy, and Realism in American Literature* (New York: Columbia University Press, 1982), pp. 234–48; and Elsa Nettels, *Language and Gender in American Fiction: Howells, James, Wharton, and Cather* (Charlottesville: University Press of Virginia, 1997), pp. 6, 35. For a nuanced and illuminating consideration of these issues in James, see Scott S. Derrick, *Monumental Anxieties: Homoerotic Desire and Feminine Influence in 19th Century US Literature* (New Brunswick, NJ: Rutgers University Press, 1997), chapters 3–4. I should say that, especially recently, Henry James scholarship has devoted a great deal of close, sophisticated attention to the issue of masculinity in his texts, and hence represents one among other counter-examples to the generalizations that I make in the sentences immediately following this note. See, for instance, Sara Blair, *Henry James and the Writing of Race and Nation* (Cambridge University Press, 1996); Alfred Habegger, *Henry James and the "Woman Business"* (Cambridge University Press, 1989); and Eve Kosofsky Sedgwick, *Epistemology of the Closet* (Berkeley: University of California Press, 1990). Also see the articles by Leland Person cited in my bibliography.
31 For instance, Sandra Gilbert stresses the mythic and classical resonances (Aphrodite, Phaedra) that Chopin gives to Edna's awakening femininity. Patricia S. Yeager investigates the glimpses of a never-quite-spoken "feminocentric" language that the novel fleetingly imagines. Margit Stange's astute historicist reading sets Edna within the emerging women's rights concept of female self-ownership. Michele Birnbaum emphasizes the whiteness of Edna's femininity, and in particular how her development of a seemingly autonomous female self, including her access to a freer, richer sexuality, depends not only upon the physical labor but also upon the "tropological potential" of the mostly anonymous women of color populating the novel. See Michele A. Birnbaum, "'Alien Hands': Kate Chopin and the Colonization of Race," in *Subjects and Citizens: Nation, Race and Gender from Oroonoko to Anita Hill*, ed. Michael Moon and Cathy Davidson (Durham, NC: Duke University Press, 1995); Sandra M. Gilbert, "Introduction: the Second Coming of Aphrodite," in *The Awakening* by Kate Chopin (New York: Penguin, 1986); Margit Stange, "Personal Property: Exchange Value and the Female Self in *The Awakening*," in *The Awakening*, ed. Nancy A. Walker (Boston: Bedford Books, 1993); Patricia Yeager, "'A Language Which Nobody Understood': Emancipatory Strategies in *The Awakening*," *Novel* 20, no. 3 (1987).
32 Toril Moi, "Appropriating Bourdieu: Feminist Theory and Pierre

Bourdieu's Sociology of Culture," *New Literary History* 22, no. 4 (1991), pp. 1035–6.

33 Edith Wharton, *Twilight Sleep* (New York: Scribner, 1997), p. 307.

34 *Bodies That Matter*, p. 23.

I WILLIAM DEAN HOWELLS AND THE ROOTS OF REALIST TASTE

1 James Cox, "*The Rise of Silas Lapham*: the Business of Morals and Manners," in *New Essays on "The Rise of Silas Lapham,"* ed. Donald E. Pease (Cambridge University Press, 1991), p. 110.

2 Useful studies on the development of the middle classes in nineteenth- and early twentieth-century America that also include attention to issues of cultural distinction (and which I don't refer to elsewhere in the chapter) include Burton J. Bledstein, *The Culture of Professionalism: the Middle Class and the Development of Higher Education in America*, 1st. edn. (New York: Norton, 1976); Stuart M. Blumin, *The Emergence of the Middle Class: Social Experience in the American City, 1760–1900* (Cambridge University Press, 1989); Karen Halttunen, *Confidence Men and Painted Women: a Study of Middle-Class Culture in America, 1830–1870* (New Haven: Yale University Press, 1982); Robert H. Wiebe, *The Search for Order, 1877–1920* (Westport, CT: Greenwood Press, 1980).

3 Cady refers to Howells's "open warfare with the principalities and powers of the later Gilded Age in America." Edwin Harrison Cady, *The Road to Realism; the Early Years, 1837–1885, of William Dean Howells* (Syracuse University Press, 1956), p. 243.

4 Brodhead, *Cultures of Letters*, pp. 115–41; Kaplan, *The Social Construction of American Realism*, pp. 44–64.

5 Ibid., pp. 47–55

6 Matthew Arnold, *Culture and Anarchy*, ed. Samuel Lipman (New Haven: Yale University Press, 1994), pp. 68–73.

7 See William Dean Howells, "Matthew Arnold and 'Distinction' in America" (1888), in *Selected Literary Criticism*, vol. 2 *1886–1897*, ed. Donald Pizer (Bloomington: Indiana University Press, 1993), pp. 94–100.

8 A. Dwight Culler, ed., *Poetry and Criticism of Matthew Arnold* (Boston: Houghton Mifflin, 1961), p. 323.

9 William Dean Howells, "Short Story Collections: Hamlin Garland" (1891), review of *Main-Travelled Roads*, in *Selected Literary Criticism*, vol. 2 *1886–1897*, ed. Donald Pizer (Bloomington: Indiana University Press, 1993), pp. 185–7.

10 William Dean Howells, "Literary Criticism" (1866), in *Selected Literary Criticism*, vol. 1 *1859–1885*, ed. Ulrich Halfmann (Bloomington: Indiana University Press, 1993), p. 61. America's regional dialects had been constituted as an object of educated knowledge – but not, I would argue, as an object of cultivated *taste* – at least since the 1848 publication of Bartlett's *Dictionary of Americanisms*. See Elsa Nettels, *Language, Race, and Social Class in Howells's America* (Lexington, KY: University Press of Kentucky, 1988), er I.

11 William Dean Howells, "Dialect in Literature" (1895), in *Selected Literary Criticism*, vol. 2 *1886–1897*, ed. Donald Pizer (Bloomington: Indiana University Press, 1993), p. 221.

12 Nancy Glazener's impressively thorough, archivally based study of the periodicals in which "realism" first appeared and in which it was most vigorously promoted and debated agrees that "a taste for realism, that supposedly most inclusive of literary movements, could become a mark of distinction." See Glazener, *Reading for Realism*, p. 49. See also her excellent discussion of distinction in the context of late nineteenth-century American culture on pp. 20–3. However, Glazener finds a "conflict" between realism's quasi-democratic project of "offering, or simulating, some contact with the ungenteel" and the "emphasis on realists' subtlety and refinement [that] confirmed realism's suitability as an object of connoisseurship." Although the former may indeed, as she suggests, have "risked compromising" the latter, I propose the category of realist taste, promoted by Howells, as his productive and culturally powerful solution to this conflict (Glazener, *Reading for Realism*, p. 120).

13 This position was most cogently articulated by Leo Marx, "The Vernacular Tradition in American Literature," in *Studies in American Culture; Dominant Ideas and Images*, ed. Joseph J. Kwiat and Mary C. Turpie (New York: Johnson Reprint Corp., 1971). But until recently it was an underlying assumption of most critical discussion of American realism. See Bridgman's superb study of American writers' increasing incorporation of dialect and vernacular speech into literary style: Richard Bridgman, *The Colloquial Style in America* (New York: Oxford University Press, 1966).

14 For examples of this position, see Nettels, *Language, Race, and Social Class in Howells's America*, p. 105; Brodhead, *Cultures of Letters*; William C. Fischer, Jr., "William Dean Howells: Reverie and the Nonsymbolic Aesthetic," *Nineteenth-Century Fiction* 25 (1970–1), pp. 1–30; and Kaplan, *The Social Construction of American Realism*.

15 Wilson, *White Collar Fictions*, p. 101.

16 Howells, "Dialect in Literature," p. 219.

17 Ibid., pp. 219–20. For additional discussion of this critical writing, see Nettels, *Language, Race, and Social Class in Howells's America*, pp. 64–7.

18 Arnold, *Culture and Anarchy*, p. 78.

19 Howells, "Dialect in Literature," p. 221.

20 William Dean Howells, "Standard and Taste in Fiction; Mary E. Wilkins" (1887), in *Selected Literary Criticism*, vol. 2 *1886–1897*, ed. Donald Pizer (Bloomington: Indiana University Press, 1993), p. 65.

21 Henry James also positions dialect and vernacular language as a terrain on which "initiated" readers of literature can demonstrate a distinction between themselves and other readers who are less initiated, who have less cultural range and sophistication. Consider the following introduction of Basil Ransom in *The Bostonians*, whose initial publication overlapped with that of *The Rise of Silas Lapham* in the *Century Magazine* (during 1885):

He came, in fact, from Mississippi, and he spoke very perceptibly with the accent of that country. It is not in my power to reproduce by any combination of characters this charming dialect; but the initiated reader will have no difficulty in evoking the sound, which is to be associated in the present instance with nothing vulgar or vain . . .

As with the "realist taste" for American vernaculars that Howells's fiction and criticism elaborates, this passage from *The Bostonians* suggests that "initiated" readers who have developed a knowledge of various American dialects should be able to evoke the "sound" of a given dialect from Mississippi. At the same time, these readers can assume the elite evaluative role implicit in James's notation that, at least "in the present instance," the Mississippi dialect does not sound vulgar. In a characteristic move, however (and one that certainly separates him from other dialect writers of the period), James chooses not to try to represent Basil Ransom's actual dialect, even though he goes on to stress both its importance for fully grasping Basil's character and the dialect's striking sensory qualities. Here, James's decision not to depict Basil's dialect has the effect of making the "initiated readers" he mentions into an even more exclusive group: his gesture resembles the gesture made by French restaurants in the US that do not translate their menus into English (if you are too uninitiated to know already what a Mississippi dialect would sound like, do not expect remedial tutoring here). See Henry James, *The Bostonians* (Oxford University Press, 1984), pp. 2–3. For a richly contextualizing reading of the quoted passage, see Walter Benn Michaels, "Local Color," *Modern Language Notes* 113, no. 4 (1998), pp. 734–56.

Making the *Century Magazine* of 1884 and 1885 an epicenter of finely honed and explicitly articulated taste for literary dialect, excerpts from Mark Twain's *Adventures of Huckleberry Finn* also appeared in it. When *Huck Finn* was published as a book, Twain added his famous explanatory note calling attention to his "painstaking" delineation of seven different dialects.

22 William Dean Howells, *The Rise of Silas Lapham* (New York: Harper & Row, 1958), p. 53. Further page references will appear in the text.

23 For some other remarks on Howells's use of extra quotation marks around non-standard speech, see Nettels, *Language, Race, and Social Class in Howells's America*, p. 37. One might also recall here Edith Wharton's comment in *A Backward Glance* about her and her family's everyday speech: "Any really expressive slang was welcomed with amusement – but used as slang, as it were between quotation marks, and not carelessly admitted into our speech." Contrasting her own domestic speech habits with "those who picked up the slang of the year without having any idea that they were not speaking in the purest tradition," Wharton came to believe even as a girl that "you could do what you liked with the language if you did it consciously, and for a given purpose." See Edith Wharton, *A Backward Glance* (New York: Charles Scribner's Sons, 1964), pp. 50–1.

Although Bromfield speaks fluent Italian, even high-society philanthropists consider him useless as a translator in the slums, as Miss Kingsbury teasingly explains: "We did think of Mr. Corey ... but we reflected that he probably would not talk with them at all; he would make them keep still to be sketched, and forget all about their wants."

25 This inability to cultivate the realist taste that first attracts Tom to the Lapham family is involved in Howells's prediction that neither Nanny nor Lily will ever marry, and thus becomes part of how Howells effectively marginalizes picturesquing as a kind of barren femininity or old-maidness.

26 Critics have recently suggested a link between late nineteenth-century regionalist writing, especially that focused on rural New England, and nostalgia for past American communities of supposedly greater racial (Anglo-Saxon) "purity." See Brodhead, *Cultures of Letters*; Amy Kaplan, "Nation, Region, and Empire," in the *Columbia History of the American Novel*, ed. Emory Elliot (New York: Columbia University Press, 1991); and the essays in June Howard, ed. *New Essays on "The Country of the Pointed Firs"* (Cambridge University Press, 1994).

27 Nancy Glazener's fascinating discussion of the opposition between Italian and Dutch painting in nineteenth-century American culture, which she develops in relation to *The Marble Faun*, is also pertinent here (Glazener, *Reading for Realism*, pp. 66–75).

28 Lawrence W. Levine, *Highbrow/Lowbrow: the Emergence of Cultural Hierarchy in America* (Cambridge, MA: Harvard University Press, 1988), p. 68.

29 Ibid., pp. 52, 72–3.

30 William Dean Howells, *The Rise of Silas Lapham*, ed. Don L. Cook (New York: Norton, 1982), p. 100.

31 Quoted in Levine, *Highbrow/Lowbrow*, p. 73.

32 On solitary reading as a signifier of cultural distinction in the late nineteenth century, see Bledstein, *The Culture of Professionalism*. For a Foucauldian perspective, see D. A. Miller's chapter on *David Copperfield* in D. A. Miller, *The Novel and the Police* (Berkeley: University of California Press, 1988), pp. 192–220.

33 Litvak, *Strange Gourmets*, p. 9.

34 John Seelye, "The Hole in Howells/the Lapse in *Silas Lapham*," in *New Essays on "The Rise of Silas Lapham,"* ed. Donald E. Pease (Cambridge University Press, 1991), pp. 56.

35 I take the terms "simple, natural, and honest" from a well-known 1886 "Editor's Study," in which Howells laid out the objects of American literary realism.

36 Kenneth Schuyler Lynn, *William Dean Howells; an American Life* (New York: Harcourt Brace Jovanovich, 1971), p. 296.

37 Jonathan Freedman's reading of late nineteenth-century British aestheticism demonstrates its "taste" orientation towards a real of negativity, although (it seems to me) a negative real not so focused on the social as Howells's was. Speaking of Pater, Freedman writes "The 'real' is here redefined as the experience of temporality itself, a perception that is inevitably linked to a sense of entropy and loss. What is 'really real' for Pater, in

other words, is not just the experience of time, but the sense of attenuation and exhaustion that it brings" (Freedman, *Professions of Taste*, p. 14).

38 Bourdieu, *Distinction*, p. 65.

39 Quoted in Mildred Howells, *Life in Letters of William Dean Howells* (Garden City, NY: Doubleday, 1928), p. 417.

40 Two recent critical works analyze Howells's self-irony, especially as it bears on the figure of Basil March, along lines of thought that at several points resonate closely with my own: Thomas Peyser, "The Culture of Conversation," in *Utopia and Cosmopolis: Globalization in the Era of American Literary Realism* (Durham, NC, and London: Duke University Press, 1998), especially pp. 96–8 and 119–20; and, Charles Harmon, "*A Hazard of New Fortunes* and the Reproduction of Liberalism," *Studies in American Fiction* 25, no. 2 (1997), especially pp. 186–93. Neither of these works argues as I do that the particular sort of Basil-Marchean liberalism in question is, in part, a "taste" that operates strategically as an assertion of cultural distinction relative to other middle-class positions. Both Peyser's and Harmon's works appeared only after I had completed the current chapter.

41 Howells, *Life in Letters*, p. 416.

42 The most cogent and thorough discussion to date of Howells and race is Kenneth W. Warren, *Black and White Strangers: Race and American Literary Realism* (University of Chicago Press, 1993).

43 William Dean Howells, *The Quality of Mercy*, ed. David J. Nordloh and James P. Elliott, *A Selected Edition of William Dean Howells*, vol. 18 (Bloomington: Indiana University Press, 1979), p. 79.

44 Sanford Marovitz emphasizes "a startling inconsistency" between Howells's professed sociopolitical beliefs and what Marovitz sees as Howells's "irrefutable satisfaction over his own more or less enviable position in the literary and social environment." But Marovitz fails to recognize how Howells's sincere "frustration over this internal conflict" may also have been culturally productive, even advantageous, for him. See Sanford Marovitz, "Howells and the Ghetto: 'The Mystery of Misery'," *Modern Fiction Studies* 16 (1970), p. 351.

45 Quoted in Nettels, *Language, Race, and Social Class in Howells's America*, p. 186.

46 Howells, *Life in Letters*, p. 419. A motif of the Altrurian writing is how plutocratic conditions prevent any American individual from truly imagining – let alone living – a life in accord with Altruria's own principles.

47 William Dean Howells, *The World of Chance: a Novel* (New York: Harper, 1893), p. 208.

48 On Howells's response to Tolstoy's attempt to "live as a peasant," see Sarah B. Daugherty, "Howells, Tolstoy, and the Limits of Realism: the Case of *Annie Kilburn*," *American Literary Realism* 19, no. 1 (1986).

49 William Dean Howells, *A Hazard of New Fortunes* (New York: Meridian, 1994), p. 346. Further page references will appear in the text.

50 Howells, *The World of Chance*, p. 129.

51 William Dean Howells, *Novels, 1886–1888: The Minister's Charge, April Hopes,*

Annie Kilburn (New York: Library of America, 1989), p. 331. Further page references will appear in the text.

52 See Warren, *Black and White Strangers: Race and American Literary Realism*, pp. 80–4.

53 This sort of rosy-glasses-shedding moment is central to Michael Davitt Bell's understanding of what "realism" meant to Howells and his contemporaries (Bell, *Problem of American Realism*, p. 54).

54 Andrew Ross, *No Respect: Intellectuals & Popular Culture* (New York: Routledge, 1989), p. 80.

55 Here is where I would disagree with Wai-chee Dimock's account of the subversive role played by *incommensurability* in Howells's realist economy (Wai-chee Dimock, "The Economy of Pain: Capitalism, Humanitarianism, and the Realist Novel," in *New Essays on "The Rise of Silas Lapham,"* ed. Donald E. Pease [Cambridge University Press, 1991], pp. 67–90). Rather than a disruption to that economy, *incommensurability* in *The Minister's Charge* is integral to the novel's hierarchical distribution of cultural prestige. It is Sewell's ability to recognize a certain inevitable lack of fit (and of fitness) in social arrangements – and wryly to smile at it – that gives him his special distinction. The fact that Sewell assimilates a recognition of tragic incommensurability to his everyday life (his everyday comments at the breakfast table, etc.) accounts also, I believe, for what seems to me a shift in Howells's own feelings toward him as a character. In *The Rise of Silas Lapham* Sewell is the somewhat boring voice of austere justice, an admirable and necessary figure for the point that Howells wishes to makes about the "economy of pain" that Dimock perceptively analyzes, but not at all engaging as a character. In *The Minister's Charge*, Howells's engines of affection and identification seem much more engaged with Sewell. In the latter book, for instance, Sewell continually makes jokes at his own expense – always a sign of both intelligence and likeability in Howells.

56 Both Sewell and Annie Kilburn begin with the protagonists regretting their own deviations from the simpler form of realist taste – in the process of compensating for these deviations they confront the challenges that result in their elaborating the later version of realist taste.

57 Although I do not discuss it here, *April Hopes* (1887–8) is also about confronting the reality of a painful disjunction – age difference, although that novel's comedic marriage plot does mean that the book ultimately issues in a more-or-less happy solution (Howells, *Novels*, 1886–1888).

58 At a party supposed to promote "social union" in *Annie Kilburn*, Howells privileges the ironic viewpoint of a character who looks "around at the straggling work people, who represented the harmonisation of the classes, keeping to themselves as if they had been there alone" (ibid., p. 771).

59 Carl Smith has argued that the conviction and execution of the Haymarket defendants was advertised to the public of Chicago and the nation as offering closure to the preceding period of social trauma. See Carl S. Smith, *Urban Disorder and the Shape of Belief: the Great Chicago Fire, the Haymarket Bomb,*

and the Model Town of Pullman, (University of Chicago Press, 1995), p. 2. Howells's opposition, thus, represented not only his sense of justice but also his disposition against closure.

60 William Dean Howells, *Their Silver Wedding Journey* (New York: Harper & Brothers, 1909), pp. 52–3. Further page references will be given in the text.

61 Freedman, *Professions of Taste*, p. 113.

62 Ibid., p. 80.

63 On Arnold's influence in America, see Freedman, *Professions of Taste*.

64 Already, in the Marches' first appearance in Howells's 1872 *Their Wedding Journey*, the fact that they are experienced tourists of Europe contributes to their newly developing "realist taste" for the customs and speech of American regions (see *Their Wedding Journey*, pp. 6, 56, 65, and 153). Moreover, although they often tend towards picturesquing gestures (for instance, they are drawn to Native Americans selling artifacts at roadside stands) that Howells will increasingly condemn, they also are self-ironic about their tendency (*Their Wedding Journey*, pp. 7, 85–6).

65 Ibid., p. 161.

66 Ibid., p. 174.

67 Richard Rorty, *Contingency, Irony, and Solidarity* (Cambridge University Press, 1989), pp. 40–6.

68 I should note that March sometimes appeals to what may sound like universal absolutes, whether he associates them with Christ or with the idea of "complicity" that Howells returns to again and again during this period – that is, the idea that "everybody's mixed up with everybody else," so that the actions of humans around the world affect one another's lives in powerful but often unpredictable ways. But almost always March's invocations both of Christianity and of universal "complicity" turn out to be ways of emphasizing what he casts as a constitutive uncertainty in human events, which he, Basil March, is virtually unique in recognizing and ruefully accepting.

69 Dimock, "The Economy of Pain," p. 73.

70 Ibid., pp. 74–5.

71 See also how, in *Impressions and Experiences* (1896), the conscious awareness that New York's "conditions" *differ* radically from block to block marks the cognitive superiority of Howells's first-person flaneur over both the rich and the poor. William Dean Howells, *Impressions and Experiences* (Freeport, NY: Books for Libraries Press, 1972), pp. 225–6, 246–81.

72 Slavoj Žižek's reconceptualization of how "ideological fantasy" works for an increasing number of subjects in contemporary postindustrial societies perfectly captures Basil March's relation to this "magical calculus" that Dimock argues was "central . . . to the workings" of nineteenth-century capitalism – a "calculus" whereby those who lived under the *most* difficult material conditions were seen as possessing the *least* vulnerability to suffering from them (Dimock, "The Economy of Pain," p. 73). As Žižek explains, the classic Marxist account of ideology suggests that people "misrecognize" the social reality of which their actions form a part. Hence,

"demystifying" their illusions about that reality and their own role in it is seen as a crucial step in bringing about revolutionary change. By contrast, Žižek believes that contemporary societies are full of people who have attained significant distance on the "official" stories that their own societies tell about themselves. Yet most of these same people still *act* as if they believed these stories. (An example might be people who still participate in official celebrations of American Independence Day even though they recognize what a distorted picture of the nation's history is presented by these official celebrations.) Although of course there may be a multitude of reasons that people can give for why they still *act* as if they believe an ideological fantasy (convenience, economic self-interest, wanting their kids to enjoy the fireworks, to name a few), Žižek wants to call attention to how an ideological fantasy can continue to structure someone's actions even when he or she has consciously stopped believing in it. For such subjects, Žižek suggests, the ideological fantasy has not been abolished. Instead, its *site* has shifted. *People* may not believe, but their *actions* believe for them. To the extent that this model already describes Basil March in the nineteenth century, Basil March is psychically and culturally ahead of his times. See Slavoj Žižek, *The Sublime Object of Ideology* (London and New York: Verso, 1989), pp. 28–33.

73 Lynn, *William Dean Howells; an American Life*, p. 53.
74 Rorty, *Contingency, Irony, and Solidarity*, p. xvi.
75 Edwin Harrison Cady, *The Realist at War; the Mature Years, 1885–1920, of William Dean Howells* (Syracuse University Press, 1958), p. 66.
76 In assuming the self-righteous high ground against what he calls Howells's "suppression of knowledge" about the dark problems of late nineteenth-century American life, Andrew Delbanco misses the dimension of Howells's work that self-consciously thematizes, even theorizes, the sort of "forgetting" that Basil performs here (Andrew Delbanco, "Howells and the Suppression of Knowledge," *Southern Review* 19, no. 4 [1983]).
77 Howellsian conjugality calls attention to the unexplored gender asymmetry embedded in the public/private distinction that Rorty's celebration of ironic liberalism relies on. Although Rorty's text scrupulously refers to its privileged ironist figure as "she," Howells's books remind us of how intertwined with bourgeois marriage the public/private opposition is. As is the case with other nineteenth and twentieth-century husbands, part of Basil's cultural superiority to his wife inheres in his ability to pass back and forth between public and private realms, or even to inhabit the two realms simultaneously. Rorty never confronts the extent to which this historically male ability defines his liberal ironist.
78 Bell, *Problem of American Realism*, p. 37.
79 William Dean Howells, "A She Hamlet," in *Literature and Life* (New York: Harpers, 1902), p. 140.
80 Ibid., p. 138. Alfred Habegger sees an increasing effeminacy, a move away from the heartier masculinity of a Silas Lapham, in the "constant

self-checking or self-holding" characteristic of so many post-1886 Howells protagonists. For Habegger, this move away from aggressively self-confident men, which he associates with Howells's own status as "sissy" in American culture, partially explains what he sees as "the lifeless quality that becomes more and more evident in his novels after *Silas Lapham* (Habegger, *Gender, Fantasy, and Realism in American Literature*, p. 234). I disagree: in his novels after *Lapham*, Howells starts to delineate a new form of realist masculinity, one whose phallic status depends on a clear-eyed awareness of limits, blockages, and other forms of negativity.

2 THE "FACTS OF PHYSICAL SUFFERING"

1 Henry James, *The Wings of the Dove* (New York: Penguin, 1986), pp. 106, 317. Further page references will appear in the text.

2 See Freedman, *Professions of Taste*, pp. 207–10 on Densher's differentiation from Susan Shepherd Stringham, an authoress who writes for periodicals. On James and the sentimental tradition, see Habegger, *Henry James and the "Woman Business."*

3 Thomas L. Haskell, *The Authority of Experts: Studies in History and Theory* (Bloomington: Indiana University Press, 1984), pp. xxix, 180–225.

4 James, *The American Scene*, p. 90.

5 Caroline Mercer and Sarah Wangensteen trace the tendency of critics including Susan Sontag, Leon Edel, and F. O. Matthiessen to assume, despite contrary evidence in the novel, that Milly has consumption. Milly, Mercer and Wangensteen point out, clearly lacks "the destructive physical prostration, the coughing and foul breath associated with such a state as TB, a disease James knew well." See Caroline G. Mercer and Sarah D. Wangensteen, "'Consumption, Heart Disease, or Whatever': Chlorosis, a Heroine's Illness in *The Wings of the Dove*," *Journal of the History of Medicine* 40 (1985), p. 278. For various discussions of how a characteristically Jamesian "absence" informs the author's portrayal of Milly, see Nicola Bradbury, "'Nothing That Is Not There and the Nothing That Is': the Celebration of Absence in *The Wings of the Dove*," in *Henry James: Fiction as History*, ed. Ian F. A. Bell (New York: Vision and Barnes & Noble, 1984); Peter Brooks, *The Melodramatic Imagination: Balzac, Henry James, Melodrama, and the Mode of Excess* (New Haven: Yale University Press, 1976), pp. 170–96; Ruth Bernard Yeazell, *Language and Knowledge in the Late Novels of Henry James* (University of Chicago Press, 1976), pp. 16–36; Laurence Bedwell Holland, *The Expense of Vision: Essays on the Craft of Henry James* (Baltimore: Johns Hopkins University Press, 1982), pp. 259, 314–27; Alan Bellringer, "The Narrator as Center in *The Wings of the Dove*," Modern Fiction Studies 6 (1960); and F. R. Leavis, *The Great Tradition* (Garden City, NY: Doubleday, 1954), p. 193. With the partial exception of Bellringer, none of these critics connects the "emptiness" (Leavis's term) in James's depiction of Milly to the way in which her "facts of physical suffering" resist representation.

6 Elaine Scarry, *The Body in Pain: the Making and Unmaking of the World* (New York: Oxford University Press, 1985), p. 10. Albeit to a different end, Joann P. Krieg also notes "the metaphoric interchange of disease and money" in the novel. See Joann P. Krieg, "Health Is Capital: Henry James' *The Wings of the Dove*," in *Money: Lure, Lore, and Literature*, ed. John Louis DiGaetani (Westport, CT: Greenwood Press, 1994), p. 111.

7 John Goode, "The Pervasive Mystery of Style: *The Wings of the Dove*," in *The Air of Reality: New Essays on Henry James* (London: Methuen, 1972), p. 268.

8 Scarry, noting "the simple and absolute incompatibility of pain and the world," describes how "pain begins by being 'not oneself' and ends by having eliminated all that is 'not itself'" (Scarry, *Body in Pain*, pp. 50, 54).

9 Ross Posnock's *The Trial of Curiosity*, however, as well as Sara Blair's *Henry James and the Writing of Race and Nation*, have forced a welcome reconsideration of this conventional criticism about James's lack of interest in representing the poor. See Ross Posnock, *The Trial of Curiosity: Henry James, William James, and the Challenge of Modernity* (New York: Oxford University Press, 1991). For a very helpful discussion of the conflict between James and H.G. Wells around this question and some of that conflict's repercussions on subsequent literary criticism, see Raymond Williams, *The English Novel from Dickens to Lawrence* (New York: Oxford University Press, 1970), pp. 125–39. And, for an argument about James and the social that has unexpected continuities with that of Williams, see J. Hillis Miller, *The Ethics of Reading: Kant, De Man, Eliot, Trollope, James, and Benjamin*, the Wellek Library Lectures at the University of California, Irvine (New York: Columbia University Press, 1987).

10 See, Howard, *Form and History in American Literary Naturalism*, pp. 104–41, on how the figure of the slum operates in American literary naturalism. Some critics have read *Kate* as a figure for naturalistic determinism in *The Wings of the Dove*. See Lee Clark Mitchell, *Determined Fictions: American Literary Naturalism* (New York: Columbia University Press, 1989), pp. 199, 209; and Goode, "The Pervasive Mystery of Style," pp. 251–2.

11 In *The Princess Casamassima*, the physical paralysis of Rosy Muniment – she cannot leave her small room – is repeatedly made to resonate with the oppressive constraints on London's poor that is the novel's vexed topic. Diane Price Herndl provides much useful information about an increasing cultural tendency in late nineteenth-century Anglo-American culture to draw links between illness and poverty. She also describes an increasing tendency to consider illness (women's, in particular) as representing "a failure or perversity of will." I would argue that the Regent's Park scene at least hints at a critique of this latter cultural tendency, despite Herndl's assertion that Henry James had a "fundamental inability to envision an invalidism in which willfulness is not a significant part." I hear some sarcasm, for example, in Milly's conceiving herself as performing some healthy action "as with a sudden flare of the famous 'will power' she had heard about, read about, and which was what her medical adviser had mainly thrown her back

on" (and which of course was a central category in William James's psychology). See Diane Price Herndl, *Invalid Women: Figuring Feminine Illness in American Fiction and Culture, 1840–1940* (Chapel Hill: University of North Carolina Press, 1993), pp. 150–3, 90.

12 Henry James uses London's underclass to help evoke the effects of Milly's illness. Yet the park scene also suggests why the novelist tended to avoid representing the poor directly in his novels. Milly appeals to her author by "the *act* of living." The preface, explaining the novel's "drama," emphasizes that "the process of life gives way fighting, and often may so shine out on the lost ground as in no other connection" (p. 36). For James, the course of Milly's disease constitutes "the lost ground" against which, with the rich girl "on her feet," the figure of her struggle for life "shines out." The poor, by contrast, seem for James actually to blend into the ground and "smutty grass" of Regent's Park. Perhaps, for James, no one is so dead as the very poor. They are so materially constrained that they cannot but become indistinguishable from ground, unable to attain the status of figure or character.

13 See Henry James, *The Notebooks of Henry James*, ed. F. O. Matthiessen and Kenneth B. Murdock (Oxford University Press, 1947), p. 174; Brooks, *The Melodramatic Imagination*, p. 193; Bellringer, "The Narrator as Center in *The Wings of the Dove*," p. 22; and Christof Wegelin, *The Image of Europe in Henry James* (Dallas: Southern Methodist University Press, 1958), p. 524.

14 Dorothea Krook-Gilead, *The Ordeal of Consciousness in Henry James* (Cambridge University Press, 1967), p. 215.

15 Brooks, *The Melodramatic Imagination*, p. 170.

16 David Bruce McWhirter, *Desire and Love in Henry James: a Study of the Late Novels* (Cambridge University Press, 1989), p. 128.

17 Leo Bersani, *A Future for Astyanax: Character and Desire in Literature* (New York: Columbia University Press, 1984), p. 142.

18 James, *The Notebooks of Henry James*, p. 174.

19 For discussions (all of which remain at a fairly general level) of what critics tend to label Densher's passivity (as much of an old chestnut as Milly's "absence"), see Holland, *The Expense of Vision: Essays on the Craft of Henry James*, especially p. 290; Bersani, *A Future for Astyanax: Character and Desire in Literature*, pp. 139–41; Tony Tanner, *Henry James: the Writer and His Work* (Amherst: University of Massachusetts Press, 1985), pp. 112–13; Michael Moon, "Sexuality and Visual Terrorism in *The Wings of the Dove*," Criticism 28 (1986), pp. 433–5; Marcia Ian, "The Elaboration of Privacy in *The Wings of the Dove*," *English Literary History* 51, no. 1 (1984), p. 129; and Yeazell, *Language and Knowledge in the Late Novels of Henry James*, pp. 16–22. For an argument claiming, I believe incorrectly, that James employs the character of Densher to privilege action over passivity, thus revising earlier novels such as *The American*, see Robert L. Caserio, "The Story in It: *The Wings of the Dove*," in Modern Critical Views: Henry James, ed. Harold Bloom (New York: Chelsea House, 1987).

20 Scarry is apropos here: "The felt-characteristics of pain – one of which is

its compelling vibrancy or its incontestable reality or simply its 'certainty' –
can be appropriated away from the body and presented as the attributes of
something else . . . [T]he sheer material factualness of the human body will
be borrowed to lend that cultural construct the aura of 'realness' . . . "
(Scarry, *Body in Pain*, p. 14).

21 My ideas about the role played in Densher's "realist disposition" by rigorous ignorance has been influenced both by Scarry's claim that "the tor-
turer's blindness is his power" (Scarry, *The Body in Pain*, p. 57), and by Eve
Sedgwick's work on "ignorance effects" and power in *Epistemology of the Closet*
(esp. pp. 4–8).

22 I am indebted here to Andrzej Warminski's reading of determinate nega-
tion in Nietzsche's *Birth of Tragedy*. Andrzej Warminski, *Readings in
Interpretation: Hölderlin, Hegel, Heidegger* (Minneapolis: University of
Minnesota Press, 1987), especially pp. xlvii–li.

23 James punningly says of Densher in Venice, "His *business*, he had settled, as
we know, was to keep *perfectly still*" (p. 418; my italics). See Sara Blair's fascinating reading of James's treatment of Venice, inaction, and forms of masculinity in early essays about that city (Blair, *Henry James and the Writing of Race
and Nation*, pp. 46–59).

24 Consider James's animation, in *The American Scene*, of his Cambridge *alma
mater*, the "Harvard organism brooding, exactly, through the long vacation,
brooding through the summer night, on discriminations, on insistences, on
sublime and exquisite heresies to come" (James, *The American*, p. 58). Ruth
Bernard Yeazell observes both that, in late James, characters are only rarely
allowed to sleep, and that their sleeplessness occurs as part of a "struggle of
the intelligence" (Yeazell, *Language and Knowledge in the Late Novels of Henry
James*, pp. 16–18). One might think here, for instance, of Isabel Archer's
"extraordinary meditative vigil," which transpires "far into the night" and
which James calls "obviously the best thing in" *The Portrait of a Lady*. (My
thanks to Michael Martin for suggesting the latter connection.)

25 For James, the Johns Hopkins University Hospital achieves a special prestige for its collation of these same categories: a close association with bodies
in pain (because it is a working hospital) and a pervasive air of stillness and
thought (because it is part of a university). James wonders, "Why should the
great Hospital, with its endless chambers of woe, its whole air as of *most*
directly and advisedly facing, as the hospitals of the world go, the question
of the immensities of pain – why should such an impression actually have
turned, under the spell, to fine poetry, to a mere shining vision of the conditions, the high beauty of applied science?" He answers his own question
by noting that the hospital partook, "in its own way, of the University
glamour." That "University glamour" helps the hospital to transmute the
materiality of pain into a version of high culture: in the hospital wards, "the
passive rows, the grim human alignments . . . became . . . cool 'symphonies
in white'" (James, *The American Scene*, pp. 228–9).

26 See Bourdieu, *Distinction*, pp. 226–56. Defining itself not only against the

vast acquisition of wealth that he forgoes in the last scene but also against the widely recognizable and easily comprehended position of "a public man" such as Lord Mark (whose very title announces his symbolic role in a formalized hierarchy), Densher's mode of realist prestige offers an alternative as well to those emergent forms of public celebrity that James decried in works ranging from *The Bostonians* to *The Reverberator* to *The American Scene.*

27 Densher understands that Milly's Palazzo Leporelli has served her as a kind of substitute body, a last refuge as her own body accelerates its "physical break-down" (p. 423). Milly has told him, "it will be my life – paid for as that. It will become my great gilded shell." Hence his horror at the expression that Susan Stringham uses to him late in the novel – "she has turned her face to the wall" – by which Stringham means that Milly "has given up all power to care again, and that's why she's dying" (pp. 421, 454). The expression suggests a final turning-in toward the inescapable confines of Milly's dying body. When Stringham adds that Milly now just "lies there stiffening herself," "stiffening" (which might otherwise suggest some kind of resistance to death) evokes rigor-mortis (p. 425). When read next to the figure-of-speech that immediately precedes it, "stiffening" brings out the sense in which to turn one's face to the wall, or to the shrinking confines a dying body allows, is to prepare for the more literal *turn*, or metamorphosis, into the dead matter of which a wall is composed. (In this context, see also the moment when, in response to Lord Mark's probe about her health, Milly "spoke, as by a sudden *turn*, with a slight *hardness*" [p. 349; my italics].)

28 Sharon Cameron recognizes Densher's final "thought" about Milly's letter as the "notable exception" to her larger argument that in the novel "thinking is not private and it is not internal." She points out that this final thought of Densher's seems "as if intentionally veiled from our [the readers'] view." See Sharon Cameron, *Thinking in Henry James* (University of Chicago Press, 1989), p. 152.

29 Although it is tempting to perceive a self-reflexive commentary on his own sentences in certain of James's formulations about Densher: "It brought him then more to the point, though it did so at first but by making him, on the hearthrug before her, with his hands in his pockets, turn awhile to and fro" (p. 486).

30 The association that this chapter has explored between doing nothing and cultural capital might be further useful in understanding an important configuration in Anglo-American modernism. Densher's determinate negation of action not only allows the obvious observation that, as a Jamesian protagonist somewhat like Strether from *The Ambassadors*, he is a precursor to the vexedly passive bachelors Hugh Selwyn Mauberly and J. Alfred Prufrock. It also opens the novel into high modernist literature's much wider investigation of, but also investment in (indeed "taste" for), a self-conscious doing nothing, whether Beckett's burlesque version in *Waiting for Godot* or Eliot's Anglicanized version in the *Four Quartets.* James's tone

describing Densher seems to oscillate between prefiguring both these two extremes. As repeatedly happens to Beckett's Vladimir and Estragon, "it just seemed to blaze at [Densher] that waiting was the games of dupes" (p. 254), but it also seems that, like them, he can do nothing else. On the other hand, as if anticipating the speaker of "Burnt Norton," Densher rigorously, even religiously, quests for "the real, the right stillness" (p. 444).

31 Jonathan Freedman's discussion of *The Wings of the Dove* in *Professions of Taste* helped me to recognize the extent to which James criticizes Densher throughout the novel (Freedman, *Professions of Taste*, pp. 202–28). For Scott Derrick, as well, *Wings* "is a novel arguably more interested in exposing Densher's imagination than in celebrating it" (Derrick, *Monumental Anxieties*, p. 130). As Freedman correctly notes, however, whatever exposure or criticism James subjects Densher to does not prevent, indeed in certain ways makes it easier, for James to adopt postures and practices homologous with Densher's (Freedman, *Professions of Taste*, pp. 225–6). I differ from Freedman in my sense that Densher's various silences and passivities signal more than simply his "acquiescence" in the mercenary behavior that he pretends to separate himself from: Densher's "I do nothing" constitutes the paradoxical form by which he *actively forwards* that behavior.

32 At work here is a version of the gendered "logic of paradox" that Sara Blair describes, in which "James's sympathetic engagement with women's experience" serves as a means for him "to secure his own access to male and public forms of power." Blair's primary example comes from the preface to *The Portrait of a Lady*, where James positions Isabel, the preface's "female 'frail vessel,'" as a "space that he and his text authoritatively and ironically inhabit; femininity effects the reflexive author's transportation from literal to figurative meaning, from innocence to knowledge, from felt experience to more deeply felt fine awareness." See Sara Blair, "In the House of Fiction: Henry James and the Engendering of Literary Mastery," in *Henry James's New York Edition: the Construction of Authorship*, ed. David McWhirter and John Carlos Rowe (Stanford University Press, 1995), pp. 65, 70. Scott Derrick's fine reading of Densher's ultimate "enshrining of Milly Theale" as his masculinity's "stabilizing 'other'" is also pertinent here (Derrick, *Monumental Anxieties*, p. 140), as is Susan Mizruchi's deeply informed discussion of *The Awkward Age* (Mizruchi, *Science of Sacrifice*, pp. 189–266).

33 Henry James, *Roderick Hudson*, ed. Geoffrey Moore (New York: Penguin, 1986), p. 37. See Sharon Cameron's discussion of this passage (Cameron, *Thinking in Henry James*, pp. 47–53).

34 James, *Roderick Hudson*, p. 37.

35 Ibid., p. 37.

36 On the shifting gender alignments of Densher and Kate, see Julie Olin-Ammentorp, "'A Circle of Petticoats': the Feminization of Merton Densher," *Henry James Review* 15, no. 1 (1994).

3 THE "GENUINE ARTICLE": CREDIT AND ETHNICITY IN *THE RISE OF DAVID LEVINSKY*

1 James, *The American Scene*, p. 98. Recently, Posnock and Blair have both mounted rich and persuasive arguments against the received reading of James's description of his Lower East Side visit as demonstrating his elitist distaste for Jews and other immigrants. Posnock, in particular, defends James against the charge of antisemitism by suggesting that his ghetto visit participates in the larger project of *The American Scene*. Posnock reads the latter volume as a complexly ambivalent but nonetheless "calculated act of affiliation with the new century and its endless possibilities" (p. 12); the Lower East Side's Jews, Posnock argues, figure the latter for James. See Posnock, *The Trial of Curiosity: Henry James, William James, and the Challenge of Modernity*, pp. 7–14 and Blair, *Henry and the Writing of Race and Nation*, pp. 178–85. Drawing on James's personal correspondence, as well as on *The Golden Bowl*, Everett Carter's "Realists and Jews" argues against any notion of James as antisemitic. I have found Jonathan Freedman's balanced "Henry James and the Discourses of Antisemitism" most useful in my own thinking about the issue. See Everett Carter, "Realists and Jews," *Studies in American Fiction* 22, no. 1 (1994) and Jonathan Freedman, "Henry James and the Discourses of Antisemitism," in *Between "Race" and Culture: Representations of "the Jew" in English and American Literature*, ed. Bryan Cheyette (Stanford University Press, 1996).

2 Shari Benstock, *No Gifts from Chance: a Biography of Edith Wharton* (New York: Charles Scribner's Sons; Toronto: Maxwell Macmillan Canada, 1994), pp. 387–8.

3 Abraham Cahan, *The Rise of David Levinsky* (New York: Harper & Row, 1960), p. 3. Further page references will appear in the text.

4 Louis Harap, *The Image of the Jew in American Literature: From Early Republic to Mass Immigration*, 1st. edn. (Philadelphia: Jewish Publication Society of America, 1974), p. 419. My attention was drawn both to this phenomenon in *Levinsky* criticism and to this specific quote by Richard S. Pressman's excellent article, "Abraham Cahan, Capitalist; David Levinsky, Socialist" in *Styles of Cultural Activism: From Theory and Pedagogy to Women, Indians, and Communism*, ed. Philip Goldstein (Newark: University of Delaware Press, 1994), pp. 134–151.

5 In his essay "Bourdieu's Refusal," John Guillory also criticizes this automatically inverse relationship often presumed in Bourdieu's writing. It is worth mentioning that a plus–minus assumption about intellectual prestige and financial wealth parallel to Bourdieu's crops up frequently in Henry James's stories about writers and artists. "The Next Time," for instance, illustrates this assumption with almost allegorical, even a parodic, neatness, as the best-selling writer Mrs. Highmore insists that only if she manages to write a book that *fails* to make money (as she never can manage to do, no matter how hard she tries) will it possibly count as an artistic success to those few whose judgment really matters. Ralph Limbert, by contrast, never can write

"trash," despite his own best efforts, so his books never achieve commercial success. (David McWhirter drew my attention to the James connection here.)

6 In Anzia Yezierska's 1925 *Bread Givers*, Reb Smolinsky's vast Talmudic learning and his unrelenting commitment to continuing his holy studies keep his family impoverished and humiliated after they immigrate to America. All of his learning, so valued in Russia, makes him nothing but a *schnorrer* (beggar) in his landlady's scornful eyes. Talmud study does not pay rent nor even count towards doweries for the family's long-suffering daughters. See Anzia Yezierska, *Bread Givers* (New York: Doubleday, 1975).

7 Ross Posnock analyzes the politically progressive efficacy of Du Bois's investment in multiple forms of doubleness. In developing his very convincing portrayal of Du Bois's "remarkably hybrid sensibility," however, Posnock too readily accepts Du Bois's own critique of Washington as defined by a constraining "singleness of vision." Posnock is surely right that such a stance, especially as manifested in Washington's own explicit anti-intellectualism, played a crucial role in Washington's popularity among powerful white Americans (Posnock, *Color and Culture*, pp. 37, 58–9). Nonetheless, although Washington's own published writing does not *thematize* doubleness as Du Bois's does, Washington nonetheless adopted it as a political and, as Houston Baker has argued, a linguistic strategy. See Houston A. Baker, *Modernism and the Harlem Renaissance* (University of Chicago Press, 1987), pp. 25–47; and Louis R. Harlan, *Booker T. Washington: the Making of a Black Leader, 1856–1901* (London, New York: Oxford University Press, 1975), pp. i–iii. In the context of my own argument about "realer-than-thou" prestige, it is also worth pointing out that the conflict for cultural authority between Washington and Du Bois often took the form of a dispute over who was better qualified to designate the bottom-line realities of black life in turn-of-the-century America. Each became identified with a contrasting vision of what Washington called "the real needs and conditions of our people."

8 David Engel, "The 'Discrepancies' of the Modern: Towards a Revaluation of Abraham Cahan's *The Rise of David Levinsky*," *Studies in American Jewish Literature* 2 (1982), p. 37.

9 It might be helpful for considering relational class-aligned moments within Levinsky, as well as for complicating Bourdieu's model of how sociocultural differences get staged, briefly to point out that there is no reason not to read Frederic Jameson's by-now classic insistence on the oppositionality of class definition – "classes must always be apprehended relationally . . . and class struggle is always dichotomous" – back into the field from which his paradigm of *The Political Unconscious* is derived: dynamically related sites, or moments, within the individual subject. See Frederic Jameson, *The Political Unconscious: Narrative as a Socially Symbolic Act* (Ithaca, NY: Cornell University Press, 1981), p. 83.

10 See Bourdieu, *Distinction*, p. 196.

11 Abraham Cahan and Moses Rischin, *Grandma Never Lived in America: the New Journalism of Abraham Cahan* (Bloomington: Indiana University Press, 1985), p. 451.

12 Abraham Cahan, *Yekl and Imported Bridegroom and Other Stories of the New York Ghetto* (New York: Dover, 1970), p. 2. Further page references will appear in the text.

13 My thinking about Levinsky's unstable temporal position has been influenced by Paul de Man, "The Rhetoric of Temporality," in *Blindness and Insight: Essays in the Rhetoric of Contemporary Criticism, Theory and History of Literature* (Minneapolis: University of Minnesota Press, 1983) and D. A. Miller, "Balzac's Illusions Lost and Found," *Yale French Studies* 67 (1984).

14 That language can replace even the bodily act of eating in the slot aligned with materiality is emphasized by moments such as Levinsky's happiness when he "really had no need of my culinary notes" any longer (notes he had taken about the intricacies of expensive restaurant cuisine): "I had many occasions to eat in high-class restaurants and I was getting to feel quite at home in them" (p. 293). Here, instead of achieved distance from bodily consumption serving to show Levinsky's distinction, his rejecting his own *writing*-about-food, *writing* on which he was formerly dependent, registers his increase in cultural status.

15 Wilson, "Picasso and Pâté De Foie Gras: Pierre Bourdieu's Sociology of Culture," p. 59.

16 See Ibid. In a recent article on Stephen Crane's *Maggie: a Girl of the Streets*, Howard Horwitz analyzes an intellectually compromised "sociological paradigm" that, he contends, develops in turn-of-the-century American sociology and continues to shape aspects of contemporary critical theory. Turn-of-the-century sociologists and contemporary theorists alike, Horwitz argues, seek to exempt themselves from the "mud" of determinism and partiality that they otherwise find pervasive and inescapable. In predictably reaching the moment where they assume their own distance and hence freedom, however, sociologists and theorists internalize a predetermined script of liberalism, which is the widely held belief that one's own consciousness can transcend its environment. Unlike Levinsky in Cahan's novel, however, Horwitz's argument about Stephen Crane does not seem aware that it too repeats this claim to transcendence, or at the very least to distance and distinction, when it celebrates Crane's literary critique of the sociological paradigm. Crane's "trap" for sociological readers may indeed trip up those who repeat the gesture of claiming emancipation from internalized scripts while failing to recognize that they themselves follow such a script. But from what point does Horwitz imply that Crane sets this "trap" if not from some point external to it? In recognizing that those who pose themselves as distinct from "mud" fall back, in that very moment, into another version of it, wouldn't Horwitz's Crane be claiming for himself the distinction of recognizing misrecognition, and thus placing himself back under the sign of the "sociological," as Horwitz here defines it? By contrast, the

specifically literary-realist distinction that, I believe, Levinsky represents involves continually foregrounding (or at least recognizing) one's own inescapable implication in the same "mud" that one denounces. See Howard Horwitz, "Maggie and the Sociological Paradigm," *American Literary History* 10, no. 4 (1998).

17 It should be pointed out that, because of the excess resulting from the impossibility of entirely intending every context in which one's language may act, one can never fully situate one's own interests to the moment, or identify with certainty the motives of any given use of language. See Jacques Derrida, *Limited Inc* (Evanston, IL: Northwestern University Press, 1988). If, as recent criticism correctly insists, no one can ever get entirely "outside" his or her own interests, neither can anyone ever get entirely "inside" them.

18 Critics have either assigned to Levinsky or Cahan or have claimed for themselves the cultural credit that Levinsky earns here by being critical of his own practices. The former set includes Cushing Strout ("Levinsky earns our sympathy for his plain prosaic honesty in accounting for his success") and Louis Harap, who concludes that "the best part of Cahan" deserved "great artistic satisfaction and comfort" from his "fictionalized evaluation of himself as a conflicted person who chose success over integrity, a career as an exploiter . . . over a career . . . devoted to maintaining human dignity and integrity." See Cushing Strout, "Personality and Cultural History in the Novel: Two American Examples," *New Literary History* 1 (1970), p. 436; and Harap, *The Image of the Jew in American Literature*, pp. 518–24. Readers who reserve to themselves the credit Harap gives Cahan's "best part" include Sanford Marovitz ("The Secular Trinity of Lonely Millionaires: Language, Sex, and Power in *The Rise of David Levinsky*," *Studies in American Jewish Literature* 2 [1982]) and H.W. Boynton who, reviewing the novel when it first came out, doubts "whether Mr. Cahan appreciates the spiritual obscenity of the creature he has made; embodiment of all the contemptible qualities an enemy of the Yiddish Jew could charge him with" (quoted in Harap, *The Image of the Jew in American Literature*, p. 519). By positioning Cahan's text as antisemitic, Boynton gains some cultural credit for himself but misses an opportunity to analyze the scapegoating he calls attention to. He could have noted how the "contemptible qualities" of which Levinsky is supposedly an "embodiment" are in fact central and generalized mechanisms of capital accumulation.

19 If only by noticing recurrences of the word "wretched," it becomes possible to connect with this resistant identity as a Russian immigrant other categories that I have argued Levinsky puts in the slot of the material. For example, the possibility of his having "talked too much" on the train leads to Levinsky's self-description, "I was wretched," and he elsewhere refers to his immigrant speech as "my wretched English" (pp. 330, 130).

20 Levinsky himself should be credited, so to speak, as the first of the readers of his rise to point to the benefits he receives from the Levinsky Antomir Benefit Society: "All this, I confess, was not without advantage to my

business interests . . ." Indeed, he articulates as well as any critic might a possible "protest against the whole society as an organization of 'slaves' [meaning] that the society makes meek, obedient servants of my employees and helps me fleece them" (pp. 377, 519). Levinsky's "confess[ion]," however, about the "advantage to my business interests" of his "honorary" membership in the society, provides from those business interests (what Barbara Johnson in another context has called) "the distance of mentioning" (oral response, Cornell University, April 1990). Levinsky's own thematization of his exploitative business strategies provides an opening to some of the difficult questions about antisemitism surrounding this text. Potentially disturbing, for example, is the way in which my own argument about Levinsky's accumulation of several intertwined forms of capital bears a resemblance to classic antisemitic tracts describing conspiratorial Jewish accumulations of wealth and influence. Yet much of the value and even brilliance of Cahan's novel lies in its compressed account of what can be seen as the much larger historical transition of people from the folk to the bourgeoisie. This means that *The Rise of David Levinsky* should be read as a powerfully distilled performance of the far more general historical mechanisms of capitalism, the formation of modern bourgeois subjects, and the sociocultural hierarchies instituted in both phenomena (see also Pressman, "Abraham Cahan, Capitalist; David Levinsky, Socialist," pp. 148–9). To read the novel as separate from this immanent context is an error that can encourage scapegoating (i.e., Levinsky and the Jews are uniquely profit-hungry, manipulative, devious). That scapegoating move has shadowed the novel even since before it was published as a novel. The first installment of its serialized version in *McClure's Magazine* (1913) was preceded by an article a month earlier by Burton J. Hendrick, entitled "The Jewish Invasion of America," which blames Jews for various structural changes in American industry and finance. In Hendrick's last paragraph, he announces the upcoming serialization: "Mr. Abraham Cahan will show, by concrete example, the minute workings of that wonderful machine, the Jewish brain," which enables Jews "so easily [to] surpass or crowd out" others. See Burton J. Hendrick, "The Jewish Invasion of America," *McClure's Magazine* 40, no. 5 (March 1913), p. 165.

21 What Levinsky identifies as the breakthrough achievement of the Jewish garment industry, and what primarily makes his personal fortune, depends on this same logic: iterating a "genuine article" with rich connotations of authenticity, but one that can also be sold at a devalued price. "The ingenuity and unyielding tenacity of our [Russian Jewish] managers, foremen, and operatives had introduced a thousand and one devices for making by machine garments that used to be considered possible only as the product of handiwork" (p. 443). Note that, for Levinsky, this industrial achievement ("ready-made" clothing identical to that which used to require expensive, individual handiwork) is just as marked by a broken-off but preserved ethnic specificity as is sorrel soup, or as are any examples of the "the old Ghetto

way" that he reproduces in his New York factory. On the relation between industrialism and the "authentic" during the early twentieth-century, see Miles Orvell, *The Real Thing: Imitation and Authenticity in American Culture, 1880–1940* (Chapel Hill: University of North Carolina Press, 1989).

It's also worth noting here that Levinsky's dubbing New York's City College as "the genuine article" in education has suggestive parallels with his comments about silk dresses: City College combines a "quality" American standard with wide availability and with ethnic identification (City College's student body was 75 percent Jewish by 1913). Even his physical description of City College, with its "red, ivy-clad walls, mysterious high windows, humble spires" resonates with his description of "the ready-made silk dress which . . . [is] as tasteful in its lines, color scheme, and trimming as a high-class designer can make it" (pp. 168, 443). The descriptions resonate not only in their shared emphasis on visual lines, color and "trimming" but also phonically: *"red,* iv*y-*clad *walls"*; *"ready-*made *silk."*

22 Regarding "literal translation," consider also the debates of the period about "sight dialect" in novels and short stories, a form of dialogue mostly reserved for class and racial others which differs from standard English only in that phonetic spelling is employed to depict it (see Nettels, *Language, Race, and Social Class in Howells's America,* pp. 62–71). Bourdieu's insights in *Distinction* might suggest that writers' use of phonetic spelling for lower-class speech signifies lower-class speakers' inability to distance themselves from some "literal" or "natural" language, a distancing which is achieved for the more literate by their deployment of language's formal elements (such as silent letters or blatantly unmotivated letter–phoneme connections). The difference in positions between the hotel guests and Levinsky might, then, be analogized with that between the "sight dialect" assigned to racial and class others on the one hand and, on the other hand, the practice of "simplified spelling" advocated by a number of intellectuals (see e.g. H. L. Mencken, *The American Language: an Inquiry into the Development of English in the United States,* 4th edn. [New York: Knopf, 1936], pp. 400–1).

Also interesting in this context is Cahan's reprise, for Mencken's 1945 edition of *The American Language,* of his oft-played role earlier in this century as guide through the Yiddish Ghetto for such American intellectuals as Hutchins Hapgood. (One result was Hapgood's popular 1902 book, *The Spirit of the Ghetto.*) Cahan, responsible for an appendix about Yiddish in Mencken's 1945 volume, guides the reader through interpenetrations of Yiddish and English idioms.

23 Conversely, Levinsky also enjoys deciding whether "the illiterate wife of a baker" in fact has an "intelligent" relation to the English phrases with which she "interspersed her unsophisticated Yiddish" (English phrases such as "rare technique" and "bee-youtiful tone"): "At first I thought that she was prattling these words parrot fashion, but I soon realized that, to a considerable extent, at least, she used them intelligently" (p. 368).

24 For examples of the claim that Levinsky's loneliness primarily allegorizes

Jewish-American alienation, see Isaac Rosenfeld, "*David Levinsky*: the Jew as American Millionaire," in *An Age of Enormity* (Cleveland, OH: World Publishing Company, 1962); Leslie Fiedler, "Genesis: the American-Jewish Novel through the Thirties," *Midstream* 4, no. 3 (1958); Ronald Sanders, *The Downtown Jews; Portraits of an Immigrant Generation* (New York: Harper & Row, 1969); Engel, "The 'Discrepancies' of the Modern"; and Richard J. Fein, "*The Rise of David Levinsky* and the Migrant Self," *Studies in American Jewish Literature* 2 (1976).

25 Considered together, the empty "who" that Levinsky implicitly casts as the motive for his continued money-making, and the association he makes between Jewish women and bodily or linguistic materiality, intriguingly anticipate key aspects of post-World War II stereotypes of the "Jewish-American Princess" wife. According to this misogynist stereotype, Jewish women embody a kind of empty materialism, an intimate association with material goods but also a spiritual and emotional lack (not to mention intellectual vapidity). For male subjects, conceiving themselves to be intimately associated with (or even married to) a figure personifying both materialism and emptiness can serve something of the same purposes that is served for Levinsky when he produces these categories as internal aspects of himself. The so-called "Jewish-American Princess" wife provides an intimately present ground against which the male subject can locate contrasting dimensions of himself.

4 WHAT NONA KNOWS

1 Elizabeth Ammons describes Wharton as "sickened by the flapper." See Elizabeth Ammons, *Edith Wharton's Argument with America* (University of Georgia Press, 1980), p. 184.
2 Edith Wharton, *The Letters of Edith Wharton*, ed. R. W. B. Lewis and Nancy Lewis (New York: Charles Scribner's Sons, 1988), p. 461.
3 Ibid., p. 483.
4 Ibid., p. 472.
5 Ann Douglas, *Terrible Honesty: Mongrel Manhattan in the 1920s*, 1st. edn. (New York: Farrar Straus & Giroux, 1995), p. 81; Dale M. Bauer, *Edith Wharton's Brave New Politics* (Madison: University of Wisconsin Press, 1994), p. 10.
6 Jennie Ann Kassanoff, "The Fetishized Family: the Modernism of Edith Wharton" (Diss., Princeton University, 1993), p. 25.
7 Wharton, *The Letters of Edith Wharton*, p. 472.
8 Edith Wharton, *Twilight Sleep* (New York: Scribner, 1997), p. 12. Further page references will appear in the text.
9 Kaplan, *The Social Construction of American Realism*, p. 13.
10 Edith Wharton, *The Marne* (New York: Appleton, 1918), p. 44; Edith Wharton, *A Son at the Front* (New York: Charles Scribner's Sons, 1923), p. 194.
11 Bentley, *Ethnography of Manners*, pp. 70, 87, 91.
12 Dexter Manford's identification with lawful authority is far more complete,

for instance, than that of *Summer*'s Lawyer Royall, who despite his acknowledged brilliance and flashes of impressive force remains nonetheless a frustrated, semi-disgraced country lawyer. See Edith Wharton, *Summer*, 1916 (New York: Penguin, 1993).

13 In the higher-education news media, as I revised this chapter, were the tragic events involving an alleged affair between College President George C. Roche III and his daughter-in-law. When rumors of the affair began circulating, Lissa Roche committed suicide and, as *The Chronicle of Higher Education* put it, the position of George Roche, who had been an "icon of traditional values in education," came "crashing down," leaving a "stunned" community. See Martin Van der Werf, "A Scandal and a Suicide Leave a College Reeling," *The Chronicle of Higher Education*, November 19, 1999, A53–A55. This was preceeded, of course, by the much larger-scale convulsions within the nation's governing structure associated with President Clinton's quasi-incestuous affair with Monica Lewinsky, a young White House intern who, the media continually reiterated, was virtually the same age as Clinton's own daughter Chelsea.

14 Juliet Flower MacCannell, *The Regime of the Brother: After the Patriarchy, Opening Out* (London and New York: Routledge, 1991), p. 16.

15 Wharton, *The Letters of Edith Wharton*, p. 346; Edith Wharton, *Fighting France: From Dunkerque to Belfort* (New York: Charles Scribner's Sons, 1918), p. 51.

16 Wharton, *A Backward Glance*, p. 6.

17 Wharton, *A Son at the Front*, pp. 90, 192, and 334.

18 Ibid., pp. 192, 226, 192–3.

19 Ibid., 153.

20 Kassanoff, "Fetishized Family," pp. 329–331.

21 Alan Price, *The End of the Age of Innocence: Edith Wharton and the First World War*, 1st. edn. (New York: St. Martin's Press, 1996), p. 173.

22 Wharton, *A Backward Glance*, p. 356.

23 Kassanoff, "Fetishized Family," p. 329.

24 Sigmund Freud, *Beyond the Pleasure Principle*, ed. James Strachey (New York: Norton, 1960), p. 33.

25 Dennis A. Foster, *Sublime Enjoyment: On the Perverse Motive in American Literature* (Cambridge University Press, 1997), p. 4.

26 Wharton, *A Backward Glance*, p. 6.

27 MacCannell, *The Regime of the Brother*, p. 16. Part of what makes Wharton's earlier writing so interesting is that, although the law remains in place, it is often not immediately obvious who embodies the social order's "symbolic, law-giving, life-preserving function." In *The House of Mirth*, I would contend, it is not the old-monied Gus Trenor or Tony Dorset; rather, Selden and Rosedale combine to embody this function. Selden as guarantor and guardian of "the republic of the spirit"; Rosedale as figure of vital power who wishes no other use for it than to invest in and support the social order.

28 Bauer, *Edith Wharton's Brave New Politics*, p. 90.

29 Žižek, *The Sublime Object of Ideology*, p. 45.

30 Wharton, *House of Mirth*, p. 301.
31 Wharton, *The Letters of Edith Wharton*, p. 451.
32 Douglas, *Terrible Honesty*, pp. 146–7.
33 Calling Pauline's personal bathroom a "biological laboratory" may evoke the eugenics movement that Wharton attacked throughout the 1920s (see Bauer, *Edith Wharton's Brave New Politics*). Pauline's bathroom is a laboratory for the hygienic elimination of waste.
34 Pauline lobbies for "concave tiling" in her husband's office because it can be "fitted to every cove and angle, so that there were no corners anywhere to catch the dust" (p. 55).
35 Bauer, *Edith Wharton's Brave New Politics*, p. 102.
36 Sandra M. Gilbert and Susan Gubar, *No Man's Land: the Place of the Woman Writer in the Twentieth Century* (New Haven: Yale University Press, 1988), p. 131.
37 Elizabeth Ammons, "Edith Wharton and Race," in *The Cambridge Companion to Edith Wharton*, ed. Millicent Bell (Cambridge University Press, 1995), p. 84n3.
38 Jacqueline Rose's discussion of Sylvia Plath and Plath criticism has helped my thinking here. See Jacqueline Rose, *The Haunting of Sylvia Plath* (Cambridge, MA: Harvard University Press, 1992), pp. 3–10.
39 Including even time itself: her "facial-massage artist"'s cancellation of their appointment at the last minute makes clear that Pauline's subdivided time is itself a form of twilight sleep, indeed one of those "handles of reality" onto which she clings so as not to risk plunging into an unassimilable real. The cancellation leaves her with an unscheduled hour, making Pauline feel "surrounded by a sudden void, into which she could reach out on all sides without touching an engagement or an obligation . . . An hour – why there was no way of measuring the length of an empty hour! It stretched away into infinity like the endless road in a nightmare; it gaped before her like the slippery sides of an abyss" (p. 117).
40 In its entry on "jazz," the *Random House Historical Dictionary of American Slang* cites an issue of the *Journal of Abnormal and Social Psychology* from 1927, *Twilight Sleep*'s year of publication: "Used both as a verb and a noun to denote the sex act, it has long been common vulgarity among Negroes in the South, and it is very likely from this usage that the term 'jazz music' was derived. It is almost unbelievable that such vulgarity could become so respectable, but it is true nevertheless" (p. 260). Warwick Wadlington pointed out "jazz"'s original meaning to me.
41 One could certainly find external evidence that would help to support such a view. Wharton's praise to F. Scott Fitzgerald of *The Great Gatsby*'s Wolfsheim as "your *perfect* Jew" is well known (Wharton, *The Letters of Edith Wharton*, p. 482).
   In addition, in an unpublished 1927 letter to Gailliard Laipsley, Wharton makes plain her feelings about Harlem and about the fascination that young white Americans, including artists and intellectuals, were beginning to show for it:

Have you read [Carl Van Vechten's] "Nigger Heaven"? It is so nauseating (& such rubbish too) that I despair of the Republic –

I thought the whole thing was made up, but the other day Mr. & Mme. Bourdet (of "La Prisonniere") came to lunch, & they told me they had been to New York . . . & had been taken by the "Jeunes" into nigger society in Harlem "et que cétait comme dans la livre." And now I must stop & be sick – (Quoted in Bauer, *Edith Wharton's Brave New Politics*, p. 58).

42 Ammons, "Edith Wharton and Race," pp. 77–82; Bauer, *Edith Wharton's Brave New Politics*, pp. 58–63.

43 See Jennie A. Kassanoff, "Extinction, Taxidermy, Tableaux Vivants: Staging Race and Class in *The House of Mirth*," *PMLA* 115 (2000), pp. 60–74.

44 See Walter Benn Michaels, *Our America: Nativism, Modernism, and Pluralism* (Durham, NC: Duke University Press, 1995), p. 7.

45 Ibid., 1–16.

46 MacCannell, *The Regime of the Brother*, p. 16.

47 My thanks to Warwick Wadlington and Sabrina Barton for helping me to clarify my thoughts about racial panic in Wharton's novel.

48 Cathy Caruth, *Unclaimed Experience: Trauma, Narrative, and History* (Baltimore: Johns Hopkins University Press, 1996), pp. vii–viii. For a nuanced exploration of differing modes in which a trauma may be witnessed, see Alyssa Harad, "An Invitation to Witness: Trauma, Literary Testimony, and the Reader," forthcoming dissertation.

49 Wharton, *The Letters of Edith Wharton*, p. 408.

50 Benstock, *No Gifts from Chance*, p. 379.

51 There is some dispute about when the "Beatrice Palmato" outline and fragment were actually written – it may even have been as late as 1935 – but the pertinent titles appear in her notebooks by 1920. See R. W. B. Lewis, *Edith Wharton: A Biography*, 1st. edn. (New York: Harper & Row, 1975), p. 544.

52 The "Beatrice Palmato" writing is reprinted as appendices in biographies of Wharton by Lewis and Benstock, as well as in Gloria Erlich, *The Sexual Education of Edith Wharton* (Berkeley: University of California Press, 1992).

53 One intriguing exception is *The Shadow of a Dream*. See William Dean Howells, *The Shadow of a Dream and An Imperative Duty*, in *A Selected Edition of William Dean Howells*, ed. Ronald Gottesman, David J. Nordloh, and Martha Banta, vol. 17. (Bloomington: Indiana University Press, 1970).

54 Howells, *A Hazard of New Fortunes*, p. 61.

55 James, *The Wings of the Dove*, p. 503.

56 Wharton, *A Backward Glance*, p. 2.

57 Quoted in Price, *End of Innocence*, p. 166.

58 Ibid., pp. 166, 158.

59 Edith Wharton, *French Ways and Their Meaning* (New York: Appleton, 1919), p. 100.

60 Wharton, *The Letters of Edith Wharton*, p. 408.

61 Ibid., p. 412.

5 FROM REALITY, TO MATERIALITY, TO THE REAL (AND BACK
AGAIN): THE DYNAMICS OF DISTINCTION ON THE RECENT CRITICAL
SCENE

1 Howells, "Short Story Collections: Hamlin Garland," p. 186.
2 Andrew Ross, *No Respect: Intellectuals and Popular Culture* (New York:
   Routledge, 1989), p. 231.
3 The 788-page volume titled simply *Cultural Studies* collects *some* of the conference papers, and conveys a good sense of the conference's magnitude
   and scope. See Lawrence Grossberg, Cary Nelson, and Paula A. Treichler,
   eds., *Cultural Studies* (New York: Routledge, 1992).
4 Ibid., pp. 278, 83–4.
5 Paul de Man, *Allegories of Reading: Figural Language in Rousseau, Nietzsche, Rilke,
   and Proust* (New Haven: Yale University Press, 1979), p. 283. Michael Fried's
   tour-de-force rereading of Stephen Crane's corpus is paradigmatic of the
   continuing operative force even within deconstructive criticism of "realer-
   than-thou" claims. Fried's claim to distinction as a reader of Crane rests on
   his claim to have developed a unique access to a level of "actual" reality in
   Crane's texts that has hitherto been ignored. As Fried explains, he would
   shift attention away from the "'manifestly' social subject" of Crane's writings. Instead of reading Crane for his naturalistic depictions of the real
   world he lived in, Fried would trace out the appearances in Crane's text of

   > those things that, *before all*, actually lay before Crane's eyes: the written words
   > themselves, the white, lined sheet of paper on which they were inscribed, the marks
   > made by his pen on the surface of the sheet, even perhaps the movements of his
   > hand wielding the pen in the act of inscription.

   Fried would separate himself from other readers (Crane's "narratives . . .
   hitherto have wholly escaped being read in these terms," he insists) by
   ceasing to look at the "manifest" ways in which Crane's work only *seems* to
   touch reality – its claim to represent social spaces in the real world – in order
   to approach the "*before all*," "actual" real of Crane's writing. Fried variously
   refers to this before-all real as "the text's reality as writing," the "materiality of writing," and the "materiality of inscription." See Michael Fried,
   Realism, Writing, Disfiguration: On Thomas Eakins and Stephen Crane (University
   of Chicago Press, 1987), pp. 136, 17–18, 20, 28.
6 Henry James, *The Awkward Age*, ed. Ronald Blythe (New York: Penguin,
   1987), p. 6.
7 Evan Carton and Gerald Graff, "Criticism since 1940," in *The Cambridge
   History of American Literature*, ed. Sacvan Bercovitch (New York: Cambridge
   University Press, 1996), p. 313.
8 John Guillory, *Cultural Capital: the Problem of Literary Canon Formation*
   (University of Chicago Press, 1993). Specific page references will appear in
   the text.
9 Trilling may also help add to the plausibility of my earlier suggestion of
   close parallels between the treatment of intellectual prestige in works by

Henry James and Abraham Cahan, two writers who, as mentioned in the preface, might have initially struck readers as more likely to represent opposed literary perspectives. Trilling descended from the same period of mass immigration that brought Abraham Cahan to the United States. His early writing about literature and culture appeared in the *Menorah Journal* which emerged out of that early twentieth-century Jewish intellectual milieu in New York City upon which Cahan had exercised a formative influence. As we saw above, Henry James's glimpses of this Jewish intellectual scene during his 1903 visit to New York provoked for him a disturbing vision of the obliteration of "the light of our language as literature has hitherto known it." Ironically, however, the elevation of James's own critical status to the exalted canonical position he still occupies was in large part accomplished, during the 1940s and 50s, through the writings of Lionel Trilling and other New York Jewish heirs to the ferment and intensity of Cahan's intellectual milieu, such as Irving Howe and Philip Rahv. There are of course many different answers to the question of how New York Jewish literary intellectuals could move over the course of just a few decades from representing, for James himself, the "agency of future ravage" on Anglo-American "letters" to acting as passionately effective advocates for his novels and stories. I suggest that at least one answer, however, must involve the attraction for literary intellectuals such as Trilling of the similar models for deriving intellectual prestige from a particular relation to nitty-gritty reality that could be found both in the elegantly polished masterpieces of James and in fiction such as that of Cahan's, replete with borscht and Yiddish-American dialect.

10 Jonathan Freedman, "Trilling, James, and the Uses of Cultural Criticism," *Henry James Review* 14, no. 2 (1993), p. 144.

11 Lionel Trilling, *The Liberal Imagination: Essays on Literature and Society* (Garden City, NY: Doubleday 1954), page references will appear in the text; Thomas Bender, "Lionel Trilling and American Culture," *American Quarterly* 42, no. 2 (1990), p. 324; Michael E. Nowlin, "'Reality in America' Revisited: Modernism, the Liberal Imagination and the Revival of Henry James," *Canadian Review of American Studies* 23, no. 3 (1993), p. 2.

12 See Michael Nowlin's related claim that "for Trilling, 'reality' is precisely the mind-body dialectic." Ibid., p. 17.

13 On Trilling and dialectics, see Gregory Jay, "Hegel and Trilling in America," *American Literary History* 1, no. 3 (1989).

14 Trilling's realer-than-thou claim against Dreiser's critical defenders also insists that they fail properly to judge literary representations even of the "simple" reality upon which they stake their critical authority. "It has been taken for granted," Trilling says, that whoever finds any fault at all in the "roughness and ungainliness" of Dreiser's style "wants a prettified and genteel style (and is objecting to the ungainliness of reality itself)." This, however, "is mere fantasy. Hawthorne, Thoreau and Emerson were for the most part remarkably colloquial . . . their prose was specially American in

quality, and, except for occasional lapses, quite direct and simple. It is Dreiser who lacks the sense of colloquial diction – that of the Middle West or any other . . . [H]e is full of flowers of rhetoric and shines with paste gems" (Trilling, *The Liberal Imagination*, p. 26).

15 In *New York Jew*, Alfred Kazin puts it that just as Trilling admired Matthew Arnold for smiting the philistines, so Trilling took it upon himself to smite the "liberals." Both smitings are performed in the service of *intra*-middle class competition. Qt. Charles Shapiro, "On Our Own: Trilling vs. Dreiser," in *Seasoned Authors for a New Season: the Search for Standards in Popular Writing*, ed. Louis Filler (Bowling Green, OH: Bowling Green University Press, 1980), p. 153.

16 *The Opposing Self: Nine Essays in Criticism* (New York: Viking Press, 1955), p. 82. Further page references will appear in the text.

17 Trilling quotes the "odors of the shop" phrase from progressive historian Charles Beard's dismissive criticism of Henry James.

18 I would argue further that their ability to combine two different tactics for asserting a superior purchase on reality – that is, both the "less easily accessible than you think" and the "right in front of your eyes" tactics – also helps to explain the fact that poststructuralist modes of thought continue to play a defining role in such recently prominent areas of inquiry as queer studies and postcolonial criticism, despite the fact that so many commentators have declared the moment of "theory" (by which they almost invariably mean poststructuralist theory) to be over.

19 "Hypogram and Inscription," in *The Resistance to Theory* (Minneapolis: University of Minnesota Press, 1986), p. 27. Further page references will be given in the text.

20 See Jonathan Culler, *On Deconstruction: Theory and Criticism after Structuralism* (New York and Ithaca: Cornell University Press, 1982), p. 66.

21 Cynthia Chase, *Decomposing Figures: Rhetorical Readings in the Romantic Tradition* (Baltimore: Johns Hopkins University Press, 1986), p. 100.

22 Ibid., pp. 104–5.

23 De Man, *Allegories of Reading*, p. 293.

24 Butler, *Bodies That Matter*; Judith P. Butler, *Gender Trouble: Feminism and the Subversion of Identity, Thinking Gender* (New York: Routledge, 1990). Page references to *Bodies That Matter* will appear within the text.

25 Eve Kosofsky Sedgwick, "Queer Performativity: Henry James's *The Art of the Novel*," *Journal of Lesbian and Gay Studies* 1, no. 1 (1993), p. 1.

26 Joan Copjec, *Read My Desire: Lacan against the Historicists* (Cambridge, MA: MIT Press, 1994), p. 207. Further page references will appear within the text.

27 James Mellard, "Lacan and the New Lacanians: Josephine Hart's *Damage*, Lacanian Tragedy, and the Ethics of *Jouissance*," *PMLA* 113, no. 3 (1998), p. 395.

28 Ironically, Copjec's sense of the academy's dynamics of intellectual prestige seems informed by the very same warlike model of culture, described by

Foucault in an interview, that she quotes only in order to take great issue with. Foucault says, "it is not to the great model of signs and language that reference should be made, but to war and battle" (Copjec, *Read My Desire*, p. 4).

29 Copjec's specification of the Foucault texts that have had the most pernicious influence on "the academy" – "*Discipline and Punish, The History of Sexuality*, and Foucault's essays and interviews of the mid to late 1970s" – suggests that, although both Foucault and Lacan are French, "the academy" whose distributions of prestige most concern Copjec is still the American one (p. 4). This particular work of Foucault's was most taken up during his time lecturing at Berkeley and it has the status of founding documents for American "new historicist" criticism.

30 The first of these poststructuralist orientations, towards a "real" materiality that is nonetheless never empirically accessible, might count as one somewhat unexpected way in which poststructuralist arguments take after the realist dispositions that we found elaborated in works by Howells, James, and Cahan. Each in its own way, the realer-than-thou claims made in those earlier texts emphasize distance and deferral. Basil March, the Reverend Sewell, and other protagonists of Howells's later novels distinguish themselves, for instance, by recognizing the "real" of irresolvable contradictions and contingencies in American social relations. James's Merton Densher maintains certain rigorous ignorances concerning Milly Theale's "incurable pain." Cahan's David Levinsky locates the realest moments of his life in his unrecoverable youth.

31 In this context, the possible multilingual puns on Nona's name become particularly resonant: not only negativity ("no," "*non*," etc.), but also (as Warwick Wadlington suggested to me) "nun" (*nonne* means nun in German and, archaically, in French). We might say that Nona imagines herself as one among other "nuns of no" or, better, "nuns who *know* no."

32 Wharton, *Twilight Sleep*, pp. 69, 276.

Bibliography

Ammons, Elizabeth. *Edith Wharton's Argument with America*. Athens, GA: University of Georgia Press, 1980.
  Conflicting Stories: American Women Writers at the Turn into the Twentieth Century. Oxford University Press, 1992.
  "Edith Wharton and Race." In *The Cambridge Companion to Edith Wharton*, ed. Millicent Bell. Cambridge University Press, 1995. 66–88.
Andrews, William L. "William Dean Howells and Charles W. Chesnutt: Criticism and Race Fiction in the Age of Booker T. Washington." *American Literature* 48 (1976): 327–39.
Anesko, Michael. *"Friction with the Market": Henry James and the Profession of Authorship*. Oxford University Press, 1986.
Armstrong, Paul B. *The Challenge of Bewilderment: Understanding and Representation in James, Conrad, and Ford*. Ithaca: Cornell University Press, 1987.
Arnold, Matthew. *Culture and Anarchy*, ed. Samuel Lipman. New Haven: Yale University Press, 1994.
Auchard, John. *Silence in Henry James: the Heritage of Symbolism and Decadence*. University Park: Pennsylvania State University Press, 1986.
Baker, Houston A. *Modernism and the Harlem Renaissance*. University of Chicago Press, 1987.
Banta, Martha. *Taylored Lives: Narrative Productions in the Age of Taylor, Veblen, and Ford*. University of Chicago Press, 1993.
Bauer, Dale M. *Edith Wharton's Brave New Politics*. Madison: University of Wisconsin Press, 1994.
Bederman, Gail. *Manliness and Civilization: a Cultural History of Gender and Race in the United States, 1880–1917*. University of Chicago Press, 1995.
Beer, Janet. *Edith Wharton: Traveller in the Land of Letters*. New York: St. Martin's Press, 1990.
Bell, Michael Davitt. *The Problem of American Realism: Studies in the Cultural History of a Literary Idea*. University of Chicago Press, 1993.
Bellringer, Alan. "The Narrator as Center in *The Wings of the Dove*." *Modern Fiction Studies* 6 (1960): 131–44.
  "*The Wings of the Dove*: the Main Image." *Modern Language Review* 74 (1979): 12–25.
Bender, Thomas. *New York Intellect: a History of Intellectual Life in New York City, from 1750 to the Beginnings of Our Own Time*. New York: Knopf, distributed by Random House, 1987.

"Lionel Trilling and American Culture." *American Quarterly* 42, no. 2 (1990): 324–47.

Benert, Annette L. "Edith Wharton at War: Civilized Space in Troubled Time." *Twentieth Century Literature* 42, no. 3 (1996): 322–44.

Benstock, Shari. *No Gifts from Chance: a Biography of Edith Wharton*. New York: C. Scribner's Sons; Toronto: Maxwell Macmillan Canada, 1994.

Bentley, Nancy. *The Ethnography of Manners: Hawthorne, James, Wharton*. Cambridge University Press, 1995.

Berenson, Mary, Barbara Strachey, and Jayne Samuels. *Mary Berenson: a Self-Portrait from Her Letters and Diaries*. London: V. Gollancz, 1983.

Bersani, Leo. *A Future for Astyanax: Character and Desire in Literature*. New York: Columbia University Press, 1984.

Birnbaum, Michele A. "'Alien Hands': Kate Chopin and the Colonization of Race." In *Subjects and Citizens: Nation, Race and Gender from "Oroonoko" to Anita Hill*, ed. by Michael Moon and Cathy Davidson. Durham, NC, and London: Duke University Press, 1995. 319–41.

Blair, Sara. "In the House of Fiction: Henry James and the Engendering of Literary Mastery." In *Henry James's New York Edition: the Construction of Authorship*, ed. David McWhirter and John Carlos Rowe. Stanford University Press, 1995. 58–73.

Henry James and the Writing of Race and Nation. Cambridge University Press, 1996.

Blake, Casey Nelson. *Beloved Community: the Cultural Criticism of Randolph Bourne, Van Wyck Brooks, Waldo Frank, and Lewis Mumford*. Chapel Hill, NC: University of North Carolina Press, 1990.

Bledstein, Burton J. *The Culture of Professionalism: the Middle Class and the Development of Higher Education in America*. 1st. edn. New York: Norton, 1976.

Blumin, Stuart M. *The Emergence of the Middle Class: Social Experience in the American City, 1760–1900*. New York: Cambridge University Press, 1989.

Boardman, Arthur. "Social Point of View in the Novels of William Dean Howells." *American Literature* 39 (1967): 42–59.

Borus, Daniel. *Writing Realism: Howells, James, and Norris in the Mass Market*. Chapel Hill, NC: University of North Carolina Press, 1989.

Bourdieu, Pierre. *Outline of a Theory of Practice*. Cambridge University Press, 1977.

Distinction: a Social Critique of the Judgment of Taste, trans. Richard Nice. Cambridge, MA: Harvard University Press, 1984.

The Field of Cultural Production: Essays on Art and Literature, ed. Randal Johnson. New York: Columbia University Press, 1993.

Bradbury, Nicola. "'Nothing That Is Not There and the Nothing That Is': the Celebration of Absence in *The Wings of the Dove*." In *Henry James: Fiction as History*, ed. Ian F. A. Bell. New York: Vision and Barnes & Noble, 1984. 82–97.

Bridgman, Richard. *The Colloquial Style in America*. New York: Oxford University Press, 1966.

Brodhead, Richard H. *The School of Hawthorne.* New York: Oxford University Press, 1986.

Cultures of Letters: Scenes of Reading and Writing in Nineteenth-Century America. University of Chicago Press, 1993.

Brooks, Peter. *The Melodramatic Imagination: Balzac, Henry James, Melodrama, and the Mode of Excess.* New Haven: Yale University Press, 1976.

Brown, Bill. "The Popular, the Populist, and the Populace – Locating Hamlin Garland in the Politics of Culture." *Arizona Quarterly* 50, no. 3 (1994): 89–110.

Burnham, John C. *How Superstition Won and Science Lost: Popularizing Science and Health in the United States.* New Brunswick: Rutgers University Press, 1987.

Bushman, Richard L. *The Refinement of America: Persons, Houses, Cities.* 1st. edn. New York: Knopf, distributed by Random House, 1992.

Butler, Judith P. *Gender Trouble: Feminism and the Subversion of Identity.* New York: Routledge, 1990.

Bodies That Matter: On the Discursive Limits of "Sex". New York: Routledge, 1993.

Cady, Edwin Harrison. *The Road to Realism; the Early Years, 1837–1885, of William Dean Howells.* Syracuse University Press, 1956.

The Realist at War; the Mature Years, 1885–1920, of William Dean Howells. Syracuse University Press, 1958.

Cahan, Abraham. *Yekl and the Imported Bridegroom and Other Stories of the New York Ghetto.* 1896. New York: Dover, 1970.

The Rise of David Levinsky. 1917. New York: Harper & Row, 1960.

Cahan, Abraham, and Moses Rischin. *Grandma Never Lived in America: the New Journalism of Abraham Cahan.* Bloomington: Indiana University Press, 1985.

Calhoun, Craig, Edward LiPuma, and Moishe Postone, eds. *Bourdieu: Critical Perspectives.* University of Chicago Press, 1993.

Cameron, Sharon. *Thinking in Henry James.* University of Chicago Press, 1989.

Campbell, Charles. "Realism and the Romance of Real Life: Multiple Fictional Worlds in Howells' Novels." *Modern Fiction Studies* 16 (1970): 289–302.

Campbell, Donna. *Resisting Regionalism: Gender and Naturalism in American Fiction, 1885–1915.* Athens, OH: Ohio University Press, 1997.

Carby, Hazel V. "Policing the Black Woman's Body in an Urban Context." *Critical Inquiry* 18, no. 4 (1992): 738–55.

Carnes, Mark C., and Clyde Griffen. *Meanings for Manhood: Constructions of Masculinity in Victorian America.* University of Chicago Press, 1990.

Carter, Everett. "Realists and Jews." *Studies in American Fiction* 22, no. 1 (1994): 81–91.

Carton, Evan, and Gerald Graff. "Criticism since 1940." In *The Cambridge History of American Literature,* ed. Sacvan Bercovitch. New York: Cambridge University Press, 1996.

Caruth, Cathy. *Unclaimed Experience: Trauma, Narrative, and History.* Baltimore: Johns Hopkins University Press, 1996.

Caserio, Robert L. "The Story in It: *The Wings of the Dove.*" In *Modern Critical*

Views: Henry James, ed. Harold Bloom. New York: Chelsea House, 1987. 189–214.

Chametzky, Jules. *From the Ghetto: the Fiction of Abraham Cahan.* Amherst: University of Massachusetts Press, 1977.

Chase, Cynthia. *Decomposing Figures: Rhetorical Readings in the Romantic Tradition.* Baltimore: Johns Hopkins University Press, 1986.

Collins, James. "Language, Subjectivity, and Social Dynamics in the Writings of Pierre Bourdieu." *American Literary History* 10, no. 4 (1998): 725–32.

Copjec, Joan. *Read My Desire: Lacan against the Historicists.* Cambridge, MA: MIT Press, 1994.

Cowley, Malcolm, and Robert Cowley. *Fitzgerald and the Jazz Age.* New York: Scribner, 1966.

Cox, James. "*The Rise of Silas Lapham*: the Business of Morals and Manners." In *New Essays on "The Rise of Silas Lapham,"* ed. Donald E. Pease. Cambridge University Press, 1991. 107–28.

Culler, A. Dwight, ed. *Poetry and Criticism of Matthew Arnold.* Boston: Houghton Mifflin, 1961.

Culler, Jonathan. *On Deconstruction: Theory and Criticism after Structuralism.* New York and Ithaca: Cornell University Press, 1982.

Dauber, Kenneth. "Realistically Speaking: Authorship in the Late Nineteenth Century and Beyond." *American Literary History* 11, no. 2 (1999): 378–90.

Daugherty, Sarah B. "Howells Reviews James: the Transcendence of Realism." *American Literary Realism* 18 (1985): 147–67.

"Howells, Tolstoy, and the Limits of Realism: the Case of *Annie Kilburn*." *American Literary Realism* 19, no. 1 (1986): 21–41.

"The Ideology of Gender in Howells' Early Novels." *American Literary Realism* 25, no. 1 (1992): 2–19.

"William Dean Howells and Mark Twain: the Realism War as a Campaign That Failed." *American Literary Realism* 29, no. 1 (1996): 12–28.

de Man, Paul. *Allegories of Reading: Figural Language in Rousseau, Nietzsche, Rilke, and Proust.* New Haven: Yale University Press, 1979.

"The Rhetoric of Temporality." In *Blindness and Insight: Essays in the Rhetoric of Contemporary Criticism.* Minneapolis: University of Minnesota Press, 1983. 187–228.

"Hypogram and Inscription." In *The Resistance to Theory.* Minneapolis: University of Minnesota Press, 1986. 27–53.

Dearborn, Mary V. *Love in the Promised Land: the Story of Anzia Yezierska and John Dewey.* New York: Free Press, 1988.

Delbanco, Andrew. "Howells and the Suppression of Knowledge." *Southern Review* 19, no. 4 (1983): 765–84.

Derrick, Scott S. *Monumental Anxieties: Homoerotic Desire and Feminine Influence in 19th Century US Literature.* New Brunswick, NJ: Rutgers University Press, 1997.

Derrida, Jacques. *Limited Inc.* Evanston, IL: Northwestern University Press, 1988.

Dickstein, Morris. "The City as Text: New York and the American Writer." *TriQuarterly* 83 (1991): 183–206.

Dimock, Wai-chee. "The Economy of Pain: Capitalism, Humanitarianism, and the Realistic Novel." In *New Essays on "The Rise of Silas Lapham"*. ed. Donald E. Pease. Cambridge University Press, 1991. 67–90.

Residues of Justice: Literature, Law, Philosophy. Berkeley: University of California Press, 1996.

Douglas, Ann. *Terrible Honesty: Mongrel Manhattan in the 1920s*. New York: Farrar Straus & Giroux, 1995.

Drucker, Sally Ann. "Yiddish, Yidgin, and Yezierska: Dialect in Jewish-American Writing." *Yiddish* 6 (1987): 99–113.

Duffy, John-Charles. "'I Would Not Presume to Decide': Gender and Ambivalence in Howells' *Indian Summer*." *American Literary Realism* 30, no. 1 (1997): 20–33.

Dupree, Ellen Phillips. "Wharton, Lewis, and the Nobel Prize Address." *American Literature* 56, no. 2 (1984): 262–70.

Dwight, Eleanor. *Edith Wharton: an Extraordinary Life*. New York: Abrams, 1994.

Edel, Leon. *Henry James, a Life*. 1st. edn. New York: Harper & Row, 1985.

Engel, David. "The 'Discrepancies' of the Modern: Towards a Revaluation of Abraham Cahan's *The Rise of David Levinsky*." *Studies in American Jewish Literature* 2 (1982): 36–60.

Erlich, Gloria C. *The Sexual Education of Edith Wharton*. Berkeley: University of California Press, 1992.

Euripides. *Iphigenia in Tauris* Trans. Robert Potter, 2000 [cited January 3, 2000]. Available from http://www.vt.edu/vt98/academics/books/euripides/ip_tauris.

Farrell, John P. *Revolution as Tragedy: the Dilemma of the Moderate from Scott to Arnold*. Ithaca: Cornell University Press, 1980.

Fedorko, Kathy A. *Gender and the Gothic in the Fiction of Edith Wharton*. Tuscaloosa: University of Alabama Press, 1995.

Fein, Richard J. "*The Rise of David Levinsky* and the Migrant Self." *Studies in American Jewish Literature* 2 (1976): 1–4.

Felman, Shoshana. "Education and Crisis, or the Vicissitudes of Teaching." In *Trauma: Explorations in Memory*, ed. Cathy Caruth. Baltimore: Johns Hopkins University Press, 1995. 13–61.

Fiedler, Leslie. "Genesis: the American-Jewish Novel through the Thirties." *Midstream* 4, no. 3 (1958): 21–33.

Fischer, William C., Jr. "William Dean Howells: Reverie and the Nonsymbolic Aesthetic." *Nineteenth-Century Fiction* 25 (1970–1): 1–30.

Fisher, Philip. *Hard Facts: Setting and Form in the American Novel*. Oxford University Press, 1985.

Foster, Dennis A. *Sublime Enjoyment: On the Perverse Motive in American Literature*. Cambridge University Press, 1997.

Foucault, Michel. *The History of Sexuality*, vol. 1: *An Introduction*, trans. Robert Hurley. New York: Vintage, 1980.

Fowler, Virginia C. "Milly Theale's Malady of Self." *Novel* 14 (1980): 57–75.

Fracasso, Evelyn E. *Edith Wharton's Prisoners of Consciousness: a Study of Theme and Technique in the Tales.* Westport, CT: Greenwood Press, 1994.

Freedman, Jonathan. "The Quickened Consciousness": Aestheticism in Howells and James." Diss., Yale University, 1984.

Professions of Taste: Henry James, British Aestheticism and Commodity Culture. Stanford University Press, 1990.

"Trilling, James, and the Uses of Cultural Criticism." *Henry James Review* 14, no. 2 (1993): 141–50.

"Henry James and the Discourses of Antisemitism." In *Between "Race" and Culture: Representations of "the Jew" in English and American Literature,* ed. Bryan Cheyette. Stanford University Press, 1996. 62–83.

Freud, Sigmund. *Beyond the Pleasure Principle,* ed. James Strachey. New York: Norton, 1960.

Fried, Michael. *Realism, Writing, Disfiguration: On Thomas Eakins and Stephen Crane.* University of Chicago Press, 1987.

Froula, Christine. "The Daughter's Seduction: Sexual Violence and Literary History." *Signs* 11, no. 4 (1986): 621–44.

Fryer, Judith. *Felicitous Space: the Imaginative Structures of Edith Wharton and Willa Cather.* Chapel Hill, NC: University of North Carolina Press, 1986.

Gallagher, Jean. "The Great War and the Female Gaze: Edith Wharton and the Iconography of War Propaganda." *Lit: Literature, Interpretation, Theory* 7, no. 1 (1996): 27–49.

Gallop, Jane. *Around 1981: Academic Feminist Literary Theory.* New York and London: Routledge, 1992.

Gambrell, Alice. *Women Intellectuals, Modernism, and Difference: Transatlantic Culture, 1919–1945.* Cambridge University Press, 1997.

Garland, Hamlin. "Howells." In *American Writers on American Literature,* ed. John Albert Macy. New York: H. Liveright, 1931. 285–97.

Main-Travelled Roads. 1890. Lincoln: University of Nebraska Press, 1995.

Gilbert, Sandra M. "Introduction: the Second Coming of Aphrodite." In *The Awakening by Kate Chopin.* New York: Penguin, 1986. 7–34.

Gilbert, Sandra M., and Susan Gubar. *No Man's Land: the Place of the Woman Writer in the Twentieth Century.* New Haven: Yale University Press, 1988.

Gilman, Sander L. *Jewish Self-Hatred: Anti-Semitism and the Hidden Language of the Jews.* Baltimore: Johns Hopkins University Press, 1986.

Glazener, Nancy. *Reading for Realism: the History of a US Literary Institution, 1850–1910.* Durham, NC: Duke University Press, 1997.

Goldberg, David Joseph. *Discontented America: the United States in the 1920s.* Baltimore: Johns Hopkins University Press, 1999.

Goode, John. "The Pervasive Mystery of Style: *The Wings of the Dove.*" *The Air of Reality: New Essays on Henry James.* London: Methuen, 1972.

Goodman, Susan. "Competing Visions of Freud in the Memoirs of Ellen Glasgow and Edith Wharton." *Colby Library Quarterly* 25, no. 4 (1989): 218–31.

Edith Wharton's Women: Friends and Rivals. Hanover, NH: University Press of
    New England, 1990.
Goodwyn, Janet. *Edith Wharton: Traveller in the Land of Letters.* Basingstoke:
    Macmillan, 1990.
Graff, Gerald. *Professing Literature: an Institutional History.* University of Chicago
    Press, 1987.
Graff, Gerald, and Michael Warner. *The Origins of Literary Studies in America: a
    Documentary Anthology.* New York: Routledge, 1989.
Greenwald, Elissa. "I and the Abyss: Transcendental Romance in *The Wings of
    the Dove.*" *Studies in the Novel* 18, no. 2 (1986): 177–92.
Grossberg, Lawrence, Cary Nelson, and Paula A. Treichler, eds. *Cultural Studies.*
    New York: Routledge, 1992.
Guillory, John. *Cultural Capital: the Problem of Literary Canon Formation.* University
    of Chicago Press, 1993.
"Bourdieu's Refusal." *Modern Language Quarterly* 58, no. 4 (1997): 367–98.
Habegger, Alfred. *Gender, Fantasy, and Realism in American Literature.* New York:
    Columbia University Press, 1982.
Henry James and the "Woman Business". Cambridge University Press, 1989.
Hadley, Kathy Miller. *In the Interstices of the Tale: Edith Wharton's Narrative Strategies.*
    New York: Lang, 1993.
Hale, Nathan G., ed. *Freud in America,* vol. 1 *The Beginnings of Psychoanalysis in the
    United States, 1876–1917.* Oxford University Press, 1971.
Freud in America, vol. 2 *The Rise and Crisis of Psychoanalysis in the United States:
    Freud and the Americans, 1917–1985.* Oxford University Press, 1995.
Halttunen, Karen. *Confidence Men and Painted Women: a Study of Middle-Class
    Culture in America, 1830–1870.* New Haven: Yale University Press, 1982.
Hapgood, Hutchins. *The Spirit of the Ghetto.* Cambridge, MA: Belknap Press of
    Harvard University Press, 1967.
Harad, Alyssa. "An Invitation to Witness: Trauma, Literary Testimony, and the
    Reader." Diss., University of Texas at Austin, forthcoming.
Harap, Louis. *The Image of the Jew in American Literature: From Early Republic to Mass
    Immigration.* 1st. edn. Philadelphia: Jewish Publication Society of America,
    1974.
Harap, Louis, and American Jewish Archives. *Creative Awakening: the Jewish
    Presence in Twentieth-Century American Literature, 1900–1940s.* New York:
    Greenwood Press, 1987.
Harlan, Louis R. *Booker T. Washington: the Making of a Black Leader, 1856–1901.*
    London and New York: Oxford University Press, 1975.
Booker T. Washington: the Wizard of Tuskegee, 1901–1915. New York: Oxford
    University Press, 1983.
Harmon, Charles. "*A Hazard of New Fortunes* and the Reproduction of
    Liberalism." *Studies in American Fiction* 25, no. 2 (1997): 183–95.
Harris, Neil. *Cultural Excursions: Marketing Appetites and Cultural Tastes in Modern
    America.* University of Chicago Press, 1990.

Hart, John E. "The Commonplace as Heroic in *The Rise of Silas Lapham.*" *Modern Fiction Studies* 8 (1962–3): 375–83.

Haskell, Thomas L. *The Emergence of Professional Social Science: the American Social Science Association and the Nineteenth-Century Crisis of Authority.* Urbana: University of Illinois Press, 1977.

The Authority of Experts: Studies in History and Theory. Bloomington: Indiana University Press, 1984.

Hemingway, Ernest. "A Clean, Well-Lighted Place." In *The Short Stories of Ernest Hemingway.* New York: Simon & Schuster, 1995. 379–83.

Hendrick, Burton J. "The Jewish Invasion of America." *McClure's Magazine* 40, no. 5 (March 1913): 125–65.

Hertz, Neil. *The End of the Line: Essays on Psychoanalysis and the Sublime.* New York: Columbia University Press, 1985.

Hofstadter, Richard. *Social Darwinism in American Thought.* Rev. edn., Boston: Beacon Press, 1955.

Holbrook, David. *Edith Wharton and the Unsatisfactory Man.* London: Vision, 1991.

Holland, Laurence Bedwell. *The Expense of Vision: Essays on the Craft of Henry James.* Baltimore: Johns Hopkins University Press, 1982.

Horwitz, Howard. *By the Law of Nature: Form and Value in Nineteenth-Century America.* New York: Oxford University Press, 1991.

"Maggie and the Sociological Paradigm." *American Literary History* 10, no. 4 (1998): 606–38.

Howard, June. *Form and History in American Literary Naturalism.* Chapel Hill, NC: University of North Carolina Press, 1985.

ed. *New Essays on "The Country of the Pointed Firs".* Cambridge University Press, 1994.

Howe, Irving. *World of Our Fathers.* New York: Simon & Schuster, 1976.

Howells, Mildred. *Life in Letters of William Dean Howells.* Garden City, NY: Doubleday, 1928.

Howells, William Dean. "Literary Criticism." 1866. In *Selected Literary Criticism,* vol. 1 *1859–1885,* ed. Ulrich Halfmann. Bloomington: Indiana University Press, 1993. 60–2.

The Rise of Silas Lapham. 1885. New York: Harper & Row, 1958.

The Rise of Silas Lapham. 1885. ed. Don L. Cook. New York: Norton, 1982.

Novels, 1886–1888: The Minister's Charge, April Hopes, Annie Kilburn. New York: Library of America, 1989.

"Standards and Taste in Fiction; Mary E. Wilkins." 1887. In *Selected Literary Criticism,* vol. 2 *1886–1897,* ed. Donald Pizer. Bloomington: Indiana University Press, 1993. 60–7.

"Editor's Study." *Harper's New Monthly Magazine* (1888): 314–18.

"Matthew Arnold and 'Distinction' in America." 1888. In *Selected Literary Criticism,* vol. 2 *1886–1897,* ed. Donald Pizer. Bloomington: Indiana University Press, 1993. 94–100.

A Hazard of New Fortunes. 1890. New York: Meridian, 1994.

"Short Story Collections: Hamlin Garland." 1891. In *Selected Literary Criticism*, vol. 2 *1886–1897*, ed. Donald Pizer. Bloomington: Indiana University Press, 1993. 185–7.

The Quality of Mercy. 1892. *A Selected Edition of William Dean Howells*, ed. David J. Nordloh and James P. Elliott, vol. 18. Bloomington: Indiana University Press, 1979.

The Shadow of a Dream and An Imperative Duty. 1892. *A Selected Edition of William Dean Howells*, ed. Ronald Gottesman, David J. Nordloh, and Martha Banta, vol. 17. Bloomington: Indiana University Press, 1970.

The World of Chance: a Novel. New York: Harper, 1893.

"Are We a Plutocracy?" *The North American Review*, no. 158 (1894): 185–96.

"Equality as the Basis of Good Society." *The Century Magazine* 51, no. 29 (1895): 63–7.

"Dialect in Literature." 1895. In *Selected Literary Criticism*, vol. 2 *1886–1897*, ed. Donald Pizer. Bloomington: Indiana University Press, 1993. 219–23.

Impressions and Experiences. 1896. Freeport, NY: Books for Libraries Press, 1972.

"Who Are Our Brethren?" *The Century Magazine* 52, no. 29 (1896): 932–6.

"An Opportunity for American Fiction." Review of Thorstein Veblen, *The Theory of the Leisure Class. Literature*, May 20, 1899 and June 3, 1899, 525; 79–80.

Their Silver Wedding Journey. 1899. New York: Harper & Brothers, 1909.

The Coast of Bohemia. New York: Harper and Brothers, 1901.

"A She Hamlet." In *Literature and Life*. New York: Harpers, 1902. 132–40.

Ian, Marcia. "The Elaboration of Privacy in *The Wings of the Dove.*" *English Literary History* 51, no. 1 (1984): 107–36.

Jacobson, Matthew Frye. *Whiteness of a Different Color: European Immigrants and the Alchemy of Race.* Cambridge, MA: Harvard University Press, 1998.

James, Henry. *Roderick Hudson.* 1874, ed. Geoffrey Moore. New York: Penguin, 1986.

The Portrait of a Lady. 1882. Oxford University Press, 1981.

The Bostonians. 1886. Oxford and New York: Oxford University Press, 1984.

The Princess Casamassima. 1886. Harmondsworth: Penguin Classics, 1986.

The Awkward Age. 1899, ed. Ronald Blythe. New York: Penguin, 1987.

The Wings of the Dove. 1902. New York: Penguin, 1986.

The American Scene. 1907. Bloomington: Indiana University Press, 1968.

The Notebooks of Henry James, ed. F. O. Matthiessen and Kenneth B. Murdock. Oxford University Press, 1947.

James, Henry, and William Dean Howells. *Letters, Fictions, Lives: Henry James and William Dean Howells*, ed. Michael Anesko. Oxford University Press, 1997.

Jameson, Fredric. *The Political Unconscious: Narrative as a Socially Symbolic Act.* Ithaca, NY: Cornell University Press, 1981.

Jay, Gregory. "Hegel and Trilling in America." *American Literary History* 1, no. 3 (1989): 565–90.

Johnson, Barbara. "Moses and Monotheism." Paper presented at the A. D. White Professor-at-Large Lecture Series, Cornell University April 1990.

The Feminist Difference: Literature, Psychoanalysis, Race, and Gender. Cambridge, MA: Harvard University Press, 1998.

Kaplan, Amy. *The Social Construction of American Realism.* University of Chicago Press, 1988.

"Nation, Region, and Empire." In *The Columbia History of the American Novel,* ed. Emory Elliot. New York: Columbia University Press, 1991. 240–66.

Kassanoff, Jennie A. "The Fetishized Family: The Modernism of Edith Wharton." Diss., Princeton University, 1993.

"Extinction, Taxidermy, Tableaux Vivants: Staging Race and Class in *The House of Mirth.*" *PMLA* 115, no. 1 (2000): 60–74.

Kasson, John F. *Rudeness and Civility: Manners in Nineteenth-Century Urban America.* New York: Hill & Wang, 1990.

Kilcup, Karen L., and Thomas S. Edwards. *Jewett and Her Contemporaries: Reshaping the Canon.* Gainesville, FL: University Press of Florida, 1999.

Kirschner, Don S. *The Paradox of Professionalism: Reform and Public Service in Urban America, 1900–1940.* New York: Greenwood Press, 1986.

Klinkowitz, Jerome. "Ethic and Aesthetic: the Basil and Isabel March Stories of William Dean Howells." *Modern Fiction Studies* 16 (1970): 303–22.

Kress, Susan. "Women and Marriage in Abraham Cahan's Fiction." *Studies in American Jewish Literature* 3 (1983): 26–39.

Krieg, Joann P. "Health Is Capital: Henry James' *The Wings of the Dove.*" In *Money: Lure, Lore, and Literature,* ed. John Louis DiGaetani. Westport, CT: Greenwood Press, 1994. 111–20.

Krook-Gilead, Dorothea. *The Ordeal of Consciousness in Henry James.* Cambridge University Press, 1967.

Laclau, Ernesto, and Chantal Mouffe. *Hegemony and Socialist Strategy: Towards a Radical Democratic Politics.* London: Verso, 1985.

Larson, Magali Sarfatti. *The Rise of Professionalism: a Sociological Analysis.* Berkeley: University of California Press, 1977.

Lasch, Christopher. *The New Radicalism in America, 1889–1963: the Intellectual as a Social Type.* New York: Knopf, 1965.

Lears, T. J. Jackson. *No Place of Grace: Antimodernism and the Transformation of American Culture, 1880–1920.* University of Chicago Press, 1994.

Leavis, F. R. *The Great Tradition.* Garden City, NY: Doubleday, 1954.

Leonard, Garry M. "The Paradox of Desire: Jacques Lacan and Edith Wharton." *Edith Wharton Review* 7, no. 2 (1990): 113–6.

Levine, Lawrence W. *Highbrow/Lowbrow: the Emergence of Cultural Hierarchy in America, the William E. Massey, Sr., Lectures in the History of American Civilization, 1986.* Cambridge, MA: Harvard University Press, 1988.

Lewis, David L. *When Harlem Was in Vogue.* New York: Penguin, 1997.

Lewis, R. W. B. *Edith Wharton: a Biography.* 1st. edn. New York: Harper & Row, 1975.

Litvak, Joseph. *Strange Gourmets: Sophistication, Theory, and the Novel.* Durham, NC: Duke University Press, 1997.

Loesberg, Jonathan. "Bourdieu's Derrida's Kant: the Aesthetics of Refusing Aesthetics." *Modern Language Quarterly* 58, no. 4 (1997): 417–36.

Lynn, Kenneth Schuyler. *William Dean Howells; an American Life*. New York: Harcourt Brace Jovanovich, 1971.

MacCannell, Juliet Flower. *The Regime of the Brother: After the Patriarchy*. London and New York: Routledge, 1991.

Machor, James L. *Readers in History: Nineteenth-Century American Literature and the Contexts of Response*. Baltimore: Johns Hopkins University Press, 1993.

Marovitz, Sanford. "Howells and the Ghetto: 'The Mystery of Misery'." *Modern Fiction Studies* 16 (1970): 345–62.

"The Secular Trinity of Lonely Millionaires: Language, Sex, and Power in *The Rise of David Levinksy*." *Studies in American Jewish Literature* 2 (1982): 20–35.

Marx, Leo. "The Vernacular Tradition in American Literature." In *Studies in American Culture; Dominant Ideas and Images*, ed. Joseph J. Kwiat and Mary C. Turpie. New York: Johnson Reprint Corp., 1971.

McHale, Brian. "Free Indirect Discourse: a Survey of Recent Accounts." *PTL: A Journal for Descriptive Poetics and Theory of Literature* 3 (1978): 249–87.

McKee, Patricia. *Producing American Races: Henry James, William Faulkner, Toni Morrison*. Durham, NC: Duke University Press, 1999.

McWhirter, David Bruce. *Desire and Love in Henry James: a Study of the Late Novels*. Cambridge University Press, 1989.

Henry James's New York Edition: the Construction of Authorship. Stanford University Press, 1995.

Mellard, James. "Lacan and the New Lacanians: Josephine Hart's *Damage*, Lacanian Tragedy, and the Ethics of *Jouissance*." *PMLA* 113, no. 3 (1998): 395–407.

Mencken, H. L. *The American Language: an Inquiry into the Development of English in the United States*. New York: 4th. edn. Knopf, 1936.

Supplement I. The American Language: an Inquiry into the Development of English in the United States. New York: Knopf, 1945.

Mercer, Caroline G. and Wangensteen, Sarah D. "'Consumption, Heart Disease, or Whatever': Chlorosis, a Heroine's Illness in *The Wings of the Dove*." *Journal of the History of Medicine* 40 (1985): 259–85.

Michaels, Walter Benn. *The Gold Standard and the Logic of Naturalism: American Literature at the Turn of the Century*. Berkeley: University of California Press, 1987.

Our America: Nativism, Modernism, and Pluralism, Post-Contemporary Interventions. Durham, NC: Duke University Press, 1995.

"Local Colors." *Modern Language Notes* 113, no. 4 (1998): 734–56.

Miller, D. A. *The Novel and the Police*. Berkeley: University of California Press, 1988.

"Balzac's Illusions Lost and Found." *Yale French Studies* 67 (1984): 164–81.

Miller, J. Hillis. *The Ethics of Reading: Kant, De Man, Eliot, Trollope, James, and Benjamin*. New York: Columbia University Press, 1987.

Mitchell, Lee Clark. *Determined Fictions: American Literary Naturalism.* New York: Columbia University Press, 1989.

Mizruchi, Susan L. *The Science of Sacrifice: American Literature and Modern Social Theory.* Princeton University Press, 1998.

Moi, Toril. "Appropriating Bourdieu: Feminist Theory and Pierre Bourdieu's Sociology of Culture." *New Literary History* 22, no. 4 (1991): 1017–49.

Montgomery, Maureen E. *Displaying Women: Spectacles of Leisure in Edith Wharton's New York.* New York: Routledge, 1998.

Moon, Michael. "Sexuality and Visual Terrorism in *The Wings of the Dove.*" *Criticism* 28 (1986): 427–43.

Murphy, Brenda. "American Realism and the Limits of Critical Theory." *Modern Language Studies* 16, no. 4 (1986): 81–5.

Nettels, Elsa. *Language, Race, and Social Class in Howells's America.* Lexington, KY: University Press of Kentucky, 1988.

Language and Gender in American Fiction: Howells, James, Wharton, and Cather. Charlottesville: University Press of Virginia, 1997.

North, Michael. *The Dialect of Modernism: Race, Language, and Twentieth-Century Literature.* New York: Oxford University Press, 1994.

Nowlin, Michael E. "'Reality in America' Revisited: Modernism, the Liberal Imagination and the Revival of Henry James." *Canadian Review of American Studies* 23, no. 3 (1993): 1–29.

"Edith Wharton as Critic, Traveller, and War Hero." *Studies in the Novel* 30, no. 3 (1998): 444–51.

O'Hara, Daniel T. "Between Marx and Freud: the Authority of the Commonplace in Cultural Criticism Today." *Contemporary Literature* 28, no. 3 (1987): 409–15.

Olin-Ammentorp, Julie. "'A Circle of Petticoats': the Feminization of Merton Densher." *Henry James Review* 15, no. 1 (1994): 38–54.

Oostrum, Duco van. *Male Authors, Female Subjects: the Woman Within/Beyond the Borders of Henry Adams, Henry James and Others.* Amsterdam: Rodopi, 1995.

Orvell, Miles. *The Real Thing: Imitation and Authenticity in American Culture, 1880–1940.* Chapel Hill, NC: University of North Carolina Press, 1989.

Parrish, Timothy L. "Haymarket and Hazard: the Lonely Politics of William Dean Howells." *Journal of American Culture* 17, no. 4 (1994): 23–32.

"Howells Untethered: the Dean and 'Diversity'." *Studies in American Fiction* 23, no. 1 (1995): 101–17.

Pease, Donald E. "The Cultural Office of Quentin Anderson." *South Atlantic Quarterly* 89, no. 3 (1990): 583–622.

Person, Leland S. "Henry James, George Sand, and the Suspense of Masculinity." *PMLA* 106, no. 3 (1991): 515–28.

"James's Homo-Aesthetics: Deploying Desire in the Tales of Writers and Artists." *The Henry James Review* 14, no. 2 (1993): 188–203.

"Reading Sexuality: the Object Lesson of James's Master." *Arizona Quarterly* 53, no. 4 (1997): 23–27.

Petty-Schmitt, Chapel, with George Arms, James Barbour, and Robert E.

Fleming. "Criticism of William Dean Howells: a Selected Checklist." *American Literary Realism* 20, no. 3 (1987–8): 69–92.

Peyser, Thomas. *Utopia and Cosmopolis: Globalization in the Era of American Literary Realism*. Durham, NC, and London: Duke University Press, 1998.

Pittenger, Mark. "A World of Difference: Constructing the Underclass in Progressive America." *American Quarterly* 49, no. 1 (1997): 26–65.

Pizer, Donald. *Hamlin Garland's Early Work and Career*. New York: Russell & Russell, 1969.

Realism and Naturalism in Nineteenth-Century American Literature. Rev. edn. Carbondale: Southern Illinois University Press, 1984.

The Theory and Practice of American Literary Naturalism: Selected Essays and Reviews. Carbondale: Southern Illinois University Press, 1993.

The Cambridge Companion to American Realism and Naturalism. New York: Cambridge University Press, 1995.

Documents of American Realism and Naturalism. Carbondale: Southern Illinois University Press, 1998.

Porter, Carolyn. *Seeing and Being: the Plight of the Participant Observer in Emerson, James, Adams, and Faulkner*. Middletown, CT: Wesleyan University Press, 1981.

Posnock, Ross. *The Trial of Curiosity: Henry James, William James, and the Challenge of Modernity*. New York: Oxford University Press, 1991.

Color and Culture: Black Writers and the Making of the Modern Intellectual. Cambridge, MA: Harvard University Press, 1998.

Pressman, Richard S. "Abraham Cahan, Capitalist; David Levinsky, Socialist." In *Styles of Cultural Activism: From Theory and Pedagogy to Women, Indians, and Communism*, ed. Philip Goldstein. Newark: University of Delaware Press, 1994. 134–51.

Price, Alan. *The End of the Age of Innocence: Edith Wharton and the First World War*. New York: St. Martin's Press, 1996.

Price Herndl, Diane. *Invalid Women: Figuring Feminine Illness in American Fiction and Culture, 1840–1940*. Chapel Hill, NC: University of North Carolina Press, 1993.

Raphael, Lev. *Edith Wharton's Prisoners of Shame: a New Perspective on Her Neglected Fiction*. New York: St. Martin's Press, 1991.

Robertson, Michael. *Stephen Crane, Journalism, and the Making of Modern American Literature*. New York: Columbia University Press, 1997.

Rorty, Richard. *Contingency, Irony, and Solidarity*. Cambridge University Press, 1989.

Rose, Jacqueline. *The Haunting of Sylvia Plath*. Cambridge, MA: Harvard University Press, 1992.

"Jeffery Masson and Alice James." *Oxford Literary Review* 8, no. 1–2 (1986): 185–92.

Rosenfeld, Isaac. "*David Levinsky*: the Jew as American Millionaire." In *An Age of Enormity*. Cleveland, OH: World Publishing Company, 1962.

Ross, Andrew. *No Respect: Intellectuals and Popular Culture*. New York: Routledge, 1989.

Ross, Dorothy. *The Origins of American Social Science: Ideas in Context.* Cambridge University Press, 1991.

Rowe, John Carlos. *The Theoretical Dimensions of Henry James.* Madison, WI: University of Wisconsin Press, 1984.

Russett, Cynthia Eagle. *Darwin in America: the Intellectual Response, 1865–1912.* San Francisco: W. H. Freeman, 1976.

Sanders, Ronald. *The Downtown Jews; Portraits of an Immigrant Generation.* New York: Harper & Row, 1969.

Scarry, Elaine. *The Body in Pain: the Making and Unmaking of the World.* New York: Oxford University Press, 1985.

Scharnhorst, Gary F. "Maurice Thompson's Regional Critique of William D. Howells." *American Literary Realism* 9 (1976): 57–63.

Sears, Sallie. *The Negative Imagination; Form and Perspective in the Novels of Henry James.* Ithaca, NY: Cornell University Press, 1968.

Sedgwick, Eve Kosofsky. *Epistemology of the Closet.* Berkeley: University of California Press, 1990.

"Queer Performativity: Henry James's *The Art of the Novel.*" *Journal of Lesbian and Gay Studies* 1, no. 1 (1993): 1–17.

Seelye, John. "The Rise of William Dean Howells." *The New Republic,* July 3, 1971. 23–6.

"The Hole in Howells/the Lapse in *Silas Lapham.*" In *New Essays on "The Rise of Silas Lapham"*, ed. Donald E. Pease. Cambridge University Press, 1991. 47–65

Seltzer, Mark. *Henry James and the Art of Power.* Ithaca: Cornell University Press, 1984.

Bodies and Machines. New York: Routledge, 1992.

Sensibar, Judith L. "Edith Wharton Reads the Bachelor Type: Her Critique of Modernism's Representative Man." *American Literature* 60, no. 4 (1988): 575–90.

Shapiro, Charles. "On Our Own: Trilling vs. Dreiser." In *Seasoned Authors for a New Season: the Search for Standards in Popular Writing,* ed. Louis Filler. Bowling Green, OH: Bowling Green University Press, 1980.

Simpson, Lewis P. "The Treason of William Dean Howells." In *The Man of Letters in New England and the South: Essays on the History of the Literary Vocations in America.* Baton Rouge: Louisiana State University Press, 1973. 85–127.

Singer, David. "David Levinsky's Fall: a Note on the Liebman Thesis." *American Quarterly* 19 (1967): 696–706.

Singley, Carol J. *Edith Wharton: Matters of Mind and Spirit.* Cambridge University Press, 1995.

Smith, Barbara Herrnstein. *Belief and Resistance: Dynamics of Contemporary Intellectual Controversy.* Cambridge, MA: Harvard University Press, 1997.

Smith, Carl S. *Urban Disorder and the Shape of Belief: the Great Chicago Fire, the Haymarket Bomb, and the Model Town of Pullman.* University of Chicago Press, 1995.

Smith, Henry Nash. *Democracy and the Novel: Popular Resistance to Classic American Writers.* New York: Oxford University Press, 1978.

Sprinker, Michael. *Imaginary Relations: Aesthetics and Ideology in the Theory of Historical Materialism*. London and New York: Verso, 1987.

Stange, Margit. "Personal Property: Exchange Value and the Female Self in *The Awakening*." In *The Awakening*, ed. Nancy A. Walker. Boston: Bedford Books, 1993. 201–17.

Strout, Cushing. "Personality and Cultural History in the Novel: Two American Examples." *New Literary History* 1 (1970): 423–38.

Sundquist, Eric J. *American Realism: New Essays*. Baltimore: Johns Hopkins University Press, 1982.

"Realism and Regionalism." In *Columbia Literary History of the United States*, ed. Emory Elliott. New York: Columbia University Press, 1988. 501–24.

To Wake the Nations: Race in the Making of American Literature. Cambridge, MA: Belknap Press of Harvard University Press, 1993.

Tanner, Tony. *Henry James: the Writer and His Work*. Amherst: University of Massachusetts Press, 1985.

Tanselle, G. Thomas. "The Boston Seasons of Silas Lapham." *English Journal* 48 (1959): 60–6.

Thomas, Brook. *American Literary Realism and the Failed Promise of Contract*. Berkeley: University of California Press, 1997.

Tichi, Cecelia. *Shifting Gears: Technology, Literature, Culture in Modernist America*. Chapel Hill, NC: University of North Carolina Press, 1987.

Tintner, Adeline R., and Henry D. Janowitz. "Inoperable Cancer: an Alternate Diagnosis of Milly Theale's Illness." *Journal of the History of Medicine* 42 (1987): 73–6.

Todorov, Tzvetan. "The Structural Analysis of Literature: the Tales of Henry James." In *Structuralism: an Introduction*, ed. David Robey. Oxford: Clarendon, 1973.

Trilling, Lionel. *The Liberal Imagination: Essays on Literature and Society*. Garden City, NY: Doubleday, 1954.

The Opposing Self: Nine Essays in Criticism. New York: Viking Press, 1955.

Tuttleton, James W., Kristin O. Lauer, and Margaret P. Murray. *Edith Wharton: the Contemporary Reviews*. Cambridge University Press, 1992.

Twain, Mark, and Kenneth Schuyler Lynn. *Huckleberry Finn: Text, Sources, and Criticism*. New York: Harcourt Brace & World, 1961.

Tylee, Claire M. "Imagining Women at War: Feminist Strategies in Edith Wharton's War Writing." *Tulsa Studies in Women's Literature* 16, no. 2 (1997): 317–43.

Updike, John. "A Critic at Large: Howells as Anti-Novelist." *New Yorker*, July 13, 1987. 78–88.

Van der Werf, Martin. "A Scandal and a Suicide Leave a College Reeling." *The Chronicle of Higher Education*, November 19 1999, A53–A55.

Veblen, Thorstein. *The Theory of the Leisure Class: an Economic Study of Institutions. 1899*. New York: New American Library, 1953.

The Higher Learning in America: a Memorandum on the Conduct of Universities by Business Men. 1918. Stanford: Academic Reprints, 1954.

Wadlington, Warwick. *The Confidence Game in American Literature*. Princeton University Press, 1975.
Reading Faulknerian Tragedy. Ithaca and London: Cornell University Press, 1987.
Waid, Candace. *Edith Wharton's Letters from the Underworld: Fictions of Women and Writing*. Chapel Hill, NC: University of North Carolina Press, 1991.
Walden, Daniel. "Abraham Cahan: Realism and the Early Stories." *Yiddish* 7, no. 4 (1990): 5–18.
Ward, David. *Poverty, Ethnicity, and the American City, 1840–1925: Changing Conceptions of the Slum and the Ghetto*. Cambridge University Press, 1989.
Warminski, Andrzej. *Readings in Interpretation: Hölderlin, Hegel, Heidegger*. Minneapolis: University of Minnesota Press, 1987.
Warren, Kenneth W. *Black and White Strangers: Race and American Literary Realism*. University of Chicago Press, 1993.
Washington, Booker T. *Up from Slavery*. New York: Penguin, 1986.
Watkins, Evan. "Reproduction, Reading, and Resistance." *American Literary History* 2, no. 3 (1990): 550–63.
Wegelin, Christof. *The Image of Europe in Henry James*. Dallas: Southern Methodist University Press, 1958.
Weine, Steven M. "The Witnessing Imagination: Social Trauma, Creative Artists, and Witnessing Professionals." *Literature and Medicine* 15, no. 2 (1996): 167–82.
Wershoven, Carol. *The Female Intruder in the Novels of Edith Wharton*. Rutherford, NJ: Fairleigh Dickinson University Press, 1982.
Wharton, Edith. *House of Mirth*. 1905. New York: Penguin, 1985
Summer. 1916. New York: Penguin, 1993.
Fighting France: From Dunkerque to Belfort. New York: Charles Scribner's Sons, 1918.
The Marne. New York: Appleton, 1918.
French Ways and Their Meaning. New York: Appleton, 1919.
A Son at the Front. New York: Charles Scribner's Sons, 1923.
Twilight Sleep. 1927. New York: Scribner, 1997.
A Backward Glance. 1933. New York: Charles Scribner's Sons, 1964.
The Letters of Edith Wharton, ed. R. W. B. Lewis and Nancy Lewis. New York: Charles Scribner's Sons, 1988.
The Uncollected Critical Writings, ed. Frederic Wegener. Princeton University Press, 1996.
White, Barbara A. "Neglected Areas: Wharton's Short Stories and Incest, Parts I and II." *Edith Wharton Review* 8, no. 8 (1991): 2–12.
Wiebe, Robert H. *The Search for Order, 1877–1920*. Westport, CT: Greenwood Press, 1980.
Williams, Raymond. *The English Novel from Dickens to Lawrence*. New York: Oxford University Press, 1970.
Wilson, Christopher P. *The Labor of Words: Literary Professionalism in the Progressive Era*. Athens: University of Georgia Press, 1985.

"Markets and Fictions: Howells' Infernal Juggle." *American Literary Realism* 20, no. 3 (1987–8): 2–19.

White Collar Fictions: Class and Social Representation in American Literature, 1885–1925. Athens: University of Georgia Press, 1992.

Wilson, Elizabeth. "Picasso and Pâté De Foie Gras: Pierre Bourdieu's Sociology of Culture." *Diacritics* 18 (1988): 47–68.

Wilson, Howard A. "William Dean Howell's Unpublished Letters About the Haymarket Affair." *Journal of the Illinois State Historical Society* 56, no. 1 (1963): 5–19.

Woodress, James. "Howells in the Nineties: Social Critic for All Seasons." *American Literary Realism* 25, no. 3 (1993): 18–25.

Yeager, Patricia. "'A Language Which Nobody Understood': Emancipatory Strategies in *The Awakening*." *Novel* 20, no. 3 (1987): 197–219.

Yeazell, Ruth Bernard. *Language and Knowledge in the Late Novels of Henry James.* University of Chicago Press, 1976.

Yezierska, Anzia. *Hungry Hearts.* 1921. Boston: Houghton Mifflin, 1920.

Bread Givers. 1925. New York: Doubleday, 1975.

Zanger, Jules. "David Levinsky: Master of *Pilpul*." *Papers in Language and Literature* 13 (1977): 283–94.

Žižek, Slavoj. *The Sublime Object of Ideology.* London and New York: Verso, 1989.

Index

Ammons, Elizabeth, 184n1
Anderson, Amanda, 154
antisemitism, 181n18, 182n20; *see also* James,
    Henry; Wharton, Edith
Arnold, Matthew, 18–19, 21, 40, 190n15

Banta, Martha, 158n3
Bauer, Dale, 111, 112
Beckett, Samuel, 176n30
Bederman, Gail, 163n30
Bell, Michael Davitt, 11, 46, 159n53
Bellringer, Alan, 172n5, 174n13
Benstock, Shari, 174
Bentley, Nancy, 1, 99
Berenson, Bernard, 110–11
Berenson, Mary, 126–7
Bersani, Leo, 174n17 and 19
Birmingham Centre for Contemporary
    Cultural Studies, *see* cultural studies
Birnbaum, Michele A., 163n31
Blair, Sara, 163n30, 173n9, 175n23, 177n32
Bledstein, Burton, 164n2, 167n32
Blumin, Stuart, 164n2
Bourdieu, Pierre, 6–10, 12, 32, 64, 76, 80–2,
    87–8, 132, 183n22
    Abraham Cahan, implicit critique of, 80–2,
        87–8
    distinction and cultural capital, defined,
        6–7
    and John Guillory, 132
    and literary realism, 9–11
    and poststructuralism, 9
Boyers, Robert, 132–3
Boynton, H., 181n18
Bradbury, Nicola, 172n5
Bridgman, Richard, 165n13
Brodhead, Richard, 17, 19, 160n8 and 9,
    167n26
Brooks, Peter, 55
Brown, Bill, 159n4
Bush, George, 152

Butler, Judith, 8–9, 12, 14, 131–2, 155
    "Arguing with the Real," 153–5
    Bodies That Matter, 8–9, 148–50, 153–4
    Gender Trouble, 149–50
    Joan Copjec's critique of, 149–50
    materialization, *see* materiality

Cady, Edwin, 17–18, 46
Cahan, Abraham, 4, 8, 126
    Catskills, 87
    David Levinsky, possible identification with,
        75–6
    dialect, 83–5, 92, 93–4; American slang, 85
    Grandma Never Lived in America, *see* English-
        language journalism
    Jewish-American literature, relation to, 77,
        95
    journalism: *Daily Forward*, 73–4, 78; English-
        language journalism, 83; *New York
        Commercial Advertiser*, 83
    Rise of David Levinsky, The, 8, 13, 73–6, 101
    Yekl, 13, 83, 94–5
    Yiddish culture in America, 89–93; *see also*
        real, the ethnic
Calhoun, Craig, 162n21
Cameron, Lizzie, 126–7
Cameron, Sharon, 176n28, 177n33
Carter, Everett, 178n1
Carton, Evan, 131
Caruth, Cathy, 117
Caserio, Robert, 174n19
castration, *see* psychoanalytic criticism; real,
    the
Chase, Cynthia, 142–3
Chopin, Kate, 12
civil service reform, 87
Clinton, Bill, 185n13
Copjec, Joan, 9, 131–2, 149–53
Cowie, Elizabeth, 150
Cox, James, 16–17, 21
Crane, Stephen, 53, 180n16

209

Ian, Marcia, 174n19
incest, *see* real, the, father's desire as
Iphigenia, *see* Wharton, Edith

Jameson, Frederic, 179n9
James, Henry
    American, The, 57
    American Scene, The, 1, 5, 50, 73–4, 175n24
    antisemitism, 74
    Awkward Age, The, 130–1
    Bostonians, The, 165n21
    Merton Densher, identification with, 67
    "Next Time, The," 178n5
    notebooks, 55
    Princess Casamassima, The, 53, 173n11
    Roderick Hudson, 69–70, 147
    style, 67
    Watch and Ward, 69
    Wings of the Dove, The, 48–72, 75, 81, 96, 124
James, William, 174n11
Jay, Gregory, 189n13
jazz, 97–8, 114
Jewish-American literature, *see* Cahan,
    Abraham
    talmud learning in, 77

Kafka, Franz, 135
Kaplan, Amy, 18, 99, 160n8, 165n14, 167n26
Kassanoff, Jennie, 103, 187n43
Kirschner, Don, 160n8
Krieg, Joann P., 173n6
Krook, Dorothea, 55

Lacan, Jacques, *see* Copjec, Joan; Žižek, Slavoj
Larsen, Nella, 98
Leavis, F. R., 172n5
Levine, Lawrence, 27
Levinsky, Monica, 185n13
literary criticism, 9–10, 130, 146, *see also*
    cultural studies, deconstruction, feminist
    criticism, historicist criticism, marxist
    criticism, masculinity studies, New
    Criticism, proletarian aesthetic,
    psychoanalytic criticism, queer studies,
    structuralism
literary intellectuals, 1–5, 75
    "ethnic" intellectuals, 78, 179n7
literary naturalism, 53
Litvak, Joseph, 10, 29–30
Loesberg, Jonathan, 164n24
Lynn, Kenneth, 31, 45

MacCannell, Juliet Flower, 9, 101, 150
manners, *see* real, the
Marovitz, Sanford, 168n44, 181n18

Martin, Michael, 175n24
Marx, Leo, 165n13
marxist criticism, 130, 132; *see also* Jameson,
    Frederic
masculinity and masculinity studies, *see* gender
materiality, 3, 132–3; *see also* real, the
    body, 148–9
    historical materialism and, 147
    materialization, 8–9, 153, 155–6; gender
        and, 12, 153–4; *see also* Butler, Judith
    positing, inscription, signification and,
        141–3; *see also* real, the: language and
        dialect as
    practices as, 146–7
    Rise of David Levinsky, The, 79–82
    socioinstitutional relations as, *see* real:
        relations as
    specification and, 148
    versus phenomenality, *see* real versus
        "reality"
    vulgar materialism, 144–5
McWhirter, David, 55, 70
Mellard, James M., 150
Mencken, Henry Louis, 74, 183n22
Menorah Journal, 189n9
Mercer, Caroline, 172n5
Michaels, Walter Benn, 115, 166n21
Miller, D. A., 167n32
Mitchell, Lee Clark, 173n10
Mizruchi, Susan, 2, 158n3, 177n32
modernism, 47, 97–8, 135, 176n30
Moi, Toril, 12
Moon, Michael, 174n19

Nettels, Elsa, 163n30, 164n10, 165n14 and n17,
    166n23, 183n22
New Criticism, 131
New Thought, 99
New York intellectuals, 135, 144, 189n9; *see also*
    Trilling, Lionel
North, Michael, 7
Nowlin, Michael, 189n11

Olin-Ammentorp, Julie, 177n36
Orvell, Miles, 183n21

Parrington, Vernon Louis, *see* Trilling, Lionel
Partisan Review, 135
Person, Leland, 163
Peyser, Thomas, 168n40
Pittenger, Mark, 159n6
Posnock, Ross, 160n10, 162n28, 178n1, 179n7
Porter, Carolyn, 159n6
poststructuralism, 5, 9, 131, 133, 151
Pound, Ezra, 103, 176n30